Let Us Prey

Let Us Prey

*The Plague of Narcissist Pastors
and What We Can Do About It*

REVISED EDITION

DARRELL PULS

CASCADE *Books* · Eugene, Oregon

LET US PREY
The Plague of Narcissist Pastors and What We Can Do About It
Revised Edition

Copyright © 2020 Darrell Puls. All rights reserved. Except for brief quotations in critical publications or reviews, no part of this book may be reproduced in any manner without prior written permission from the publisher. Write: Permissions, Wipf and Stock Publishers, 199 W. 8th Ave., Suite 3, Eugene, OR 97401.

Cascade Books
An Imprint of Wipf and Stock Publishers
199 W. 8th Ave., Suite 3
Eugene, OR 97401

www.wipfandstock.com

PAPERBACK ISBN: 978-1-7252-5728-3
HARDCOVER ISBN: 978-1-7252-5729-0
EBOOK ISBN: 978-1-5326-8949-9

Cataloguing-in-Publication data:

Names: Puls, Darrell, author.

Title: Let us prey : the plague of narcissist pastors and what we can do about it / Darrell Puls.

Description: Eugene, OR: Cascade Books, 2020 | Includes bibliographical references.

Identifiers: ISBN 978-1-7252-5728-3 (paperback) | ISBN 978-1-7252-5729-0 (hardcover) | ISBN 978-1-5326-8949-9 (ebook)

Subjects: LCSH: 1. Narcissism Religious aspects. | 2. Pastoral theology.

Classification: RC553.N36 L50 2020 (paperback) | RC553.N36 (ebook)

Manufactured in the U.S.A.   06/05/20

Contents

Tables

Acknowledgments

I thank my wife, Carole, for tolerating the long hours I put into this project; she recognized its value and encouraged me along the way. My gratitude also goes to those whose questions, comments, and suggestions helped sharpen the focus while at the same time filling in gaps along the way. I am indebted to Dr. Steven Sandage of Boston University for his insights, critiques, and suggestions on this complex topic. He helped sharpen the focus and more accurately describe the nuances between various interconnected mental health issues. My thanks and appreciation go to all the therapists, counselors, psychologists, and psychiatrists I conferred with, including Dr. Mike Patterson, former chair of the behavioral studies program and then provost of Corban University. Their insights proved invaluable in coming to understand how the true narcissist operates in a world very different from ours. It is a world where there is no substitute for victory even if it is at the expense of everyone around them and they crash in flames.

Since the first publication in 2017 I have collected dozens of stories volunteered by readers telling of their experiences at the hands of a narcissist pastor. They have given permission to publish the stories if I protect their identities. These stories make the revised edition more powerful and more relevant to everyone.

Finally, I thank God for the energy and tenacity it took to pursue this difficult and controversial topic through the early stages of research to the publication of this book.

Introduction to the Revised Edition

Who am I? This seems to be the central question of today's existence. We are told first to find ourselves, to know who we are, and to expand into everything we can be. We are then able, or so we are told, to answer life's deepest questions while building our lives on self-reliance and meaningful work. The message we receive is that we are autonomous and independent beings unique from everyone else. From this mantra of the modern age we are told to set our course for the far horizons as independent and powerful agents of the self.

We see this same mantra wrapped in religious language in many churches. The Christian life is often interpreted as a partnership between "God and me." It is a partnership where God wants to bless us beyond measure, to make us rich in possessions, health, and power. This is a pseudo-gospel where we are at the center of the universe.

There is a darker side to this phenomenon. In this scenario, the pastor needs to be the center of everything, the master imbued with godlike powers, the center of the church. Few go this far outwardly but the signs are there if you care to notice. They consume the energies and talents of those around them, then discard and replace them without pity or remorse. They can be charming, charismatic, pitiless, and cruel.

Please do not misunderstand. I love pastors! I have worked closely with them for more than twenty years and served as an associate pastor for three years, so I know the work from the inside. A large majority of pastors focus on the well-being of their flocks, which is as it should be. Pastoring as a calling or profession can be so unrewarding that up to 80 percent of those who start out in eager energy will leave the pastorate long before retirement. They are good, dedicated, and altruistic shepherds who do their best to feed and protect their flocks.

This book is not about them. It is about the other pastors, the ones who prey on their flocks rather than nurture them.

I have heard the statement, "He's/She's such a narcissist" more times than I care to count. Narcissism has been a hot topic of late, particularly in politics. Multiple blogs (mine included) have sprouted like spring flowers (or weeds, if you prefer) wherever the ground is fertile and a huge amount of research into pathological, destructive narcissism has been done in the last few years. The term *narcissism* is bandied about in casual conversation as if it is one of the more common features of our society. Well, it is, and it is not.

We are all narcissists to some degree, and many have observed the increase in narcissistic behaviors in our society. Who does not like to be recognized or even praised for a job exceptionally well done? We may hem and haw, "aw shucks"-ing it to near death, but behind the curtain of humility even the most modest among us secretly revel in recognition. It is good and proper to be recognized for years of hard work even if your job description was that of a single-purpose drone. It takes a certain amount of narcissism to believe that we are the people who can lead others through difficult times. We need praise, recognition, and acceptance. Without them, we feel isolated from the rest of society and may fall into deep depression.

Narcissism becomes a problem when we begin to believe that praise and recognition are our rights, and that we are superior to the rest of the pack in good looks, intellect, and accomplishments. Once the need for recognition morphs into demands for recognition and reward, the problem becomes serious. This is called entitlement. It is one of the hallmarks of the true narcissist. They believe they are superior beings—therefore, they should be recognized and rewarded for their very existence.

Normal narcissism is a motivation for many. In order to be at the top of the pack, we know that we must excel throughout school, not just fourth grade. If we work hard, our self-image is likely to be one of accomplishment, but if we fail to produce those accomplishments, the most common healthy response is disappointment, learning from what we did wrong, and then moving forward. The "normal" narcissist does this as well, though dealing with failure is a more difficult struggle. By normal narcissist I mean someone who has an abnormally high opinion of himself (most are males) without the accomplishments to back it up, but who also does not engage in pathological behaviors that are designed solely to gain recognition and power by any means available. Further along the spectrum are those who engage in pathological behaviors to use people and casually throw them away when done. At the most extreme are those whose belief in their own prowess and greatness clashes so strongly with reality that they gradually disengage from reality entirely and spend the rest of their days in delusional anger.

There is no doubt that people from around the world are reading the blog I wrote for the American Association of Christian Counselors. I have received hundreds of emails from people who state something like, "You told my story. It's like you were there! How can I can thank you? For the first time in years I know that I am not alone and that what happened was calculated and planned!" I get on average three every week and they are a source of great encouragement as well as heartache.

There is good reason to believe that the pastorate is attractive to "religious" narcissists. There is no other profession where one gets to stand in front of people every week and tell them as an expert and on God's behalf how they are to live, how their sins and shortcomings are getting in their way, and then be told over and over afterwards what a wonderful message he or she just delivered. Pastors are automatically invited into every nook and cranny of human existence, from weddings to tragic death, and are told our deepest, darkest secrets along with our aspirations for the future, are sought out for advice and then invited to dinner as the honored guest. If any job entails becoming a human repository of intimate knowledge about other people, this is it. The problem is in how pastors with dangerously high levels of narcissism use it to control, manipulate, exploit, and abuse those around them.

As I said, my concern is not those pastors who think a bit too highly of themselves. My concern is that group of pastors who seek the pulpit to glorify themselves, to gain power over others, and to exploit anyone and everyone until they are no longer useful.

The first edition contained a research study of Canadian pastors. I was dismayed to learn recently that the scoring key had been changed without authorization, leading to a complete misinterpretation of the original data. The result was the data were invalidated and have been eliminated from this edition. The conclusion that almost one-third of the pastors tested fell within the diagnostic range of Narcissistic Personality Disorder was wrong. Nobody knows what the actual percentage may be.

Narcissism is a spectrum condition, meaning that it goes from the least inclination to full-blown Narcissistic Personality Disorder (NPD). NPD is defined by both beliefs and behaviors. I have focused more on behaviors than beliefs because behaviors are visible, and beliefs are not. That does not discount beliefs, as they are the foundation of behaviors.

If the responses I have had from around the world from the first edition are any indicator, a specific percentage finding for Narcissistic Personality Disorder in pastors is unnecessary. The readers themselves have concluded that predatory narcissist pastors are to be found in far too many churches, and they have caused immense problems for everyone involved with them. You will read their stories.

Darrell Puls, December 20, 2019

1

Into Darkness

I buried my head under the darkness of the pillow and pretended it was night.
I couldn't see the point of getting up. I had nothing to look forward to.

—Sylvia Plath, *The Bell Jar*

The following is a combination of true stories. Names and
identifying details have been changed to protect the people
involved and the churches where these events took place.

David was a successful and highly regarded college professor. As a
young man he had sensed a call to ministry, but he could not see
himself in the role of a pastor and he was not at all interested in missions.
Instead, he poured himself into research and teaching graduate studies in
leadership and business administration at a highly regarded university. He
was well respected in academic circles. Married with two grown children,
he also volunteered with several community groups and had served them
in various capacities. It was a comfortable life and he looked forward to

retiring in a year or two and then sailing in the fall with his wife down the east coast from Connecticut, where they lived, to Florida, and then back to Connecticut for the summers. Financially secure, he was carefully planning his exit from the university when the senior pastor of his church asked to meet with him over lunch. David was a bit surprised when he walked into the restaurant and saw that the executive pastor was there as well.

They said they had been praying for months for someone to take over leadership of the seminary that had grown as an adjunct to the church. They said that they knew of David's plans to retire—and then told him that his was the only name that kept coming up in answer to their prayers. Obviously, they said, God was calling him into ministry as a teacher and seminary leader.

David was flattered, confused, and excited. Could this be what God was calling him to? He had always admired Pastor Bob, the senior pastor, for his many successes in ministry. Pastor Bob was tall, thin, and distinguished looking, always impeccably dressed, with a head of carefully brushed graying hair and a certain sense of distant serenity about him. He could be a very persuasive man when he wanted, and David was now the object of that persuasion.

David had spent almost his entire adult professional life researching, writing about, and teaching leadership skills to graduate students in the business administration program—and now was being offered the chance of a lifetime to place all of that knowledge and experience into use for the church where he had been a member for many years. To be the builder of something that would have a lasting impact for generations to come was an enticing offer. After prayer and discussing the entire set of possibilities with his wife, he accepted.

Even though he was still six months away from leaving the academic world, David was introduced by Pastor Bob in front of 200 members and leaders as the new chancellor of the seminary. It was official. It was only much later that David pieced everything together and understood how he had been manipulated from the outset. Intentionally or not, the pastors were playing on David's own narcissistic need to be needed, his commitment to this particular church that had brought him in out of the spiritual cold, and his experience, successes, recognition—and insecurities.

David and his wife had already downsized by selling their large custom-built executive home in anticipation of sailing back and forth between smaller, more modest homes in Florida and Connecticut after he left academic work and she retired from a family law practice. Now the plans to sail for several months each year were placed on hold and what had been intended as temporary housing took on more of an aura of permanency.

As the date of his departure from the university drew nearer, David and his wife activated financial arrangements that they had carefully made over the course of their careers; it would guarantee a living income that would only need to be supplemented by the church. Finally, he cleaned out his old office and turned in his keys. He was going to be chancellor of the rapidly growing seminary. It was an exciting time, full of promise and energy.

The first note that something might not be entirely right happened on David's first day. Pastor Bob seemed surprised to see him, which David dismissed as a momentary memory lapse. David was given an office at the church and began work. His first assignment was to create a nonprofit foundation to provide a steady financial base for the seminary, and to analyze and document all of the programs as they began the application process for accreditation. David could not think of ways in which he could feel more blessed. He was putting his all of his knowledge and experience into building the kingdom of God by training the pastors and church leaders of tomorrow.

The first indications of discord were not long in coming. It was a large church and the entire pastoral staff of eight was meeting for their weekly breakfast when Pastor Bob verbally berated another, somewhat elderly pastor in front of everyone. There was nothing loving, gentle, encouraging, or pastoral about it—the attack was vicious, unsparing, and humiliating. Being new, David expected one of the more senior pastors to intervene, but they were all avoiding eye contact. Once the attack was over, everyone resumed their conversations as if nothing had happened.

David left the meeting wondering if this type of behavior was common, as no one seemed overly upset by it, not the pastor who was attacked or even a pastor who was also a licensed therapist. Still, it did not make sense that someone who weekly preached love, kindness, and gentle correction could be so unsparing to his own staff. The non-reaction of the others was equally confusing. It was only much later that David learned that this passive acceptance was a sign of a brutalized and thoroughly intimidated staff. This was their "normal," and it was something David had encountered fewer than a dozen times in all of his years of leadership research and corporate consulting.

David had of course experienced many narcissists at every level of the corporations he consulted with, but they tended to be so obvious that they were easy to spot and counter. They tended to have grand visions that drew in other people and gave them energy to move into new territory. In fact, their narcissism was one of the primary reasons they had risen so far in the corporate world. But there was a downside that is inseparable: their constant need of more praise can lead them to make less than ethical decisions, they cannot take any form of criticism, easily fly into an almost uncontrolled rage, tend to be vicious and merciless when someone makes a mistake, but never admit or take responsibility for their own mistakes.[1] The pattern David was now experiencing was more unsettling as the senior pastor seemed to be a gentle, even painfully shy, man. The pattern would be repeated many times in the years David served as seminary chancellor.

Being new to the internal work world of churches, and giving the benefit of the doubt, David filed these things away in the back of his mind. He knew that this sort of behavior would be tolerated in the corporate world if the narcissist was a high producer or was at the very highest levels of the corporate structures, which is where the narcissists reigned supreme. His confusion came from not experiencing a covert, or shy, narcissist before and so he could not categorize the behaviors he saw. Since church staff culture was new to him he rationalized that this behavior was not the norm.

Like most people, he subscribed to the notion that churches were somehow immune from the narcissism, power struggles, and vengeance found in the corridors of power. He also knew that most men and women with strong narcissistic tendencies functioned quite well in the structured world of large corporations. David now says that, for all of his experience, he was surprisingly naïve. Thirty years of experience as a researcher, consultant, and teacher had made him wise and comfortable with secular work, but the world of church culture was entirely new.

About a year after David was hired, a young associate pastor named Hector was brought on as youth pastor. Hector was fresh out of seminary with a Master of Divinity degree. He and his wife were full of energy and ideas, and fully committed to living their faith. They started the work together, even though Melinda was at home most of the time with their two small children.

In spite of their age and experience differences, David and Hector quickly became trusted friends.

About six months into his tenure, Hector and Melinda took the high school students on a weekend camping trip into the forests of rural Connecticut. He had informed Pastor Bob of the trip beforehand, and no objections were made. But a few days after they returned, Hector came into David's office, flopped down on the couch, and began to shake. The story quickly spilled out. A parent had complained to Pastor Bob that Hector was promoting drug use. His daughter had gone to Hector and Melinda and asked if she was going to hell because she had tried marijuana. They had used this as a teaching opportunity about the dangers of drug use but said

---

1. Rijsenbilt and Commandeur, "Narcissus Enters the Courtroom."

that God could forgive this minor sin. They prayed together, asked God's forgiveness, hugged, and thought little else of it.

Subsequently, though, her father was livid. But instead of calling Hector he called Pastor Bob, and demanded that Hector be fired immediately. Pastor Bob had stormed into the middle of a meeting Hector was having with a parent and without prelude and began yelling at Hector while the parent quickly scrambled out the door. "Don't you ever put me in a place where I have to defend you! You are supposed to defend me, not the other way around!" he screamed. He went on to shout that he had never approved the camping trip and that Hector was never again to do such a thing without his written approval. The kids belonged in church on Sunday mornings, not off in some mosquito-infested swamp! He then stormed out, slamming the door behind him.

David spent hours calming Hector. Since he had never seen Pastor Bob's temper in flood stage, David thought Hector was exaggerating.

In many ways, Pastor Bob was extremely gifted and even visionary. There was no question that he had been spectacularly successful over the years and had hundreds of loyal followers, but the longer David was there the more it became obvious that something was not right. In fact, something was wrong, very wrong. Granted, Pastor Bob had taken the church from an old, wooden structure to a sprawling, multi-structure campus; he was to be granted deference for that reason alone. He had also been ordained and in full-time ministry for almost thirty years when only a small fraction of those who start as pastors will retire as pastors.

But the side of Pastor Bob that David was seeing was well hidden from public view, and the signs of something deeper and darker were there if one looked closely. Taken individually they might have indicated eccentricity or something else benign; taken together, however, distant and faint alarms began going off in the back of David's mind. No one could make a decision, no matter how mundane, without Pastor Bob's approval beforehand. Bob controlled all spending, which probably is not that unusual in a large church, but what was unusual is that there were neither a budget nor budget controls even though the annual income and expenditures were almost two million dollars. More alarmingly, there were neither financial accountability nor transparency in the church or the seminary. Having created and worked with numerous nonprofit organizations in the past, David knew how important both were to the health and welfare of the church should anyone challenge how money was being used.

Pastor Bob seemed to have a very high view of himself despite his declarations of childhood deprivation and various learning disabilities. At first it was amusing but that changed over time. No matter what the topic,

Pastor Bob spoke with great authority, including on church architecture, history, theology, psychology, and psychiatry to . . . pretty much anything and everything that mattered. He dominated conversation in every meeting, whether it was a staff meeting or a men's Bible study, whether he was leading it or not. He continually referred to various celebrities as his "wonderful, close friends."

It was clear that he was emulating several television preachers in how he constructed and conducted worship, in his vocabulary, and even in his selection of pastoral robes. Under the guise of following the ancient apostles, Pastor Bob personally selected every member of the board of directors, which he controlled. David would later learn that one board member who asked to see the budget and who talked about putting financial controls in place received a phone call the next day informing him that he was no longer on the church board. Pastor Bob justified it all by saying that the church was not a democracy; it was a theocracy and he was the head as Gods' anointed representative.

Even though Pastor Bob frequently preached about joy and laughter, he seemed to have little of either. In fact, Bob never seemed to laugh; he would smile and perhaps chuckle but no one ever heard him truly laugh. He rarely tried to tell a joke, and it usually fell flat when he did. It seemed that Pastor Bob simply did not understand what people found humorous. What he did well, however, was sarcasm aimed at undercutting whomever he chose as a target. Hector said that he could "weaponize a compliment in such a way that everyone else in the room thought he was praising me, but only he and I knew that he was slighting me. The look in his eyes when we made eye contact was unnerving."

Much more troubling was the fact that Pastor Bob would say something with total conviction and then say the opposite a few days or weeks later but with just as much sincerity—and would vehemently deny that he had ever said that which he was now contradicting. At one point, Pastor Bob angrily denied that he had announced that David was to be chancellor of the seminary—until he was reminded that he said it with fanfare in front of more than 200 people, that it had been recorded, and that he had presented David a name plate for David's office door with the word *Chancellor* on it. David was becoming more concerned and confused, as what he was seeing behind the scenes was often contrary to what Pastor Bob preached from the pulpit. He had never run into this behavior before in a pastor, and it was baffling. David's need to believe in Pastor Bob overrode his own observations and increasing concern.

Pastor Bobs' preaching was fascinating—at first. David will never deny his debt of gratitude to Bob for it was he who broke through David's layers of resistance and drew him back into the church after having left it many years before. Bob's preaching seemed simple and winsome, but over time David began to notice how repetitive it was, and how shallow. Pastor Bob justified it by saying that this was a "seeker's" church where they needed to present a positive message that did not get caught up in the finer points of theology. That was fine, but the sermons seemed to have more pop psychology than theology much of the time.

To David, for the seminary to grow meant engaging with the community and with other churches. They did neither but focused all of their outreach energies into the poorest remote villages of Burundi in central Africa. They would do short mission trips to remote villages and perhaps dig a well, but always preached at the villagers that they needed Jesus, ignoring the fact that most were already Christians. It seemed to be their only outreach ministry. When asked why the church did nothing for the hungry or poor in the local community, Pastor Bob demanded he be shown one hungry child from the area, and flatly stated that the poor in the community were far better off than the poor in any other country—and were not actually all that poor as they had TVs and cell phones.

Even though the church had little to no contact with other area churches, Bob often bragged about how young pastors would come to him for guidance and how other churches were patterning themselves after "his" church. David wondered how this could be since they had been steadily losing attendees on Sunday morning for the last few years and Pastor Bob rarely had anything good to say about any other churches in the area. Even so, Pastor Bob had built a sense of uniqueness in the staff and congregation that allowed him to ignore and even disrespect other churches. He said they were special, anointed by God to be a pillar of fire for others to follow—except to David more and more it seemed that the fire was mostly smoke and no one was following. Bob often referred to the church as being his, which is not unusual, but there seemed to be an element of ownership as if the church were his personal possession.

Though the signs were accumulating, it all remained an enigma to David. He had seen these kind of behaviors in corporations, of course, but always in extraverted personalities; he was blinded by the prevailing assumption that this could not be the case in the church. After all, pastors are called by God! However, by then David was deep into expanding the seminary and so he kept his thoughts to himself. He simply did not see that he was slowly sinking into a very unhealthy church culture. In a moment of candor, David admits that he did not want to see it. He denied the reality of what was happening like the rest of the pastoral staff and focused on his work.

Meanwhile, on the surface, all was well between Pastor Bob and Hector. However, when Hector and Melinda left for their annual vacation a few months after the camping incident, Pastor Bob called a special meeting of the church board from which all staff were excluded. In it he claimed that Hector was disrespectful, poorly trained, and not a leader. He claimed that the youth groups were shrinking (they were rapidly growing) and that Hector needed to go. The board voted on the spot to fire him.

Hector and Melinda returned home on Saturday evening and were in the congregation the next morning when Pastor Bob announced that Hector had resigned due to a moral failure. Hundreds of eyes turned to stare at him or refused to look in his direction. Pastor Bob stared at him with a half-grin. Stunned, all Hector and Melinda could do was rush out. The lock on Hector's office door had been changed and all of his belongings were neatly packed in boxes in the hall. Later he tried to confront Pastor Bob but was refused entry. A board member told Hector that Pastor Bob had it on good authority that he was having multiple affairs and took action to protect the church. The humiliation was too much. Hector fell into a deep and crippling depression. The reason given for firing him was an absolute lie and he was never given an opportunity to defend himself. He has not only left ministry, he has left the church completely, a bitter and broken man. His marriage did not survive.

David was shocked. It made no sense that Hector and Melinda would be sitting in the congregation if they had any idea Pastor Bob was going to announce Hector's resignation for moral failure. It made no sense, but Hector refused to speak about it, Melinda and their children and moved away as quickly as they could, and Hector simply disappeared.

Pastor Bob was getting older and both staff and leaders often remarked what a difficult time he would have when he retired, as the church was his life—he had no hobbies or interests outside of the church, even to the detriment of his family. Then it became apparent that he did not intend to retire, even though he was now reaching normal retirement age.

His signal to everyone was a sermon series on Martin Luther, the man who set out to have a debate within the Roman Catholic Church but inadvertently started the Reformation and changed the world. Pastor Bob capped the series by having his middle name changed from James to Martin Luther (something I later discovered is more common than I thought). It was becoming increasingly clear that Pastor Bob was tightening his grip on the church at a time when most would be searching for their replacement and looking forward to retirement. There is an interesting twist here that few would think of as anything more than simple vanity or confusion: every time Pastor Bob talked about having his middle name changed, it was by a judge with ever-higher authority. The level of the judge always rose in the retelling. First, it was a superior court judge, then an appellate judge, then a federal judge, and finally a state supreme court justice. Was senility creeping in, did he not know the difference, or was he deliberately lying? David did not know, but increasingly Pastor Bob was becoming the butt of jokes told quietly in the corners.

Then David sealed his own fate. Pastor Bob had asked him to fill in for him at a community prayer breakfast where Bob was scheduled to speak. It was no secret that Bob was losing energy and at times was becoming a bit confused, so David drew from his experience and said before about 150 men and women that all churches needed to have a succession plan in the event a long-term pastor retired, was suddenly incapacitated, or resigned unexpectedly. He also said, "Pastor Bob is an amazing man of God, but we must always remember: even though he brought this church forth from nothing and it would not exist today without him, this is not Bob's church; this is God's church and we will need to carry it forward when Bob is gone. I pray that day does not happen for many years, but all of us are mortal." With that single statement, David shifted from being Pastor Bob's protégé to his enemy.

Things rapidly changed in their relationship. Bob had suggested David start a new degree program in servant leadership, something that was becoming popular in seminaries around the country. David made plans to attend an academic conference where servant leadership was the main topic and then was going to consult with seminary professors already in such a program. David made all of the travel arrangements but then was told a few days before he was scheduled to leave, "We're not doing that anymore." Pastor Bob simply cancelled the new degree program he was so eager for David to start and for which David had spent weeks in planning.

David was accustomed to clear corporate structures where power was carefully measured and clearly delegated. David confronted Pastor Bob. Either he was the chancellor of the seminary, or he was not. As chancellor, he needed the authority to act autonomously within the bounds of the seminary structure and budget. Pastor Bob shot back that he, not David, was in charge and that included the seminary. The title of "chancellor" meant nothing at all; it was just a nice-sounding word. Not only that, David was not growing the seminary fast enough and it should have been fully accredited by now. David replied that only twenty months had passed while accreditation normally takes at least three full years, something he had told Pastor Bob many times. The conversation seemed to end in a stalemate, but it was not the end. In fact, it was only the beginning of the end.

David received a notice from the Internal Revenue Service stating that the application for the nonprofit foundation had been withdrawn and was no longer under consideration. Without nonprofit status, the foundation could not raise funds and became meaningless. Almost two years of his work was casually discarded as if it was nothing. He was deeply hurt, but still the loyal soldier, now deeply enmeshed in a narcissistic culture and trudging on to the next challenge for the seminary, which now had more than one hundred full-time students. David believed along with so many others that Pastor Bob had the grander vision to lead them, and they were part of making it into reality. David simply refused to see that Pastor Bob was sick and that he had been pulled into the center of that sickness, nor did he want to see it because that would require admitting that he had been duped and manipulated. He had succumbed to his own narcissistic need to be needed, had allowed himself to be controlled and used—and was about to be thrown away.

Bob came into David's office unannounced and sat down. Without prelude or warning, he verbally, spiritually, and emotionally attacked David more viciously than anything he had experienced in three decades of university work and corporate consulting. This shy, quiet man of God raged for twenty or thirty minutes. David was so stunned that he could not speak. Pastor Bob berated David's abilities, his intelligence, his loyalty, and even the Prius that he drove. He attacked David's theology and humiliated him with a viciousness in his words and demeanor that left David stunned and in pain, much the same as Hector had been a year prior. Pastor Bob seemed to know David's every weakness and used each of them against him. Then Pastor Bob abruptly got up to leave—and wanted a hug! It was one of the most unsettling and confusing encounters David had ever had.

David suddenly found himself shunned. Everyone on staff avoided him and no one would speak to him except as was necessary. The seminary had been pulled back under Pastor Bob's complete control and David no longer had authority. The faculty knew it, and it was not long before the students knew it. He felt like the proverbial "dead man walking."

He was devastated. Even the pastor/therapist in the next office, who David had considered his friend, avoided him. To begin dealing with his own woundedness and confusion, David saw an outside Christian therapist, who rather quickly said that Bob saw him as a threat and would do whatever was necessary to neutralize that threat, even if it meant destroying David emotionally, spiritually, and professionally. He told David in clear and certain terms to resign and get out immediately. David was bewildered. "I had no idea how I could possibly be conceived as a threat by Pastor Bob. It made no logical sense. I just wanted to serve!"

Almost exactly three years after he arrived full of energy and hope, David resigned from his position as staff pastor. He was deeply depressed, broken-spirited, and convinced that following the call into ministry of any kind had been among the stupidest things he had ever done—the last thing he ever wanted to consider again was ministry in any form. He had no job and he had no ministry. In reality, he was barely functional. The one saving blessing was his and his wife's financial independence, which now was all they seemed to have.

David describes this period as one of the worst times of his life, a desert full of scorpions and dry bones. He could not understand what he had done wrong or why he should have been treated so badly. He had trusted Pastor Bob, the other pastors, and even the church board, and now felt betrayed by all of them. He increasingly withdrew into himself and needed solitude, which he found on the sailboat he and his wife kept moored in a marina near their home. It became his refuge.

Day after day, he would go to the marina and just sit in the boat cockpit or cabin. He would fiddle with the sails and rigging and do maintenance work, but even the thought of sailing had lost its attraction. For the first time in his adult life, and after three decades of high profile, high-pressure success, David felt like a complete failure. Bob had found his every weakness and systematically exploited them all. David had failed at many things over the years but had always looked at failure as a learning experience from which he could extract some insight and move on. Not this time. He had not failed; he *was* a failure. Full of unrelenting shame, David was now convinced that he was broken beyond repair.

There came a day when he gave up. He had nothing left.

David puts it this way: "I was praying on the boat. The marina was deserted, and I was the only one there. To be truthful, I can't say that I was really praying in the conventional sense of the word; it was more agonized wailing, screaming a demand at heaven to know why, and feeling sorry for myself. Finally, expended and exhausted, I had no words at all. As the tears poured down my face and in mid-wail, I was stopped by a voice that was as clear as anything I ever heard before or since. It said, 'Trust Me!' Startled and confused, I looked around, but I was still alone. No one was in sight. In stunned silence, I at first thought I had totally lost my sanity, but then concluded that I had just heard the voice of God, and that I must trust in what had been said and the One that said it. I chose to trust in Christ, though I had no idea where my life was going. Faith at that point was almost gone, but I decided that God was involved in all of this in ways I could not see. I once again found and tapped into the determination, or stubbornness if you want to call it that, that had brought me this far in life."

Still, David describes himself as being like a kicked puppy, needing love but afraid of further pain and injury. He would shy away from contact with Pastor Bob but refused to leave the church. On Sunday mornings, he found that he could not bring himself to enter the sanctuary when Bob was preaching, but he refused to be driven out completely. "My soul was so badly crushed that it was as if an invisible curtain would not allow me to go through the doors from lobby to sanctuary, but there also was another part of me that refused to be defeated. Instead, I would stay in the lobby throughout morning services. Something within me would not give up and my natural stubbornness became an unexpected virtue. Anger became my motivator. I wanted Bob to know that he would not and could not drive me out. I wanted him to see me back there as a constant reminder that he had not beaten me. In fact, I wanted him to understand that he had failed, though I doubt I ever accomplished any of these goals—Bob had moved on and was oblivious. He didn't care. Though I seriously contemplated leaving the church, God granted me the courage to defy everything Bob had done to me and stay. My wife, though, stopped coming to church entirely. She and I both doubted that she could contain her anger, and it was not time for confrontation."

Nevertheless, there were currents beginning to swirl ever closer to the surface and hints of greater discontent were becoming visible. Something powerful was coming into the light.

David, like many of us, has a deep need to understand why people act in the ways that they do, particularly when those ways are not just counterproductive but ultimately self-destructive. He contacted several people who he thought might have greater insight into the situation: a former colleague whose counsel he trusted, a Christian psychiatrist, and another Christian therapist. David told them everything he had observed (and much has been left out here) of how Bob interacted with others and with him. He received the same response he had gotten from his own therapist: Get out!

"Each of them said that I was dealing with Narcissistic Personality Disorder and that I needed to get out as the attacks on me would only get worse. Fortunately, I was already off the staff, but I was still an active member of the church.

"I had never heard of NPD and, being an academic, I ordered every book I could find on it. There was a pause of sorts as I caught my spiritual and emotional breath. I concentrated on building a ministry to distressed churches going through internal conflict and developmental challenges. I was gathering a new sense of self and mission and concentrated on becoming healthy again."

In the meantime, several church leaders banded together after all their efforts to rein in Pastor Bob had failed. The fight broke into the clear when more than sixty members demanded that he resign during an open church meeting. Pastor Bob had publicly stated for many years that he would immediately resign if ever there was even one vote against him, but that was not to be the case. Instead it was marked by Bob's son, who yelled after the vote as he stormed out, "You can't tell him what to do; this is HIS church!" That statement was a dawning of awareness for many that Bob truly believed that the church was his personal possession. Yes, he had built it, but he was the steward, not the owner. The frightening part was that he had declared many times that he would rather see the church destroyed than change the direction he and God (in that order) had set.

People had begun leaving in an increasing stream over the last couple of years as Pastor Bob's charisma faded. Attendance on Sunday mornings continued to drop, which Bob tried to make invisible by removing a few rows of pews and widening the spaces between the remaining ones. It did not work. Now he sometimes delivered thundering but disjointed sermons on how Satan was loose in the congregation and how those who opposed him were the minions of hell and demon possessed. He even referred to one of the godliest men David has ever known, and one of the biggest financial supporters of the church, as being Satan's personal servant.

The battle intensified and raged between those who had finally seen through the charade of godliness and those who refused to believe any of the charges. The church board split evenly between those who believed Bob could do no wrong and those who demanded he resign or retire immediately. The flood gates opened from trickle to flood stage as people left in greater and greater numbers, even though the fight itself was invisible to most; it was sensed if not seen.

In the middle of all this, David learned that he was only one of many staff Pastor Bob had hired and then driven out. Three more would follow in the next two years. As near as David can tell, he is one of only two who stayed in ministry. Some quit the church completely and are still broken and bitter.

The final one to be attacked, the pastor/therapist, eventually came to David seeking forgiveness for shunning him, saying that he had been afraid to be seen with him, as any of them who spoke to him would have been targeted next. He said they knew it was wrong to turn David into a pariah but each of them feared for their own jobs if they did not. He had been a member of the church his entire life and Pastor Bob had been his hero. He had always thought of himself as "one of the chosen," an inviolate member of the inner circle—until Bob attacked him and demanded that he choose between loyalty to him or to his marriage. Only then did David realize that Bob was taking no prisoners; he truly would rather leave scorched earth behind him than retire, and he was bent on destroying any staff who might stay if he was forced out.

In the end, Bob was forced into retirement, all the pastoral staff left, half of the congregation was gone, and the church was a spiritual shambles. The few who knew the details formed a company of the wounded and began to rebuild as they sought a true shepherd. They prayerfully and carefully sought out a new senior pastor who was spiritually and emotionally healthy. God led them to a man who was happy where he was and not looking for such a new and daunting challenge. They got him anyway. Today they are several years into the rebuilding process, have changed course, become healthier, and recently renamed the church to better fit the new direction. There is much good to remember, and relatively few know the inner story. They have come far but the journey is not over as bits and pieces of the old fight surface from time to time. Healing has begun but is not yet complete.

David left the church after the new pastor was hired and his experience has been redeemed. He now says that he has found a new depth of compassion and understanding for the suffering of others, particularly those who have gone through similar experiences.

Hector eventually went to law school in another state and now practices family law in California. He and David talk and email regularly.

Only one out of nineteen former associate or worship pastors is still in ministry.

This experience is far from unique, nor is it even unusual. David still wants to believe that what he experienced was uncommon and that narcissism so strong that it can be classified as Narcissistic Personality Disorder is very rare in pastors. However, he also knows that wanting to believe it does not make it so. Narcissist pastors are not rare. Not at all.

What follows is typical of emails I have received. This is from an associate pastor trying to survive a narcissist senior pastor.

> I am miserable and broken hearted. The trial continues here, weekly intimidation in a meeting with 15 other pastors, continual name-dropping, every goal expressed as the best and greatest, a demand that we be a loving, transparent, empathetic team, yet receiving quite the painful opposite from him, a demand for an undefined "100% loyalty" with a proclamation that "less than 50% of staff" are loyal, yet in a private meeting when I asked him where he saw me on that spectrum, he said, "I don't know." I am amazed at how seasoned pastors, deacons, and leaders can't seem to see, and continue to fall right in line with telling him

what he needs to hear. Forced retirements based on half-truths and lies continue, one every 4–6 months or so. No one in lay leadership seems to notice.

A few years ago, two students from the Christian college where I teach came to me and unloaded their burdens about how they had been forced to leave the church they had grown up in, and their families with them. They spoke of a pastor who verbally attacked anyone who dared disagree with him, who yelled at and physically threatened people, and who declared that disagreeing with him was to disagree with God. He had to be right all the time, flew into a rage at the slightest provocation, and so on. They also described a deep sense of spiritual abuse where the pastor was constantly pulling people in, making them dependent, then pushing them away and blaming them for the push. These two young women were crushed by it, and one was deeply concerned because her mother was still in that church and seemed unable to pull away.

The litany of pain and abuse was sickeningly familiar. I suggested they go online to the Mayo Clinic, one of the most respected medical organizations in the world, and search their website for Narcissistic Personality Disorder. They did, and both said that it was like reading a checklist of how the pastor behaved and related to people. One asked if I would meet with her brother, who was deeply depressed and struggling with the idea that he must have done something to provoke the attack. She also showed the information to her mother, who was still in that church; her mother acknowledged that all of it was accurate, and perhaps it was time to get out. I met with both and assured them that this was not their fault. The mother was so thoroughly victimized that she burst into sobbing when she realized that she was a victim of a ruthless and predatory pastor, saying over and over, "It's not my fault, oh thank you, Jesus, it's not my fault."

If you are caught in a church with a predatory pastor, your choices are more limited than what you may think. You can stay and suffer, stay and force the pastor out, or leave. Pray for him or her, certainly, but even the most optimistic Christian therapists do not hold much hope for repentance or recovery. There really are no other realistic options as the predatory narcissist pastor is going to do everything his way, regardless of the consequences, and will not change in any meaningful way. As much as I hate to say this, there is almost no middle ground. Toxic narcissism has one of the worst treatment records of any mental disorder—even in the extremely unlikely event that the pastor would agree to treatment—as they summarily reject the very idea that they may have a mental illness.

I am not a therapist, but, having worked with churches pastored by predatory narcissists and having been the focus of narcissistic rage myself in my ministry of church conflict interventions, I know the terrible damage they can do. In recent years, several conflicted churches I worked with presented me with pastors who exhibited the symptoms of NPD, some so strongly that there was no question about it—they were very sick. I must also note that I am not qualified to make a formal diagnosis as there are nuances and combinations within any mental illness that elude me. That is why I always consult with a licensed therapist before drawing any conclusions, let alone recommendations to a church about its pastor. I strongly recommend that anyone who works in this arena do the same for it would be a tragedy to label anyone wrongly, even if that label did not have life and career implications.

Narcissists can be chameleons of incredible proportions. They can bend and color themselves to fit almost any situation if it gives them what they need. They are often charming, intelligent, seemingly well-read, and amazingly manipulative and non-empathetic to the problems of others. They are also vindictive, spiteful, and unrelenting in their attacks against their perceived enemies. Since I was working with their churches, they saw me as a threat, but a threat with power over them. As a result, they were overly friendly to me, and several even wanted me to counsel them to help them "be a better pastor." Since that would be a conflict of interest, I sent them to a Christian therapist—who after the third one emailed me with a request to stop sending him narcissist pastors!

Just what constitutes a narcissist? Most of us have in mind the ancient Greek myth of Narcissus, who fell in love with his own reflected image. In that sense, each of us has narcissistic characteristics. Pride trumps humility and we each have an image of ourselves that we try to project to others—we want others to see us as we want to be seen and try to hide our physical blemishes and personal weaknesses. That is much of what makeup, weight loss, and fashion are all about. Some of us show off through our knowledge and vocabulary use (that's me), some preen and prance at the gym showing off their bodies, while others project their image through the car they drive, the home they live in, or expensive toys. Narcissism shows itself through each of us.

What I am writing about is something much more pathological and dangerous. There are degrees of narcissism, and what I am writing of crosses a line into very unhealthy, even dangerous, self-image and compulsive, destructive behaviors at the furthest end of the narcissistic spectrum. It can accurately be called pathological, even malignant.

I need to be clear about something: a large majority of pastors channel their narcissistic tendencies into healthy outlets and truly care for their congregations. I am not writing about them. I am writing about those who have what Sam Vaknin terms "malignant self-love," who feed off others much like a real-life emotional vampire. Vaknin details the life, conflicts, and strivings of a narcissist from the inside—he has been diagnosed with severe NPD himself, something that becomes self-evident if you go online and download his resume—his every accomplishment since junior high school is listed.

I am convinced that everyone in church leadership needs a heightened awareness of the problem, its scope, and its consequences. This includes seminary professors, board members, staff, therapists, and everyone else who works directly with pastors, or is just a member of a church.

2

What Are Narcissism and Narcissistic Personality Disorder?

The narcissist devours people, consumes their output, and casts the empty, writhing shells aside.

—Sam Vaknin, *Malignant Narcissism Revisited*

Narcissism is increasing in our society. "A telling statistic in this respect is that in 1950 twelve percent of American teenagers felt they were important, while at the end of the eighties this percentage had risen to 80 percent."[1] As this is written forty years later it seems to be at an all-time high.

We all have a budding narcissist within us. What does yours look like? Who does not like praise, being told how wonderful, gifted, and talented they are? We all preen a bit when someone compliments us, particularly when it is someone we respect or admire. It feels good to be told you have done an outstanding job or to be publicly rewarded. While there may be a sense of embarrassment that goes with it, underneath it just feels good. That is the narcissist in each of us. For that matter, not all narcissism is bad. It

1. Zondag and van Uden, "My Special Prayer," 3.

18

takes a certain bit of narcissistic self-image to step forward and lead in times of crisis. It takes a strong narcissistic urge to declare that you are the one who can lead the people through uncertain times and decipher the problems that none before you have been able to fully understand. What matters is whether the person with strong narcissistic tendencies can learn from failures as well as successes, something that most of us call accumulated wisdom, and change their behaviors accordingly.

Even those with moderately destructive narcissistic tendencies can operate well when appropriate organizational policies, control systems, counselors, peer review teams, and when both social and legal sanctions are clear and in place.[2] The problem is that the person with extreme narcissism learns little from mistakes, never becomes wise (although he certainly tries to sound it), refuses to accept that policies and rules apply to him, and rarely gains enough self-awareness to understand and counter his own urges. Even if external controls are imposed, he will not trust the reasons given for he believes that he is superior to everyone else and should be controlling them, not the other way around. It is a personality trait that preys on unsuspecting people, manipulates and uses them until they are no longer useful, and then discards them like yesterday's trash.

I first read the myth of Narcissus in junior high or early high school. Though there are two Narcissus myths, the most commonly recognized is the one told by the Greek poet, Ovid.

According to this myth, Narcissus's mother, the nymph Liriope, was worried because of his extraordinary beauty and asked the prophet Teiresias what to do regarding his future.

Teiresias responded, "If he but fail to recognize himself, a long life he may have, beneath the sun . . ."[3] Unfortunately, the nymph Echo fell madly in love with Narcissus when he was sixteen. She secretly started following him and Narcissus sensed it, asking, "Who's there?" Eventually Echo revealed herself. She tried to embrace Narcissus but he stepped away from her, refusing the overture and telling her to leave him alone. Echo was so brokenhearted that she stopped eating and gradually just faded away until nothing but an echo remained of her.

Nemesis, the Goddess of Revenge, heard the story and decided to punish Narcissus. She arranged it so Narcissus would see his reflection in a pond and fall in love with his own image. Ovid writes,

> There as he stooped to quench his thirst another thirst increased. While he is drinking he beholds himself reflected in

2. Sosik, Chun, and Zhu, "Hang On to Your Ego."

3. Ovid, *Metamorphoses*.

the mirrored pool—and loves; loves an imagined body which contains no substance, for he deems the mirrored shade a thing of life to love. He cannot move, for so he marvels at himself, and lies with countenance unchanged, as if indeed a statue carved of Parian marble. Long, supine upon the bank, his gaze is fixed on his own eyes, twin stars; his fingers shaped as Bacchus might desire, his flowing hair as glorious as Apollo's, and his cheeks youthful and smooth; his ivory neck, his mouth dreaming in sweetness, his complexion fair and blushing as the rose in snow-drift white. All that is lovely in himself he loves, and in his witless way he wants himself—he who approves is equally approved; he seeks, is sought, he burns and he is burnt. And how he kisses the deceitful fount; and how he thrusts his arms to catch the neck that's pictured in the middle of the stream! Yet never may he wreathe his arms around that image of himself. He knows not what he there beholds, but what he sees inflames his longing, and the error that deceives allures his eyes. But why, O foolish boy, so vainly catching at this flitting form? The cheat that you are seeking has no place. Avert your gaze and you will lose your love, for this that holds your eyes is nothing save the image of yourself reflected back to you. It comes and waits with you; it has no life; it will depart if you will only go.[4]

Once Narcissus figured out that his love for his own image was futile, he killed himself.

What Ovid wrote well describes the modern narcissist: he is in love with the *image* of himself, a shimmering yet fragile image he projects that has no substance and is ever beyond his grasp; it is thus impossible to love for it has no substance and never becomes real. The true narcissist offers an image of unlimited success, great vision and ideas, but with little substance behind it; what we most often interpret as unbounded self-love is actually self-hatred because the narcissist believes that his true self is worthless and damaged beyond repair. Consequently, it is only the carefully constructed and projected image of self that is deemed worthy of love, though even when love is expressed towards him the narcissist refuses to accept it, as his deep shame constantly reminds him of how worthless he is.

Extreme narcissism describes a twisted form of self-love/self-hatred that dominates all relationships as opposed to Christ's example of "you shall love your neighbor as yourself" (Matt 22:39). Though the narcissist may project an image of loving others, it is a thin and ephemeral manifestation little different from a movie projected onto a screen or seeing oneself in a

4. Ovid, *Metamorphoses*.

mirror—reversed and distorted. Not experiencing the emotion of love, the idea of loving others has no real meaning to them. They then assume that everyone else is like them, hiding behind the glittering mask of a Baroque costume ball. The challenge remains that narcissism is often more about self-hatred and personal loathing than it is about misplaced love of self.

Narcissism is hallmarked by excessive pride, which has been defined as "a self-centered attitude where one is continually expecting or demanding praise and adulation" and envy as "a persisting envy of another person or persons who enjoy special advantages or receive the admiration and recognition that one wants for oneself."[5] One researcher/clinician describes a narcissist as one who "displays excessive sense of self-importance and preoccupation with eliciting the admiration and attention of others."[6] Pride, envy, and self-aggrandizement form a bundle of contradictory defenses against fear of rejection, deep self-loathing, and rage.

Toxic narcissism is a condition that projects overpowering pride and as Proverbs reminds, "Pride goes before destruction, a haughty spirit before a fall" (Prov 16:18), and "The fear of the Lord teaches a man wisdom, and humility comes before honour" (Prov 15:33). In fact, the ancient story of Job compares pride to excrement (Job 20:6–7). Pride is one of the principal spiritual manifestations of Narcissistic Personality Disorder and is one of the seven deadly sins that Christianity has traditionally recognized.

Steven Sandage is professor of psychology of religion and theology at Boston University, and Shane Moe is a licensed family therapist. They write, "[T]he dynamics of narcissistic pride and spirituality are complex, as an intense commitment to the sacred seems to fuel narcissism."[7] This actually makes sense when you realize the depths and urgency of narcissistic neediness: if true narcissists recognize no one but themselves as god, then donning the cloaks of the sacred brings them into a position where the worship of God is also vicarious worship of themselves. Sandage and Moe put it in poignant terms: "Both yearnings for a state of narcissistic perfection and disturbing feelings of incompleteness, emptiness or unworthiness can remain prominent and influential in the minds of those who commence meditation. . . . Spiritual insights and practices prompt both narcissism and shame depending on the relational spirituality of the person involved. On the other hand, authentic forms of spirituality can be part of the transformative

---

5. Capps and Haupt, "The Deadly Sins," 801.

6. Haugk, *Antagonists in the Church*, 61.

7. Sandage and Moe, "Narcissism and Spirituality," 410.

processes that move people from narcissism towards humility and psychological maturity."[8]

The internal tensions between the need for narcissistic perfection and the certain knowledge of their incompleteness accompanied by a deep sense of emptiness creates a never-ending internal war between two mutually hostile and irreconcilable absolutes: the need for complete perfection and the fear of oblivion through failure. Because spirituality represents absolute truths in God and idealized objects such as holy texts and places, narcissists are relentlessly drawn to putting on the image of the sacred through leadership in religious organizations where they are more apt to have their needs met. It is a thin veneer.

Sandage and Moe conclude that the "empirical research to date suggests a nuanced picture of how narcissism relates to individual differences in styles of spirituality and religiosity. Some ways of relating to the sacred (e.g. intrinsic religiosity, perceiving the sacred, religious involvement and interest) seem to be negatively related to narcissism and positively related to community concern. Both intrinsic religiosity and spiritual seeking have also been positively associated with healthy forms of narcissism, while the constructs of . . . extrinsic religiosity can serve to illuminate more unhealthy forms of narcissism embedded in relational spirituality."[9]

In a later study, Sandage and others tied poor or failed adult attachment attempts to spiritual instability, which in turn is tied to spiritual grandiosity. Attachment theory describes how children attach to their parents as a required process for mental health in later life. The failure to attach separates the child from the parent emotionally and can lead to serious mental health issues as the child matures. They state that spiritual instability stems from "an implicit internal working model of mistrust, fear, disappointment and alienation which then often provokes greater felt insecurity and emotional dysregulation." While in some cases it may lead to what has been termed a "dark night of the soul," the fear, insecurity, mistrust, and shame "tend to preclude spiritual growth until they are transformed."[10]

Though they may wish for and even crave deep spirituality, and struggle to make a deep sense of spirituality real, the religiosity of the narcissist exists on the surface and is never made real in the sense of it bringing peace to mind and soul. The true narcissist knows neither.

---

8. Sandage and Moe, "Narcissism and Spirituality," 410.

9. Sandage and Moe, "Narcissism and Spirituality," 412.

10. Sandage et al., "Attachment to God," 3.

EXTREME NARCISSISM IN THE GENERAL POPULATION

Narcissistic Personality Disorder is a disease of extremes and must be defined to be understood in the context it is used in this book. While there are several psychological tests that can be used to identify incipient NPD, they all have at their center the criteria stated in the *Diagnostic and Statistical Manual of Mental Disorders IV* and the newer *DSM-5* published by the American Psychological Association. They are easy to understand and to the point:

Diagnostic Criteria for Narcissistic Personality Disorder

Narcissistic Personality Disorder: A pervasive pattern of grandiosity (in fantasy or behavior), need for admiration, and lack of empathy, beginning by early adulthood and present in a variety of contexts, as indicated by five (or more) of the following:

1. Has a grandiose sense of self-importance (e.g., exaggerates achievements and talents, expects to be recognized as superior without commensurate achievements).

2. Is preoccupied with fantasies of unlimited success, power, brilliance, beauty, or ideal love.

3. Believes that he or she is "special" and unique and can only be understood by, or should associate with, other special or high-status people (or institutions).

4. Requires excessive admiration.

5. Has a sense of entitlement (i.e., unreasonable expectations of especially favorable treatment or automatic compliance with his or her expectations).

6. Is interpersonally exploitative (i.e., takes advantage of others to achieve his or her own ends).

7. Lacks empathy: is unwilling to recognize or identify with the feelings and needs of others.

8. Is often envious of others or believes that others are envious of him or her.

9. Shows arrogant, haughty behaviors or attitudes.[11]

The DSM standards apply to pathological narcissism but also provide an excellent guide for laypersons to better understand what extreme

---

11. American Psychiatric Association, *DSM-5*, 669–70.

narcissism is and how to identify it. These are not phases through which one may pass on the way to a healthier outlook but instead are pathological drives that the narcissist believes are normal while knowing deep inside that they are not. He is compelled. As a friend commented after forgiving narcissistic abuse, "This isn't something he does; it's who he is. It's sort of like Martin Luther responding to his accusers when he said, 'Here I stand. I can do no other.' I pity him."

No one knows for certain what the percentage of people with actual Narcissistic Personality Disorder is in the general population, but it seems to be low. Most estimates range between 0.5 percent and 2.2 percent. The DSM-5 has a higher top number of approximately 6 percent[12] but that higher number may be skewed by the fact that NPD is identifiable in patients seeking mental health treatment at a rate of more than 16 percent. However, those with diagnosable NPD almost never are seeking treatment for their narcissism!

As was stated earlier, everyone has a narcissist within them. It is how these tendencies are channeled that produces a healthy or malignant outcome. In contrast to the negative descriptions of the nine diagnostic criteria, healthy narcissism can be described this way:

1. Realistic self-appraisal of abilities and limitations.

2. An ability to tolerate criticism and rejection as well as approval and praise.

3. Grandiose fantasies that motivate achievement.

4. An ability to internally control one's sense of power and constructive aggression.

5. A balanced sense of entitlement relative to others.

6. Possession of empathy and compassion. An appreciation of commitment and mutuality.

7. An ability to tolerate feelings of self-conscious emotions (envy, shame, pride) and inferiority and humiliation.[13]

The problem of NPD appears to be growing, particularly in the sense of entitlement that permeates North American society. According to Christopher Lasch in *The Culture of Narcissism*, the growth of bureaucracy, where many narcissistic personalities thrive, coupled with the decline in

---

12. American Psychiatric Association, *DSM-5*, 670.

13. Adapted from Ronningstam, *Identifying and Understanding the Narcissistic Personality*.

institutional authority, has opened space for nontoxic and toxic narcissism to thrive. The roles of fathers, teachers, and preachers are being eroded as authority figures and have lost much of their credibility in public scandals, while therapists have replaced religion and its moral constraints. From the therapist's office, love has been defined as "the fulfillment of the patient's emotional requirements."[14]

If love is defined as meetings one's emotional requirements whatever they may be, then this is indeed narcissism fulfilled for the love of self is a direct contrast to Christ's teaching, "No one has greater love than this, to lay down one's life for one's friends" (John 15:13). Not that loving oneself is wrong. After all, we am commanded to love our neighbors as much as we love ourselves. The problem is that narcissistic self-love is a mask, a deception to cover self-hatred and feelings of worthlessness of such intensity that there is little to no room for others. Giving up one's place in a long line is uncommon. Giving up one's life for another is unthinkable to those see themselves as the center of everything and who constantly demand to know what is in it for them—they simply see themselves as being too indispensable for something as unproductive as self-sacrifice.

While it is unthinkable for themselves, they will speak with great admiration and sentimentality of those who do give up everything in pursuit of a life of service to others and even urge others to follow suit. It is the *appearance* of the self-sacrifice of ministry that is part of the larger attraction. In reality, they regularly sacrifice others to meet their own needs. They seek security and will ask, "What are the pay, health benefits, housing allowance, and pension benefits that can be expected as a pastor?" Their pride has a way of slipping into conversation in the mistaken belief that they are showing a version of humility and self-sacrifice. One narcissist pastor regularly boasted how he had negotiated with God—he told God that he would be a pastor if God would agree that he would never have to move—apparently believing that God wanted him to be a pastor so badly that he had the power side in the negotiation! Of course, God agreed—what other choice was there? While it was intended to show the love and compassion of God for this poor man who desperately did not want to move to another place, it was really about him and how important he was to God.

Sigmund Freud once described the narcissistic individual as someone who was focused on "self-preservation . . . highly independent, extroverted, not easily intimidated, aggressive and unable to love or commit in close intimate relationships."[15] Freud was right, but only in a limited sense. He

14. Lasch, *The Culture of Narcissism*, 11–13.

15. Campbell and Miller, eds., *The Handbook of Narcissism*, 5.

did not detect what we will describe as covert or introverted narcissists who fly beneath the radar under a cloak of shyness and veiled humility. For that matter, extreme narcissism often is part of other mental diseases and has been connected to bipolar disorder, substance misuse, depression, and anorexia nervosa.[16]

To the narcissist, reality is self-constructed, self-protective, and self-feeding. Some narcissists have been found to focus on appearances to the neglect or even complete denial of their inner needs. Their self-image is often built on how they look. They will spend countless hours in a gym working out and checking their bodies in a mirror, and even spend every cent they have on plastic surgery to gain what they believe to be perfection. But perfection is always just one more workout or surgery away.

One spectacular example of this is a young man who wants a perfect athletic body, but without the time and commitment of going to the gym, working out, and watching his diet. Instead, he has had more than thirty plastic surgeries to place implants throughout his body that make him look like a body builder but his "muscles" are nothing more than sacks of silicone. While narcissists may look in the mirror and see the symmetry of perfection, they know it's all fake in the same way that they know their personas of competence and power are fake. In other words, their attempts at physical perfection contribute to a greater sense of being inadequate.

However, not many ministers are that seriously into their own deceptions in terms of physical beauty. Why? Many believe they are better looking than others simply as a matter of course.

Ministry is one of the most challenging of professions and the dropout rate for newer clergy is high. Richard Krejcir has been reporting on trends in ministry for more than twenty years. He writes, "Most statistics say that 60% to 80% of those who enter the ministry will not still be in it 10 years later, and only a fraction will stay in it as a lifetime career. Many pastors—I believe over 90 percent—start off right with a true call and the enthusiasm and the endurance of faith to make it, but something happens to derail their train of passion and love for the call."[17] Narcissists in particular would seem susceptible to the pressures, inconsistencies, and frustrations of pastoral ministry, even though they find it fascinating and attractive.

Krejcir argues that the day-to-day trials they must face where they are required to act in ways contrary to their nature extract emotional, relational, and financial tolls that are simply beyond their abilities to bear. A therapist will label this as "narcissistic injury" while the narcissist calls it depression

---

16. Tyrer, ed., *Personality Disorders*, 31.

17. Krejcir, "What is Going On with Pastors in America?"

or burnout. He or she may seek help for these self-diagnoses, but never for their underlying foundations of narcissism. Burnout is acceptable as it can be explained away as giving everything to the insatiable demands of ministry until there is nothing left to give, while ministry demands even more. Their depression is very similar and has the same roots. No matter how hard they have tried or how much they have sacrificed, people are always critical and unwilling to accept their superiority. There can be nothing wrong with them—depression and burnout, in this case both forms of victimhood, are always the result of others not appreciating them or their many gifts and hard work.

Narcissists are highly limited in accessing and expressing feelings, often showing wild swings between irrational rage and overemotional sentimentality. The problem at the core is that they do not actually experience a wide array of feelings, even though they must appear to and act like it. While healthy people have a full emotional range of A to Z, the narcissist, while mimicking the full range, only experiences a range of A to B or, as one wag put it, they experience the full range of emotions from A to Z, but without the intervening letters. They do not understand or experience love at more than a superficial level, they do not understand grief in others, nor are they able to experience empathy or compassion.

In fact, most of their projected emotions are an act designed to get what it is they need most: admiration and adulation from others as a means to control them. Kealy and Rasmussen write that the reason behind this vacuum is the vacuum itself: there is no real self underneath the psychological exoskeleton of narcissism.[18] We all have masks of various types that we project to others, but behind the mask of the narcissist is nothing at all like what is projected, much like pulling back the curtain to reveal the inadequate, sniveling being operating the controls of the great and mighty Oz. Thus, any feelings of tenderness or dependence, which the narcissist deems to be weakness, are interpreted as threats to be warded off.

The ability to function within the norms of accepted social graces is a challenge for the narcissist. As clergy they must act in ways that are strongly contrary to their natures. That they can do so a majority of the time gives credit to their acting abilities, but these norms tend to crack and crumble quickly under the stresses of feeling threatened and unappreciated. In particular, they do not understand and will not abide by the normal understandings of personal boundaries, which they cross at will while expecting their own sense of boundaries to be respected.

18. Kealy and Rasmussen, "Veiled and Vulnerable," 365.

Narcissists strive for power and control to bolster their deficiencies in the area of feelings and to counter the gaping abyss of toxic shame that both fuels them and threatens their destruction. They will often resort to rage to cover or protect themselves from a perceived slight or to restore their sense of power when they feel humiliated. It is common for the narcissist to explode over seemingly inconsequential slights or disagreements, and to smolder with rage. We as Christians often believe and behave as if everyone will respond to authentic love, which is a naïve proposition with the narcissist and his brother, the sociopath. No change can occur in either character or personality until control is relinquished, but control and power are so central to the narcissist that the thought of surrendering it is too terrifying even to contemplate and is immediately shoved aside. The narcissist uses power and manipulation as tools to control other people and keep them at a safe emotional distance, which in turn protects the narcissist from being used and discarded in the same manner that he uses and discards others.

This places a narcissistic pastor or church leader in direct opposition to Jesus, who said, "I am among you as one who serves" (Luke 22:27). The narcissist serves no one but himself unless he sees a personal benefit in serving others; in that case, the service lasts only as long as the benefit is strong enough to overcome what he sees as the humiliating self-abasement of serving. The narcissist serves to have his own needs met at the expense of others and expects to be served, and not to serve others more than is absolutely necessary.

While narcissists may be mentally sharp and intellectually alert, they do not have normal connections between emotion and logic; rather, their minds operate like computers in a constant balancing of advantages and disadvantages of various actions and relationships. While they may be looking closely at another person and are seemingly engaged in their story, they are matching behaviors with body language and facial expressions for future use; they are unable to perceive that individual as a bundle of emotions and needs or connect at an emotional level. In other words, their ability to read people and manipulate them is extremely high but their emotional intelligence and sensitivity are equally low.

Simon Baron-Cohen is Professor of Experimental Psychology and Psychiatry at the University of Cambridge. In *The Science of Evil*, Baron-Cohen writes, "He has no idea that his behavior only drives others farther away, and when they avoid him, he takes this as confirmation that they are bad people, that the problem is with them rather than him."[19] Applied to the narcissist, he expects others to befriend him because of who he is, but he has

19. Baron-Cohen, *The Science of Evil*, 90.

no need to befriend others unless they earn it. In fact, at least one narcissist describes other people as nothing more than 3-D cartoon characters. The implications of that statement are stunning.

One of the most prominent theories of the development of narcissism is that it is the result of being denied love and acceptance at a crucial juncture in a child's life. Whether through not caring, inattentiveness, preoccupation, or intentional cruelty, parents may reject the child at the very moment when rejection is deadliest to the child's healthy emotional development. The core of the child begins to die at that moment, unnoticed and unmourned. This wounding is invisible to the parents, who may believe that they are doing exactly the right things when in reality their response to the child's neediness is deadly to the child's emotional development. For example, a parent may not acknowledge their child's success and may even criticize or belittle it, believing that they are helping the child learn humility. To the parent it is a worthy lesson, but to the child it is a devastating rejection of all that is good in her.

Some parents use their children as sources of their own self-aggrandizement, reliving (or fulfilling fantasies of) high school athletic prowess or academic grandeur. They demand that the child be outstanding in athletics or academics in ways that they never could in order to fulfill their own narcissistic needs; the child is nothing more than the access point. This type of behavior exhibits an underlying level of insanity that confuses children in greater proportion than if the parents were suffering from a nervous breakdown. In other words, it is safer for the child if the parent suffers emotional collapse than if the parent is a narcissist and attempting to have their needs met vicariously through the accomplishments of their children. The parental façade of respectability and sanity only causes confusion in the child who then adopts narcissism as a survival strategy. Psychiatrist Alexander Lowen writes in *Narcissism: Denial of the True Self*, "The narcissist faces the risk of being overwhelmed by feelings of going wild, crazy, or mad, should his defense of denial break down. This is especially true of anger. Every narcissist is afraid of going crazy, because the potential for insanity is in his personality. This fear reinforces the denial of feelings, creating a vicious cycle."[20]

The covert (also known as shy or hidden) narcissist is perhaps the most dangerous because he is camouflaged so well that he tends to escape detection as his more extroverted peers grab the headlines. He is also the most self-destructive. Hessel Zondag recently retired as lecturer in the Psychology of Religion at the University of Tilburg in The Netherlands. In a study of Dutch clergy, he noted that vocational dissatisfaction and burnout

20. Lowen, *Narcissism*, 155.

are so prevalent among clergy who suffer from covert narcissism that they have a higher risk of suffering from stress-related illnesses, have an inability to share and empathize with their colleagues and often do not feel they are as successful in their ministry—even if they are constantly showered with accolades and a growing congregation. They often over-estimate their own abilities and performance, have a lax attitude towards professional ethics, and are notorious for violating personal boundaries. Narcissistic pastors will be those who seek the applause of a public ministry while hoping to avoid suffering because it will not fill their need for admiration.[21]

NARCISSISM AND THE ROLE OF CLERGY

Clergy lead in the drama of worship, play pivotal roles in the lives of people at the emotionally critical times of weddings, baptisms, and funerals, and Sunday by Sunday proclaim—and interpret—the Word of God. While a majority of clergy sincerely pursue the pathway of Christ, for the narcissist it's all an act but one that, as contradictory as it seems, *he believes that he believes in.* While this may explain why a narcissist would be drawn to the position of pastor/preacher, many of these actions are in direct contrast to the image of God presented in 1 Corinthians 13, which describes the ulti-mate love of God: "It does not insist upon its own way; it is not irritable or resentful; it does not rejoice in wrongdoing, but rejoices in the right. Love is patient: love is kind; love is not envious or boastful or arrogant or rude truth. It bears all things, believes all things, hopes all things, endures all things" (1 Cor 13:4–7). The narcissist may believe this intellectually but, not having experienced love, cannot conceive of love in the ways that non-narcissists do; there is no internalization, no "head to heart" connection and so he behaves just the opposite under pressure.

God requires our love and worship, but the true narcissist cannot love more than superficially. Scripture declares that we exist to glorify God. In Micah 6:8 we also read these clear and uncompromising words: "He has shown you, O mortal, what is good. And what does the LORD require of you? To act justly and to love mercy and to walk humbly with your God." The narcissist often sees godlike qualities in himself, which is contrary to all of Christian and Jewish Scripture.

Some have said that God is a narcissist and have specifically stated that Jesus was the biggest narcissist of all. After all, they argue, Jesus was just a man who claimed he could forgive sins and perform miracles, and eventu-ally stated the he and God were one. The point they miss and that undercuts

21. Zondag, "Just Like Other People," 427–28.

the foundations of their argument is that true narcissists do not experience love or empathy, both of which are foundational to compassion. Donald Capps wrote a satirical piece titled "God Diagnosed with Narcissistic Personality Disorder" for the journal *Pastoral Psychology.* Capps "diagnosed" God as suffering from NPD because God can be shown from Scripture to have exhibited all nine of the diagnostic markers for the condition.

Capps concludes however, that, unlike a narcissist, God has true empathy for the world he has created, such that it "more than rivals that of any human being." God has and shows true compassion, "not wishing that any should perish" (2 Pet 2:9). Capps concludes with the premise that the most valuable test for extreme narcissism revolves around this question: Does the person in question believe and act as if they are God?[22] That is a question that many will bridle at, but deep inside the true narcissist sees himself as godlike and God as a terrifying rival. And therein lies what may be the greatest danger of all: the narcissist does not truly see God as loving, caring, and forgiving, but instead understands God as a terrifyingly powerful rival to be diminished. We will return to this later.

Extreme narcissism is typified by a greatly exaggerated sense of self-importance and power, rigidity, the inability to admit error, a sense of personal greatness, the use of power to manipulate and control others, an inability to feel or express remorse, a lack of empathy for others, and an inability or refusal to forgive.[23] Overt narcissist pastors are highly competitive, may be charismatic and charming, and may initially attract followers. Eventually, though, the self-destructive cycle kicks in as they begin to feel threatened, which results in tearing the followers down as a means of bolstering their own fragile egos.[24] Thus they create their own problems: they attract followers as part of their deep need for admiration and often charismatic image, but then attack those same followers and drive them away, creating the need for more followers. It should not be a surprise, then, that the narcissist trusts no one as all his closest confidantes are in a continual state of flux with the exception of those who attach and subjugate themselves to the narcissist to meet their own wounded emotional needs. These are his bodyguards and acolytes. He sees them as pathetic but useful creatures who are to stand between him and outside threats.

However, it is a one-way loyalty. No matter how long they have been with him or how unswerving their loyalty, they are expendable. Just like any bodyguard, they are expected to "take a bullet for the boss" and always

22. Capps, "God Diagnosed with Narcissistic Personality Disorder."

23. Lerner, *The Object of My Affection Is in My Reflection*, 12–13.

24. Hotchkiss, *Why is it Always About You?*, 125.

watch for and defend his well-being, but "the boss" has no compunctions about sacrificing them to protect himself, or about attacking them directly at any time and for any reason he chooses. Though his "bodyguards" may be loyal to the bitter end, even they, his closest associates, are vulnerable—if the narcissist's ship is sinking and no one can save it, he will attempt to torpedo every other ship in range, including theirs. In one case, a narcissist pastor was being forced into resigning. He assured his executive that he was protecting him at the same time he was urging the board to fire the executive for incompetence.

It is commonly thought that narcissists are in love with themselves, but appearances are deceiving. A therapist who works with celebrity narcissists concludes, "Narcissism has more to do with self-*loathing* than with self-love."[25] In other words, while the narcissist pursues greatness and believes he deserves it simply because of who he is, he hates himself as unworthy and unlovable as yesterday's garbage. This constant internal tension must be released in some way, which brings on certain self-destructive tendencies, such as engaging in forbidden sexual encounters or drug and alcohol abuse. In order to counter this self-destructive tendency, the narcissist adopts an image of tremendous self-confidence coupled with stories of great success that he tells himself and others in never-ending attempts to attach himself to those he sees as having greater power and success.

It is the self-created image that the narcissist loves, even though he knows it is false, and he creates it to hide the real person whom he hates: himself. Though narcissists are the original Manchurian candidates in terms of seeking pastoral postings, there are signs along the way that scream for attention and action, which we will visit several times but from different directions.

Forgiving

Narcissists find forgiving those who they feel have slighted and wronged them nearly impossible. In fact, it is safe to say that they never forgive any slight, real or imagined. Why? Forgiveness is constructed on the ability to empathize, an ability that the narcissist does not have. Second, forgiveness opens the way to a deeper relationship where one can again be vulnerable, which the narcissist cannot accept as vulnerability is too threatening. With empathy comes the ability to release anger and resentment in healthy ways. The covert narcissist may appear to be vulnerable and empathetic to the pain of others and may even declare it, but will quickly shy away at any attempt

25. Raskin and Hall, "A Narcissistic Personality Inventory (NPI)."

to probe it. Now place that reality into the person of pastor, and the depth of the problem begins to emerge. Without forgiveness, the power of the church is greatly reduced to be a witness to the world of the transformative power of God. A church leader who cannot offer the grace of forgiveness destroys the central message of Christianity—the grace of the cross.

In order to forgive we must first believe that someone has wronged us, but we cannot forgive if we remain wrapped up in our pain and outrage. The gateway to forgiving is being able to experience empathy for those who have done us harm, and you cannot truly forgive if you cannot develop empathy for those who harmed you. Let's face it. Jesus commanded his followers to forgive and we expect our clergy to be paragons of forgiveness and mercy. The narcissistic pastor knows neither forgiveness nor mercy except as they may fit his own agenda. The failure to embody forgiveness and reconciliation by the pastor will be reflected in the members of the congregation, who will learn to mimic that same lack of empathy or leave the church, thereby destroying the spiritual foundations on which churches are built. Not only is there an inability to forgive, the narcissist experiences tremendous rage at the slightest suggestion he *should* forgive, let alone that he should apologize and ask for forgiveness.[26]

Offenses against the narcissist, real or imagined, are intolerable and are never forgiven! Years after the event, no matter how small the slight, his rage seethes just below the surface as strong as it was at first. Likewise, telling a narcissist that he should seek forgiveness is likely to trigger explosive rage in the overt narcissist and depression in the covert narcissist, for the narcissist is never wrong. Here, feeling wrongly accused, which the narcissist understands as an attack on the core of who he or she is, compels him or her to seek revenge in order to rebalance the scales of justice—except that rebalancing to the narcissist is never equal. The scales of justice must always be skewed in his favor. Narcissists get mad—and they get even!

Not only is the extreme narcissist generally unable to forgive, he is unable to even consider what it means to forgive, which is to let go of all pain, animosity, fear, and the desire for revenge, eventually replacing them with feelings of benevolence and even love.[27] Psychotherapist Nathan Schwartz-Salant writes in *Narcissism and Character Transformation*: "In fact, narcissistic rage has a special, unforgiving quality. It is striking how this rage can live on in the unconscious, seemingly untouched by events that follow the wounding situation. Years after the fact, one can be astonished to experience the rage anew, as if the precipitating event had just taken place."

26. Sandage et al., "Seeking Forgiveness," 26.
27. Puls, *The Road Home*, 43.

Schwartz-Salant goes on to state that narcissistic rage coupled with unrelenting envy at the success of others is what holds the narcissist together and gives him or her the energy to function.[28]

Envy

It is said that imitation is the sincerest form of flattery. The narcissist has imitating what he admires in others down to an art form that is intended to gain power, wealth, and prestige, thus raising him to the level of the envied person. Another form of envy is the desire to possess what someone else already has by taking it from him or her or demanding it be given to them as something they are entitled to. The narcissist is envious of anyone who he sees as having greater power, prestige, or possessions, and he wants them all. That envy then drives him to imitate or copy those things the envied person has done to give the narcissist the same limelight and prestige, often by diminishing the envied person.

Psychiatrist Regis Acosta writes, "Given that its manifestations range from the constructive imitation of other's accomplishments to the spiteful, malicious wishes for others' misfortunes (e.g., Salieri and Mozart), or attempted acts of mutilation or murder (e.g., Tonya Harding and Nancy Kerrigan), envy is certainly worth considering by psychiatrists." He goes on to say, "Examining the connection of this seemingly imperative desire—on the part of the envious person—of ridding another person of his or her possessions or attributes and its connections with narcissism is . . . given the destructive nature of envy . . . its potential for breeding criminal acts . . ."[29]

There is little that is original in all of this, as the narcissist truly does not often have the imagination for originality. He sees and takes the easy way of copying what others have done and claiming it as his own. He wants desperately to be "cutting edge" and "world class" but often does not have the capacity to achieve either. His problem is that copying what others have done is not original, he does not own it, and he knows it. The result, then, is shame that is covered by rage in the form of indignation at anyone who would dare challenge his claim of originality or his right to power and prestige.

---

28. Schwartz-Salant, *Narcissism and Character Transformation*, 41.

29. Acosta, "Envy—The Forgotten Narcissistic Issue," 52.

Revenge

Not only does the narcissist not forgive, he takes revenge. No slight can go unpunished. Indeed, no good deed goes unpunished if the narcissist sees the person doing it as a threat. In extreme cases, he will name people who have crossed him from the pulpit and tear them to shreds. In one case, an associate pastor was attacked so viciously and unexpectedly during Sunday morning worship that he attempted suicide and was placed in a mental institution for a time. He has never recovered from the public humiliation, has left all ministry, and is trying to rebuild his life. Another associate was on a mission trip in Asia. He returned home only to learn that his senior pastor had called an emergency meeting of the board and demanded that he be fired.

Not having the moral courage to do it himself, the senior pastor then had others tell the associate of his professional demise when he returned home. His office had already been cleared and his property was in neatly packed boxes. As of this writing the terminated associate pastor does not know why he was fired or why it was done with no chance to respond. When you understand the power of narcissism, the reasons it was done in secrecy are not difficult to decipher. This way, the fired pastor had no chance to challenge the senior pastor or refute any of allegations against him, both of which would have placed the senior pastor in the position of having to offer proof that he may not have had.

Given their appearance of normalcy and their ability for masking their true intentions, it can be difficult to accept or believe that everything the narcissist does is about gaining and holding onto power and prestige. However, threaten their power or prestige and you will face a rage that is as overpowering as it is unpredictable. Even though you might suspect it is coming, the powerful torrent is like being caught in a raging flash flood and all you can do is ride it out and pray you don't drown.

Decision-making

The narcissist CEO (or pastor) has a problem: all decision-making centers on them. They may appoint teams and have other staff, but the final decision in almost everything must be theirs. This keeps them bogged down by the small things, leading to frustration at not having time for the more important things. Even though they know controlling all of the details is ultimately self-defeating, they can't seem to help themselves. It is common for a church governing body to suggest that the senior pastor delegate various duties to others, but any delegation will be truncated by the need to control. When faced with a recalcitrant board of elders or deacons, they will fall back on the theological argument that the pastor is the ecclesiastical head of the church and is directly connected to God. Therefore the pastor should always have the final say. One pastor proclaimed from the pulpit that challenging him was the same as challenging God—and no one protested! Narcissists will also do everything they can to manipulate information and people prior to a board meeting to circumvent any resistance and guarantee the wanted outcome. Those who resist—and do not repent and beg forgiveness when confronted—become the enemy and are marginalized or attacked directly. If possible, he will have them removed even if they do repent.

Delegating authority

No one person can do everything well, but never tell that to the narcissist. Seeing himself as superior to all others, the narcissist simply assumes that he knows more. When he doesn't, he will simply lie about it with great, but often rambling, authority (something called "word salad"). Narcissists will "delegate" to others when pressured, but without giving proper authority to execute the task. Or will place so many limitations that it is impossible to carry out the mission. This leaves those with the task in the position of constantly going to the pastor for more authority or approval of the decision they want to make but that is not in their authority. In fact, these pastors rarely delegate anything except the most menial tasks. If they do delegate, the product and the individual or group producing it will be criticized and found to be deeply flawed. The goal is to keep everyone subservient while taking credit for their work. In one case, an associate pastor made a suggestion to the narcissist senior pastor, only to have it flatly and thoroughly rejected as stupid. Three weeks later the senior pastor introduced the idea with great fanfare as his own to the entire congregation.

It is not that narcissists do not believe that there is no "I" in team; it's that they don't believe in teams.

Impatience and Inability to Listen

One of the most common indicators is the fact that the narcissist rarely converses with you. Instead, what may start as a conversation quickly turns into a lecture from him to you, stated with great authority, no matter what the topic (unless he has no interest in it—or you—at which time you are abruptly dismissed). In its more benign forms the lecture is patronizing, condescending, or even teaching. However, disagreeing with him usually changes the tone to either an attack that is badgering, sadistic, humiliating, and full of rage and indignation, or your abrupt dismissal. This being the case, the narcissist is nothing if not self-contradictory. One moment she may be raging at you with the venom of a spitting cobra and the next will want a hug while telling you that all of this is for your own good, and then acting as if it never happened (as happened to Pastor David). While most of us find this behavior baffling, narcissists see it as normal and acceptable and cannot understand why anyone would take offense or be upset and hurt by it. After all, they are superior beings; we should be grateful for the shared wisdom!

Since they see their time as being much more important than the time of others, they are impatient and able to listen to others only for short periods (unless the person they are listening to has much greater prestige, power, or wealth, at which point their attention spans lengthen dramatically). They will then take over the conversation, steer it towards themselves regardless of the topic, and begin giving orders to or lecture the hapless listener. Once he is finished, regardless of whether the issue is disposed of, he will dismiss the other person or simply get up and leave.

Deferential and Preferential Treatment

Narcissists truly believe that they are due deferential and preferential treatment due to their uniqueness and elevated gifts. In their "specialness," they have no compunctions about walking to the head of the line and demanding the best table in a restaurant or even sitting at the head table at a banquet, flying first class even though the church can't afford it, expecting discounts on food and services, requiring the best room in a hotel, and so on. The extrovert narcissist expects to be invited to dinner and relishes the occasion, while the introverted or covert narcissist expects and relishes the invitation but will almost always refuse—all the while feeling shut out of the social life of the church.

Feeling threatened or intimidated by other talented staff

As we have seen, the narcissist will do whatever is necessary to destroy a perceived threat, even when the threat is not real. The narcissist pastor is likely to turn on the most talented underling and use him or her as a scapegoat for his own failures and insecurities, as that person most often represents the greatest threat. In fact, anyone who gets attention and praise will be seen as a threat. When the threat is perceived as great enough, that threat must be eliminated quickly and by all possible means, which often means all-out emotional assault on the targeted "threat." The assault will be unrelenting and without remorse, even though the narcissist will proclaim loud and long how bad he felt at being forced to do what he did.

The shy narcissist is more likely to use subtler means, such as undercutting the targeted person, planting doubts about their loyalties and motives, and slowly cutting them off from what they love doing. The targeted person becomes confused and discouraged as they are generally unaware of being intentionally sabotaged, and eventually leave for more promising pastures.

Either way, the threat is eliminated.

Needing to be the best and brightest in the room

This is an interesting exercise in self-promotion as the narcissist, pastor or not, is rarely the brightest or most accomplished person in the room. This is where their ability to damn people with faint praise is most useful. It is also where they are most likely to make astonishing claims about their own successes. Both the overt and covert types are adept at this, but the covert type expresses it at a lower decibel level. The covert type is more likely to hold court in a corner and interject his destructive poison against his latest scapegoat with something along the lines of, "I had high hopes for her, but . . ." He may claim authority with a phrase such as, "I've studied this my entire life and . . ."

Narcissistic vulnerability, which is often seen in clergy, leads to a characteristic defensiveness, which manifests itself in belittling others ("Have you seen the kind of car he drives? Who with any self-respect would drive something like that?") and self-belittling comments ("I've always had ADD but I still manage to read three books every week"), all the time expecting you to contradict the negative and affirm his "specialness." The narcissist often relies on sarcasm and cynicism and is often noticeable for his decided lack of a normal sense of humor or even the ability to engage in a "belly laugh." My experience is that the only time you will see a true narcissist in a belly laugh is when it is at the expense of someone else.

Table 1 summarizes many of the characteristics of narcissism and the ways in which one can recognize a narcissistic personality by some of the more common actions in each of the dispositions that dominate NPD.

TABLE 1: COMMON NARCISSISTIC BEHAVIORS

Exhibi-tionist	Grandi-ose	Self-Centered	Sense of Entitle-ment	Self-Aggran-dizing	Lack of Empathy	Explo-siveness
Actions						
Flaunting money	"I am great!"	Spends great effort on looks	Expects others to pay	Pulls rank on others	Ignores the needs of others	Explosive anger when slighted
Boasts of talents	Nominates self for positions of power	Expectation of favors without repayment	Expects gifts and tributes	Exaggerates personal role in retelling stories	Laughs at problems of others	Takes revenge
Showing off body	Must be center of attention	Takes the best for self but rarely gives to others		Associates self with persons of power or wealth	Belittles problems of others	Never forgives or admits errors
Must have the best	Seeks unearned recognition					

Adapted from David Buss and Lisa Chiodo (1991).

LACK OF EMPATHY

Let's explore the substance and place of empathy in normal human relations a bit more deeply. Empathy is the ability to understand the life and challenges of others and act accordingly. Empathy says that I intellectually understand and emotionally feel your plight. Relationships are built on mutual abilities to empathize with each other. Healthy people understand and even feel the pain of others. Given that humans begin life totally dependent upon others who empathize and care for them at their weakest and most dependent life phases, it is not surprising that this need for empathy is never outgrown. The need to understand other people, and to be understood by them, is never completely removed from healthy individuals. Simply put, we need to love and to be loved.

Theologian David Augsburger argues that in the process of becoming a fully functioning human, "a person internalizes significant others" and through the growing process learns by observing them. Augsburger goes on to say that individuals have codependent needs to mirror the empathic responses needed for relational harmony and to idealize those who have shown them empathy.[30] Many of us idealize one or both of our parents because of how empathic they were—we knew they felt our fear and frustration, and they comforted us. Those who experience this tend to be empathetic themselves. Others have a different experience where little empathy was shown them and tend to be colder and less empathetic to others. The Apostle Paul puts it more succinctly: we are all members of the body of Christ and are dependent on God and one another (1 Cor 12:12–30).

To grow as a balanced individual, one must experience frustration, shame, and rage, while at the same time being supported in an empathetic relationship that neither denies the pain nor seeks to place distance between the empathizer and the individual in pain. The pain is real, and it is okay to acknowledge it as such. In this way, we learn to deal with these occurrences in healthy and constructive ways. A parent may normally offer praise and encouragement to a child, thus feeding the narcissistic tendency, but healthy parenting helps the child place these tendencies into a perspective where they inspire and give motivation but not to the extent where they become compulsive. If this is done well, childish grandiosity can be channelled into more realistic ways of thinking.

It is well established that how we experience and interact with the world has a tremendous influence in how we develop. When someone experiences the world as unavailable, nonempathetic, and withholding understanding, particularly at a critical developmental juncture, he or she is more likely to develop insatiable narcissistic needs. Narcissism is punctuated by a decided, even total, lack of empathy for the pain, discomfort, and grief of others. Seriously, we must accept the fact that the narcissist, while faking it well for a time, has absolutely no empathy for you. He or she sees your pain and grief as opportunities to fill their own needs. While many can mimic empathy extremely well for limited periods of time, the harsh reality is this: narcissists just don't care about your pain unless it can benefit them! Like a shark, they home in on the source of blood in the water. They have no compunctions about indulging their needs while vilifying yours. It's a strange chemistry: pain and rejection only exacerbate their sense of grandiose omnipotence, entitlement, and uniqueness. One narcissist pastor summed it up quite well, however: "Jesus was rejected of men, and so am I."

---

30. Augsburger, *Helping People Forgive*, 75.

It is not uncommon to find grandiose ideas, vulnerability, and fragility simultaneously in a confusing and even paradoxical mix. When narcissists are unable to have grandiose ideas validated, they may experience severe oscillations in their levels of self-esteem and wild swings in mood from elation to devastation and rage to eerie calm in a matter of a few minutes or even seconds. In this sense, extreme narcissism may parallel bipolar disorder, and it is not uncommon for those with NPD to also have bipolar problems.

Both NPD and bipolar disorders are marked by grandiosity, but there are differences. Russ Federman writes in the online version of *Psychology Today*,

> Bipolar grandiosity occurs in conjunction with multiple other symptoms that accompany hypomania and/or mania. What's important is that hypomanic and/or manic symptoms, including grandiosity, are all mood-phase specific. As such they do not endure over time and they certainly are not present during bipolar depression where low self-esteem tends to be the dominant filter through which most self-appraisal occurs.
>
> Conversely, the narcissist's grandiose self-perception is more enduring. The experience of superiority is called into play with enough frequency that it's an integral aspect of the individual's self-perception. Consider interacting with two different individuals: one with bipolar hypomanic grandiosity and the other with narcissistic grandiosity. The interactions may actually have a similar feel to them. Perhaps the one identifiable distinction is that the bipolar individual is usually experiencing strongly elevated energy along with elevated mood whereas the grandiose narcissist will experience their inflation on a psychic level, but he or she may not feel like they have three times their normal amount of physical energy.
>
> One last key distinction: unless there is a co-morbid psychosis or delusional disorder, the narcissist's grandiosity does not usually reflect delusional properties. The messianic, Einsteinian, reincarnational manifestations of grandiosity mostly occur during manic psychosis and are not present in typical narcissism. And if, in unusual circumstances, the narcissist does experience delusional self-perceptions, then he or she lives at the more extreme end of the narcissistic personality continuum.[31]

The inability of the narcissist pastor to feel or understand the emotional lives of others creates an unbearable tension between what he knows should be and what is. Empathy is of primary importance in the process of

---

31. Federman, "The Relationship Between Narcissism and Bipolar Disorder."

healing psychic or emotional wounds, as it offers affirmation and confirmation by modeling the behavior expected by a mature, caring human being. To be authentically empathetic is to be able to connect with other human beings at their deepest emotional levels. The narcissistic mirror of empathy always shatters. It is often a good act, but an act, nonetheless.

THE FORMATION AND ROLE OF SHAME

We often speak knowingly about shame, but shame is more complex than many believe. The origins of shame are found in how well we attach as infants and children to our parents, and how that attachment is returned. If we are successful in establishing a warm and nurturing relationship with our parents and our efforts to please them and explore our world are met with love, encouragement, and understanding, unhealthy shame is less likely to form. Toxic shame tends to form and establish itself when attachment attempts are rejected and our efforts and growing in understanding are met with criticism and rejection, and even violence. This rejection leaves us in a state of isolation and abandonment where we must cope by ourselves. If the rejection is severe enough, the child may become immobilized and frozen emotionally, stunting and even stopping emotional development. We may abandon further attachment attempts after repeated rejections by those we are dependent upon, which reinforces the sense of isolation and unworthiness. Shame then allows a strong sense of being accused but accused of what we do not know.

Psychiatrist Curt Thompson writes in *The Soul of Shame*, "The notion of being accused, in its most malignant form, leads to a state symbolized by another word: contempt. This word represents deep condescension and derision."[32] The accusation, condescension and derision received from outside are then turned inward, changing the fundamental belief of guilt (I did something bad) to toxic shame (I am something bad). It is an assassination of the soul. According to Thompson, the constant resurgence of shame changes neural pathways, in effect rewiring the brain to produce more and stronger inappropriate shame responses.

The narcissistic personality is built on shame: the shame of rejection, the shame of prohibited desires, the shame of knowing that he or she is broken and worthless despite all the trappings of power and wealth they may have accumulated, and the shame of knowing they are not what they project to others. Such deep-seated shame results in contradictory beliefs and behaviors that can be destructive when acted upon, but which are also

32. Thompson, *The Soul of Shame*, 69.

almost irresistible. For example, the narcissist often has a rigid moral code and is quick to condemn all who do not agree, but it is a brittle, shame-based rigidity with which he personally struggles as he feels the urges deep within that he prohibits and condemns in himself and others.

Eventually, what is brittle shatters, leading him to succumb to those urges and experience the vicarious thrill of knowingly doing something he fervently believes is wrong. He justifies it in himself, however, as being a momentary weakness that he gives in to only because of the tremendous pressure he is under. Thus, he sees no contradiction in refusing empathy for others who do the same things he does.[33] After all, if they were as smart as he is, they would not get caught! How then can the narcissist justify it for himself while condemning the same behaviors in others? He sees himself as unique and superior with special needs that others do not have or understand; therefore, the common rules of behavior do not apply to him.

People have a difficult time understanding the paradoxical qualities of the narcissist, particularly that narcissism is more about shame and self-hatred than it is about loving oneself too much—self-aggrandizement and self-promotion are nothing more than a glittering mask covering deep wounds filled with toxic shame and self-hatred. Believing oneself to be broken, ugly, and beyond repair has been described as having "a hole in the soul." Psychiatrist Willem Martens says, "Shame is felt as an inner torment, as a sickness of the soul. It is the most poignant experience of the self by the self, a wound felt from the inside, dividing individuals from both themselves and each other."[34]

Shame encompasses an all-pervasive sense of being flawed and defective as a human being. It holds a sense of worthlessness, of failing, falling short of an idealized self. Shame has been also termed a rupture of the self with the self, which is an inner estrangement where the broken self all but banishes the unbroken self. The narcissist then becomes an object of his own contempt, an object that can't be trusted. This creates an unbearable inner tension that must be defeated. It is so intolerable that the narcissist will do everything within his power not to experience it at all. Shame, which is failure and brokenness personified, is then directed outward and projected onto others. In this, we find the making of the scapegoat that the narcissist must always have nearby. Mistakes and failures can never be "my fault," says the narcissist who cannot be wrong and who never fails; therefore, someone else must always be blamed. When something does go spectacularly wrong, the narcissist vaults into the powerful role of victim, often finding

---

33. Baron-Cohen, *The Science of Evil*, 72.
34. Martens, "Shame and Narcissism," 11.

and preaching from biblical stories of victimization to justify himself. One pastor accused of a sexual offense declared, "Joseph was wrongly accused of sexual indiscretion, but God vindicated him and God will vindicate me!" DNA testing proved otherwise.

The narcissist longs for the ability to empathize, to find grace, and to understand what it is to forgive and mistakes his own unmet needs as a call from God to enter ministry. This can lead to both spiritual perfectionism and shame-based self-punishment. There is often a "holier-than-thou effect" that allows those with intrinsic religious ambitions and practices to feel that they are superior to others because they are attempting to live by a higher moral code. This reflects a reversal of how religious humility is generally understood. It seems that cultivating humility, meaning working at becoming humble, is actually incompatible with humility.[35]

In fact, while measures of humility are difficult to establish, "there is some emerging research supporting connections between humility, spiritual transcendence, and virtues such as gratitude and forgiveness."[36] Spiritual instability, then, tends to make forgiving that much more difficult. As I have noted, narcissists do not understand what humility is, though they often can mimic it quite well under normal conditions; however, the façade shatters during crises when they cannot wiggle out of responsibility for things going wrong.

Narcissistic shame demands to be massaged and soothed, and the call process for clergy unwittingly plays into this demand. Of course, everyone applying will set themselves forth in the best possible light. In interviews the overt narcissists harness their shame energy and funnel it into being full of energy and ideas, friendly to a fault, and have their charm abilities turned up to blazing wattage, while the coverts will act humble but will be determined to impress with their intellectual accomplishments and their abilities to overcome adversity.

Upon being called to a congregation, clergy are often spoken of in terms that sound like they may be the best thing since the original apostles and the narcissist tries his best to live into it. Narcissists often are able to preach effectively (for a time), make friends quickly, and brand the congregation as theirs. However, the friends begin to depart once they realize how one-sided the "friendship" is. Congregants quickly tire at being only a prop in the narcissist's grand play, to be used and then discarded. The problem here is that the narcissist feels entitled to friends without having to do anything to earn their friendship, and shame rears up when he is rejected.

35. Sandage, Paine, and Hill, "Spiritual Barriers to Humility," 9.
36. Campbell and Miller, eds., *The Handbook of Narcissism*, 414–15.

"He feels that he has a right to be treated well, regardless of how he treats others."[37]

Their sense of entitlement gives them the right to "own" you, and it is in this sense of ownership and accompanying entitlement that things begin to fall apart. A television commercial illustrates this well. Two men are riding in a car. One asks the other if he knows any building contractors. The other responds that he knows one. The first man then tells the other to check the background references for three contractors, get bids, and set a start date for the following week.

Narcissistic pastoral friendships are shallow and fleeting unless the pastor is able to see his or her friends as subordinate and useful or too powerful to attempt manipulation. David Kealy and Brian Rasmussen argue in *Journal of Clinical Social Work*, "The self-regulatory deficit of pathological narcissism is not the grandiosity itself, but a secret fragile core that must be warded off from conscious awareness and prevented from discovery by others—and indeed from the self. Maladaptive behaviors serve to protect this weakened part of the self, often with considerable success."[38] To the narcissist, behaviors that drive others away are a normal part of their defense systems to protect their fragile core from outside threats. Friends who are too accomplished are kept at arm's length to monitor and control them, but they are usually seen as a threat and eventually isolated and discarded if they cannot be manipulated into serving the narcissist.

Overt and covert narcissists approach job interviews differently. The overts come in with a grin and a hearty handshake, are full of enthusiasm and have a plan (or so they say) to skyrocket the church into a world-class ministry. They appear confident and brimming with energy. They tend to be charismatic in their approach (which they have studied very carefully and honed to a fine art) and work hard at winning over everyone in the room. They are perceived by interviewers as more successful than non-narcissists, many of whom have great difficulty in singing their own praises where the narcissist not only sings his own praises but also expects the rest of the world to be his backup singers. The overt ones are more outspoken and tend towards the dramatic.

Covert narcissists are far more difficult to spot. Their approach is low-keyed, moderate energy, self-effacing, but confident in their abilities as "servant leaders." They may have a focus on less dramatic areas such as spiritual formation, education, and children. They will hum their own praises, but rarely does it break out into full-throated song. They often have

37. Baron-Cohen, *The Science of Evil,* 88.
38. Kealy and Rasmussen, "Veiled and Vulnerable," 358.

an underdeveloped sense of humor and tend to be the butt of their own jokes. They have a habit of being deeply hurt by perceived sleights and mask themselves behind a wall of humility. Like their overt counterpart, they have a drive to perform in front of larger and larger audiences; they may therefore possess the dream of growing a congregation but not actually have the ability—performance sags over time as they exhaust their limited repertoire of interesting things to say.

The call process is crushing to the rejected narcissist, increasing the intensity of his or her shame. Rejection at this level produces a major crisis in which she will see herself as a complete failure, unworthy of love and respect—but only for a short time. To compensate and defend against overwhelming shame she will then resurrect herself, claim the powerful mantle of victimhood, and place all of the blame on the people who rejected her, for it is obvious that they did not see her spectacular qualities and therefore are not worthy of her. God has something better for her than they could have offered!

While we all have budding narcissists within us, the difference between having narcissistic tendencies and being a true narcissist is huge. Narcissistic Personality Disorder occurs "only when these traits are inflexible, maladaptive, and persisting and cause significant functional impairment or subjective distress . . ."[39]

DISTINGUISHING THE TWO TYPES OF NARCISSISM

There are two primary types of malignant narcissism: overt and covert. Grandiosity and vulnerability are prominent in both, but they are expressed very differently. Both are fueled by shame. While the overt narcissist has no problem expressing his grandiose dreams and claims, the covert narcissist, though having the same inner drives, is more circumspect in expressing them. Professors David Kealy and Brian Rasmussen write, "The grandiose theme encompasses such parallel terms as exhibitionistic, oblivious, phallic, manipulative, and extroverted. This theme emphasizes self-inflation, callousness, and fantasies of superiority. The vulnerable [covert] theme, on the other hand, refers to feelings of helplessness, suffering, and anxiety regarding threats to the self, and reflecting inner feelings of inadequacy, emptiness, and shame. Narcissistic vulnerability involved hypervigilance to insult, and

39. American Psychiatric Association, *DSM-5*, 672.

excessive shyness or interpersonal avoidance in order to retreat from perceived threats to self-esteem."[40]

The behaviors of the covert narcissist are markedly different in many respects from the overt narcissist. In summarizing several researchers, Darren Carr concludes that covert traits include "shyness, constrained affect, appearance of empathy, use of external sources to regulate self-esteem, a pattern of interpersonal conflict leading to anger/hostility and then to shame/depression, giving the impression of labile [easily changed, unstable] mood, interpersonal anxiety (especially in developing relationships), social withdrawal and avoidance. These behaviors are derived from a psychological core organized around grandiose expectations and a sense of entitlement, which is summarily disavowed."[41]

Thus, the covert narcissist will appear to be shy, self-effacing, and humble, denying any form of envy or entitlement, but displaying both. He is much more likely to present himself as but a humble servant compared to his overt counterparts and is likely to proclaim his inadequacies more than his achievements. This is an attempt, often highly effective, to "obscure from easy detection as such, concealed by symptoms of depression, anxiety, work and relationship problems, and indeed by a more elusive presentation. . . . *The self-regulatory deficit of pathological narcissism is not the grandiosity itself, but a secret fragile core that must be warded off from conscious awareness and prevented from discovery by others—and indeed from the self.*"[42] Make no mistake, however; his achievements and glory are what count and his rage, though slower in coming, is unforgettable when unleashed.

Ecclesiastes 1:2 declares, "Vanity of vanities, says the Preacher, vanity of vanities! All is vanity!" That declaration, of course, is a condemnation of all things vain. Yet vanity is a hallmark of the narcissist. For example, being young is to the narcissist is what being beautiful is to a cover girl. The aging process is terrifying and death even worse, so he or she will seek some form of immortality through leaving an indelible personal imprint. Underneath the needs for acclamation are deep and raging currents of depression, painful self-consciousness, a preoccupation with image over substance, and the need to appear vigorous and youthful. Consequently, it is common for the narcissist to follow fashion closely, to work out at the gym, and do whatever he can to project an image of youthful vigor.

40. Kealy and Rasmussen, "Veiled and Vulnerable," 358.

41. Carr, "Relationship among Overt and Covert Narcissism," 23–24.

42. Kealy and Rasmussen, "Veiled and Vulnerable," 357–58 (emphasis in the original).

As stated earlier, there are also instances of those who changed their names to reflect a youthful vigor or a piety they desired to possess. For some reason they seem to think that being named after a saint or biblical figure will confer on them greater authority and prestige, yet it only seems to degrade the saints. Again, their desires and behaviors are often paradoxical to each other. He may brag about wearing Brooks Brothers' suits, but they are often twenty years old and threadbare. One person commented about a narcissistic pastor that he looked great from a distance but was a slob up close.

True narcissists will act on their needs in an impulsive manner similar to an addict craving their drug of choice. The narcissist is an expert at manipulating others in order to get what he or she desires by any means available, particularly deceit, lies, and deviousness. One of the more unnerving traits of narcissists is their ability to lie with absolute and convincing sincerity at one moment, and then say the exact opposite with the same sincerity shortly thereafter—and then flatly deny that they ever said the first thing at all, even if it was said in front of hundreds of people as happened to Pastor David. She will lie about anything and everything as long as it fits her needs. If cornered, she will not admit to lying but may admit to having exaggerated, but "just a little, and only for effect."

Let's further make a distinction between the more benign forms of narcissism and their malignant counterparts. Freud described "the narcissistic type as independent and not easily intimidated," as one who could take on the role of supporting others and being natural leaders.[43] In fact, narcissistic pastors are more the norm than the exception, but the difference is that a majority channel their tendencies into positive organizational frameworks whereas the malignant narcissist is concerned only about himself, sees the organization/church as the means to achieving his or her dreams and sees others as tools to be used and then discarded when no longer needed or useful. The result is that the malignant narcissistic pastor sees the church as existing to fulfill his fantasies of grandiosity and affirm his godlike qualities. Malignant narcissists are filled with a cancerous attitude that destroys any organization in which they work or on which they depend to have their needs for recognition validated, although covert narcissists may be able to survive and deflect their destructive tendencies for many years.

SPIRITUALITY AND NARCISSISM

We expect many things of our pastors. In particular, the commandments of Jesus about loving one another is problematic to the narcissist: "You

43. Lasine, *Knowing Kings*, 25.

shall love your neighbor as yourself" (Matt 19:19) and "Do to others as you would have them do to you" (Luke 6:31) are just part of the pastoral job description. Unfortunately, they are foreign and even incomprehensible to the narcissist. They will recite "love your neighbor" convincingly and often, but really have no idea what that form of love is.

Keith Campbell is department head and professor of psychology at the University of Georgia. His work has been primarily on narcissism and related traits. In noting that there is a vast difference in the ways in which narcissists express their self-love/hate, Campbell in his book *When You Love a Man Who Loves Himself* notes that "narcissists . . . are not very good at getting along with others . . . Narcissists are spectacularly bad relationship partners: they cheat, they are unsupportive, they play games, and they derogate their partners to make themselves look better. They also tend to lie, manipulate other people, and exert control and power."[44]

This is not the concept of love as expressed by Jesus, the Gospel writers, James, Peter, or Paul. Placing oneself first, which is what the narcissist mistakes for love, does not improve a relationship that requires kindness and consideration of the needs of others. Many narcissistic pastors fear and openly ridicule the success of other pastors and churches. They cannot conceive of a world in which God would richly bless anyone but themselves, particularly if the pastor he attacks is experiencing tremendous success and is also a narcissist! In particular, he finds the words of Jesus in Matthew 5:44–46, incomprehensible: "But I say to you, love your enemies and pray for those who persecute you, so that you may be sons of your Father who is in heaven; for He causes His sun to rise on the evil and the good, and sends rain on the righteous and the unrighteous. For if you love those who love you, what reward do you have? Do not even the tax collectors do the same?" This is often difficult for emotionally healthy people to understand, but to the narcissist it not only is beyond comprehension, it aptly illustrates why God must not be trusted!

The challenge of working in solitude, as most pastors often do, can cause the narcissist in particular to have difficulty responding to the needs of others. The lack of constant interaction with others limits their ability to understand why others do not know and intuitively move to meet their needs. This predisposes them to feel that they have the right to do things their way and because there is no one else in the church who can do it the "right way"—and there is only one right way: theirs! Even in a church with multiple pastors, if the senior pastor is suffering from destructive narcissism, his way is the only way. Variations are tolerated only as long as they

---

44. Campbell, *When You Love a Man Who Loves Himself,* 92.

are viewed as neutral and posing no threat or are supporting him or her. One pastor, in order to maintain control over a new associate, dictated the Scripture passages and wrote the sermons for the him on the rare times he was allowed to preach. As the associate said, there "was hell to pay" if he deviated from the script in any way.

It is difficult for the non-narcissist to comprehend how an ordained pastor might see God not as friend and comforter but rival and even enemy. Warren McWilliams, theology professor at Oklahoma Baptist University writes, "[B]ecause a narcissist is preoccupied with self, he or she suspects that God must operate from the same perspective. To a narcissist everyone else is a rival, so *God must be the supreme rival.*"[45] Accordingly, the narcissist pastor is always in a contest for supremacy with and at the same time against a God who terrifies him.

The result, says Schwartz-Salant, is that the rival must be destroyed.[46] Of course, such an overt affront against God is not tolerable in a pastor, leaving him or her to subtler devices to attain ascendency and eventual supremacy. Again, the internal tension between worshipping and banishing the same God causes a brittleness that can express itself in several ways, including projecting one's own fears and failures onto others within reach, and then destroying them in a futile act of contrition, an unfulfilling pattern that is repeated as often as his internal pressures become too strong to keep contained. As I noted earlier, one long-time pastor chewed his way through twenty-one associate pastors before his congregation became fully aware of what was happening and forced him into retirement.

Another had a history of calling associates for one- or two-year terms and then getting rid of them, or hiring students for the jobs he did not like. He then made the lives of the student interns miserable while boasting that he was giving them the chance of their lifetimes to work with a prestigious church. Of the first three student interns, two left in tears in a matter of weeks, while the third, after surviving to receive a glowing recommendation at the end of the internship, stated that he would not wish his experience on his worst enemy.

Narcissists are unable even to make emotional connections with anyone, which again contributes to their sense of isolation. They are driven in their need to find fame, and an ever-present supply of attention, flattery, and power in an attempt to replace self-loathing. The narcissist longs for recognition and celebrity status. The age of the Internet and streaming video has given almost unlimited access for narcissist pastors to reach large numbers

---

45. McWilliams, *Christ and Narcissus,* 124 (emphasis added).

46. Schwartz-Salant, *Narcissism and Character Transformation,* 41.

of people all around the world and it does not take but a few keystrokes to find them on YouTube.

Though often talented and highly intelligent, narcissists are generally unable to make it on their own and will develop relationships only with those who feed their need for admiration, are seen as having power and control in which the narcissist can bask, or those over whom they can feel superior, often by destroying them as a substitute for their own self-loathing. Because they are unable to create true intimacy with others, they often suffer from a compulsion to be needed and a desire to perform. Preaching is seen as performing and creates a pseudo-intimacy with the congregation that the narcissist mistakes for connection. They do not often understand the emotional components of ministry and certainly do not comprehend the subtleties of relational connection. What they may often have, however, is what psychoanalyst Robert Waska describes as a "designated devotee." "Even though these patients seem unable to bond with anyone and truly express their underlying feelings in a dependent manner that engages another enough to build an authentic relationship, they will often have a designated person whom they will allow themselves to feel for, depend on, and love. This is a person of their choosing and in that way can and often does change at a moment's notice."[47]

THE CHALLENGE OF COVERT NARCISSISTS TO THE CHURCH

What has been said about overt or outwardly focused narcissists holds true for covert narcissists as well, but with a twist. The covert narcissist is self-effacing, claims to be humble, even poor in spirit, and may even claim to be shy and working with a disability such as dyslexia. The challenge is that covert, or shy, narcissists are often the wolves who come in the most convincing sheep's clothing (Matt 7:15), and they are ravenous. Do not believe the adage that still waters run deep when it comes to the covert narcissist. Covert narcissists, while calm on the surface, will be seething and shallow under the surface because they have not received significant recognition and adulation. Such narcissists can be depressed, withdrawn, and anxious due to their fear that they will be further rejected.[48] They secretly long to be praised but hide this prideful desire under a veneer of false humility and grudging servanthood and will often tell you how very busy they are—but

47. Waska, "Striving Toward Useful Interpretation."

48. Leary and Hoyle, eds., *Handbook of Individual Differences in Social Behavior,* 554.

with few results for all of their activity. Having to take time from their busy schedule to help others allows them to have their egos massaged while at the same time promoting an aura of importance. Covert/shy narcissists are haunted by criticism; it causes them to feel degraded and humiliated.[49] In some ways, covert narcissists are apt to do greater damage to people and congregations than their overt colleagues because they are so much subtler and thus more difficult to spot and defend against.

The Deadly Sins of Narcissism

Calling anything a deadly sin suggests there is a moral imperative that must be addressed. While there are individual opinions as to what the deadly sins of narcissism actually are, the traditional Seven Deadly Sins seem to fit quite well:

1. Envy = the desire to have an item or experience that someone else possesses

2. Gluttony = excessive ongoing consumption of food or drink

3. Greed or Avarice = an excessive pursuit of material possessions

4. Lust = an uncontrollable passion or longing, especially for sexual desires

5. Pride = excessive view of one's self without regard to others.

6. Sloth = excessive laziness or the failure to act and utilize one's talents

7. Wrath = uncontrollable feelings of anger and hate towards another person

One of the most interesting writers on NPD is Sam Vaknin, who writes from an insider's perspective. Vaknin himself has severe NPD, which he readily acknowledges.

As noted earlier, it seems that one reason that the role of pastor might be attractive to the narcissist is the fact that a vast majority of clergy work essentially alone. Vaknin states that, even though they may be highly intelligent and capable, their inability to tolerate setbacks and criticism makes it impossible for the narcissist to work in a true team environment where team members routinely evaluate, criticize, and modify each other's work.[50] To the narcissist, exposing one's work for criticism is not something to be considered, primarily because his work is already better than everyone else's

49. Campbell and Miller, eds., *The Handbook of Narcissism*, 72.

50. Vaknin, *Malignant Self-Love*, 40.

and his lofty status precludes them from criticism. If there is a team, narcissists "lead" the team by dictating to it, which defeats the entire purpose of a team. Narcissist pastors and other leaders will liken themselves to famous but dictatorial coaches as justification for their own actions, which they see as directive but "for your own good." What the narcissist might term as a team exists only to do his bidding. Challenge his manner of leading and you will either experience a torrent of narcissistic rage or suddenly find yourself shut out of everything. They truly love the idea of the church as a theocracy with them at the head. But they are not representing God, they are replacing God.

Since the narcissist craves love but feels unworthy of it, he tends to undermine, sabotage, and challenge what love is expressed for him. He projects an image that is lovable, but it is only a mirror image, a thin and reversed manifestation of what is there just beneath the surface. The narcissist understands awe, admiration, respect, attention, or even being feared as being interchangeable with love. In obtaining what he needs, the narcissist employs everything he can think of to gain attention and admiration. Without these, he feels as if he does not exist. Underneath it all, the narcissist believes that he is weak, unworthy, ugly, and broken beyond repair. The paradox is in the fact that his ego is so brittle that he cannot even contemplate the idea that there might be something wrong with him; doing so is the equivalent of death and is to be avoided at all costs. To that extent, Vaknin writes that "all narcissists are walking scar tissue, the outcomes of various forms of abuse in early childhood or early adolescence."[51] This is the reason they will not seek treatment under any circumstance except perhaps for depression or "burnout."

No matter what, the narcissist, pastor or not, almost always believes he is being treated unfairly, and any satisfaction with new achievements or conquests is short-lived. Why? Simply put, he believes that he is entitled to everything that he wants, and it is unfair for anything to be withheld. It is his right, not privilege. Vaknin writes, "He feels that he deserves whatever he . . . extracts from others and much more besides. Actually, he feels betrayed, discriminated against and underprivileged because he believes that he is not being treated fairly, that he should get more than he does."[52] A case in point was that of a senior pastor who complained after he retired that his congregation did not so much as give him a gold watch. That was true, as far as it went; they gave him a brand new car instead!

51. Vaknin, *Malignant Self-Love*, 58.
52. Vaknin, *Malignant Self-Love*, 55.

So, you ask, if these behaviors are ultimately self-destructive, why does the narcissist persist in them? Vaknin offers an explanation that many find very difficult to accept, but which has been validated in the clinical literature numerous times: "He does not suffer from a faulty sense of causation. He is not oblivious to the likely outcomes of his actions and to the price he may have to pay. *But he doesn't care.*"[53] That concept of simply not caring is difficult for "normal" people to digest and is often met with protests of "we just need to love him more" or something similar. I honestly wish it was that simple, but it is not. Getting the praise and adulation that he needs is to him water, air, and food; it trumps everything else, and there are no substitutes.

You cannot know a narcissist at anything other than a surface level, for all he will show you is the polished veneer unless he believes that showing something else will benefit him. He may be warm and friendly on the surface, but that too is a projected image. Intimacy terrifies him and he will do everything possible to avoid it. And that is a major key in understanding. Everything the narcissist does must have a benefit built into it for him. In helping others, it will be praise for helping. In visiting the sick, it will be praise and appreciation for his time. In counseling, it may be the vicarious thrill of learning deeply held secrets and occupying the powerful position of confessor. If the benefit is not there, he will not do it unless there is no choice. This is one of the reasons why narcissist pastors will try to relegate the more unrewarding parts of ministry to subordinates—but only under the guises of empowering them or giving them opportunities to learn.

It is a challenge to understand and accept that the narcissist does not care about the outcomes of his actions, or about the people he hurts, uses, or destroys along the way. As rational people, we think that he should feel bad because that is how we feel when we learn that we have hurt someone we care about. The problem here is that we are projecting our own feelings and expectations onto someone who finds them totally alien and cannot understand them. Normal guilt requires us to confront ourselves and what we did, then move to heal the harm and change our ways so that we do not repeat it. Not the narcissist. Healthy guilt is an alien and undecipherable experience. He doesn't feel bad at all, and for a very simple reason: he is mostly disconnected from his emotions and does not even know what it is to feel sorry for someone or to feel regret because he did something that hurt another. The regret he may feel is because he was criticized or got caught, which he defends with rage or victimhood.

---

53. Vaknin, *Malignant Self-Love*, 56 (emphasis added).

I could go on, but this gives you a general picture of the narcissist pastor. I will examine how he works and interacts in the various roles of being a pastor, along with my experience with narcissist pastors, in later chapters.

3

The Work and Habits
of the Narcissist Pastor

History will be kind to me for I intend to write it.

—Winston Churchill

Churchill hit it on the head when it comes to narcissists. Narcissists write their own histories and change them as the need or mood fits. Much of their histories are fiction. They will claim all manner of successes and recognition—but never failure. Some of it will be spun out of thin air while other parts will be greatly exaggerated. Failures will disappear, only to be replaced by spectacular successes. Sometimes, the stories are true but ancient, and sometimes they are blatantly false as a "loyalty test" to see who will correct him.

In line with fluid histories, narcissists' narratives about who they are and what they believe tend to be a bit more elastic than they should be. To the narcissist, truth and reality are what he says they are at that moment and are subject to sudden change without any notice. Their histories will probably include being mentored or trained by "world-class professors" and attendance at prestigious universities or being invited to speak at major conferences. Much or all of it will be fiction.

Every leader who has a private office will do something to make it more comfortable. The narcissist, however, wants an office that impresses people as a reflection of who he is—smart, powerful, and important. The location, size, and items furnishing a pastor's office can be a strong indicator of that person's personality. Take for example, the senior pastor's office in a large church with perhaps 1,000 in attendance on Sunday morning and another 400 or so on Saturday evenings. It is not a megachurch by any means, but it is not small either. The office is in a new multi-million dollar building that houses a restaurant and commercial kitchen, gymnasium/performing arts center, a bookstore, classrooms, and offices. The office is designed to impress people, and it does.

It is on the second floor across the hall from the office of the executive pastor. Both offices are at opposite ends of the building from every other office, as if to say, "We are superior and need distance from the worker bees." From the entry door to the outside wall of windows is about thirty-five feet. Custom bookcases jammed with books line the walls and a fieldstone wall with a see-through gas fireplace separates the entry area from the more private work area. Overstuffed furniture and a conference table dominate the entry area. The outside wall of windows gives a commanding view of the campus and the valley below with double doors leading to a private balcony. Only by walking almost to the windows could anyone see his desk beyond the fireplace. The desk is piled high with books in general disarray, each with bits of paper sticking out here and there. There are more jammed bookcases, and a private restroom with a shower. Having worked in corporate conflict management for most of my career, I immediately recognize this as a typical office for the CEO of a medium-sized corporation. It is designed to proclaim the power and importance of its inhabitant[1]—just like the vanity walls I have seen in many senior management offices covered with awards and pictures of the pastor with famous people. It is a hint that all might not be well.

MORE WARNING SIGNS

According to Dr. Craig Malkin writing in *Psychology Today*, such surroundings are designed not only to impress others, but are also a means of soothing the narcissist's feelings of insecurity and inadequacy, as if to say, "I am made great by the greatness around me." Malkin affirms a series of signposts

---

1. Brown, "Narcissism, Identity, and Legitimacy," 659.

found in the research literature that serve as early warnings that you are in the presence of a narcissist.

Projected Feelings of Insecurity

Narcissists, despite their grandiosity, feel deeply insecure and inadequate. To counter this, they "project" these feelings onto others and then do their best to make these unwanted feelings part of the other person. The more you feel insecure and inadequate in his or her presence, the more comfortable and powerful the narcissist feels. Malkin writes, "Narcissists say and do things, subtle or obvious, that make you feel less smart, less accomplished, less competent."[2] They will damn you with faint praise, e.g., "You're getting better at this," in an effort to push their negative feelings onto you. According to Malkin, the narcissist brightens his or her light not by increasing his or her own wattage but by knocking out the neighboring lights to increase the surrounding darkness.

Emotion-phobia

Normal people have multiple feelings in a complex mix that ebbs and flows with the surrounding circumstances and interactions with other people. Our feelings touch others and are touched by them. Our feelings deeply influence how we see ourselves and how we connect with others, and others influence us by influencing our emotions. Our emotions impact every decision we make, no matter how rational we believe we are. Not so much the narcissist. According to Malkin, "Narcissists abhor feeling influenced in any significant way. It challenges their sense of perfect autonomy; to admit to a feeling of any kind suggests they can be affected by someone or something outside of them. The result is that they often change the subject when feelings come up, especially their own, and as quick as they might be to anger, it's often like pulling teeth to get them to admit that they've reached the boiling point—even when they're in the midst of the most terrifying tirade."[3] To the narcissist, autonomy is paramount and to feel influenced by someone else is to feel controlled and contained, things the narcissist cannot stand.

2. Malkin, "5 Early Warning Signs."
3. Malkin, "5 Early Warning Signs."

A Fragmented Family Story

A child attaches to its parents through loving interactions. Attachment theory is a concept that views early childhood-parent relationships as most significant in developing internal reasoning and emotional patterns that influence interpersonal functioning throughout life. According to Marcia Howland,

> Children and their parents go through cycles of bonding, disconnecting, and reconnecting. When done well, secure attachments form that provide emotional safety and security. When parent-child imperfections occur, how they are managed sets the tone for relational meaning. When aroused by need or danger, the conflict often causes the child to reach towards the parent for help. The response of accessible loving, protecting, reassuring, and encouraging support deactivates the stress which returns one to a state of equilibrium and balance. Protection and exploration are essential for positive development. Healthy people attach to one another in mostly secure ways. They form solid relationships based on mutual respect and trust.[4]

Narcissists know neither respect nor trust. Though they desperately want friends, they know that they have none as they constantly test and provoke others into leaving, which produces an interesting conundrum: they desperately want true friends but constantly drive away anyone who would actually befriend them in something deeper than a passing relationship. Where healthy people attach to others in healthy ways that affirm their existence as people of great value, narcissists attach to others as a means of affirming their own existence and to get from them everything they can. In fact, they are so deeply insecure that they are unable to form secure attachments.

All of this comes out in their family story. Malkin states that "insecurely attached people can't talk coherently about their family and childhood; their early memories are confused, contradictory, and riddled with gaps. Narcissists often give themselves away precisely because their childhood story makes no sense, and the most common myth they carry around is the perfect family story."[5] It's the myth of Garrison Keillor and Lake Wobegon: the women are strong, the men are good looking, and all the children are above average. Until you press them, that is. Then you will begin to hear of the rivalries and petty slights they have carried with them from their earliest memories, and which are as real today as they were decades ago.

---

4. Howland, "Correlation of Attachment Styles," 3.
5. Malkin, "5 Early Warning Signs."

Idol Worship

Narcissists tend to place rich, powerful, and famous people on pedestals, and then claim them as friends and mentors. Narcissists are name-droppers, e.g., "My good friend and mentor, Dr. T. D. Jakes . . ." Malkin goes on, "The logic goes a bit like this: 'If I find someone perfect to be close to, maybe some of their perfection will rub off on me, and I'll become perfect by association.'" This lasts as long as the idol is useful or until it turns out that it has clay feet, at which time the narcissist dismisses it and even denies ever being associated with it. Malkin adds, "Few experiences can prepare you for the vitriol of a suddenly disappointed narcissist. Look out for any pressure to conform to an image of perfection, no matter how lovely or magical the compulsive flattery might feel."[6] It's a setup to become their scapegoat when things go wrong, which they inevitably do.

A High Need for Control

The narcissist must be in control. Always. If he isn't, he will try to take control. If he cannot take control, he will exit, unless he has no choice but to remain, at which point he will either add the controlling person to his idol list or will chafe and look for a means of escape. Not being in control reminds narcissists of their vulnerability and places them in a subordinate position where they might actually have to ask permission to do or get something. Worse, their request might even be denied, leaving them standing there in humiliation. Instead, they tend to orchestrate people, resources, and events to get what they want. If there is resistance, they tend to use verbal abuse to overcome it and stay in control. Mostly, however, the means of control are much subtler. Malkin advises, "Be on the lookout for anyone who leaves you feeling nervous about approaching certain topics or sharing your own preferences. Narcissists have a way of making choices feel off-limits without expressing any anger at all—a disapproving wince, a last-minute call to preempt the plans, chronic lateness whenever you're in charge of arranging a night together. It's more like a war of attrition on your will than an outright assault on your freedom."[7]

It is not that a sign is present here and there to warn of the presence of a narcissist so much as it is the patterns and clusters of signs that you must be aware of. If you are seeing these signs over an extended period, and even if they are low intensity, pay close attention.

6. Malkin, "5 Early Warning Signs."
7. Malkin, "5 Early Warning Signs."

HALLMARKS

So how are these expressed at work for the narcissist pastor? We will lay out a foundation and then illustrate through stories of people we have worked with (names and identifying details have been changed to protect the guilty). We have already examined several of these topics on the surface, but here we will go deeper.

Academic Achievement

As noted previously, the true narcissist tends to be a mediocre student who feels entitled to high grades without having to go through the same demeaning paces as other students. He or she has a tendency not to complete projects, particularly where personal academic achievement is concerned.[8] They make terrible work teammates as they rarely complete their portions of a project and yet expect the other members to acknowledge and concede to what they see as their obvious intellectual superiority that exempts them from such mundane work. In other words, they want the majority of the credit while doing little—if any—of the work.

Covert and overt narcissists react differently to achievement failure. "In more vulnerable individuals, chronic hypersensitivity and disappointment stemming from unmet entitled expectations is intolerable enough to promote social withdrawal and avoidance in an attempt to manage self-esteem, leading to the development of overt anger and hostile expressions. These are followed by the experience of shame and depression, resulting in the impression of a rather labile [meaning readily open to change] emotional presentation."[9] For the covert or vulnerable narcissist, failure is intolerable and shameful. To the overt narcissist, however, "the degree of threat associated with negative feedback from the interpersonal arena can be blunted by their tendency to attribute such feedback to the negative attributes and shortcomings of others."[10]

Mediocrity, of course, is to be vanquished in the ever-present quest for perfection. To proclaim that she has studied a topic "my entire life" demands and confers the imprimatur of knowledge and expertise, even if she only read the front twenty or thirty pages of a book on the topic. In fact, many rarely read a complete book. As we noted earlier, several books a narcissist pastor borrowed somehow migrated onto his bookshelves with notes in the

---

8. Twenge and Campbell, *The Narcissism Epidemic*, 42.

9. Besser and Priel, "Grandiose Narcissism Versus Vulnerable Narcissism," 878.

10. Besser and Priel, "Grandiose Narcissism Versus Vulnerable Narcissism," 879.

margins for the first twenty or thirty pages, and then nothing at all. This was later discovered to be true for almost every book he claimed to have read. Many narcissists do not like to read. Some, like those I know who have Attention Deficit Disorder, not only hate to read but have a short attention span in other areas as well.

In another case, the pastor had very little theological training at all, but he happily regaled people with his profound understanding of God and human nature coming from his "deep theological training under world-class mentors." Whom he could not name, by the way. In yet another instance a pastor name-dropped several internationally known scholars as being his mentors. He also made the mistake of placing them as references when he applied for another position. In his mind he apparently was so glorious that he was convinced the pastoral search team would never actually contact them. They did. The "references" denied ever knowing him.

When the narcissist pastor is successful, he basks in the reflected light of these successful people even though he may never have met them. This was a factor in the pastor who convinced congregation members to lobby a seminary he attended for one semester to grant him an honorary doctorate. He desperately longed for academic validation and the title of "Doctor" but had no chance of ever earning the degree as he did not complete seminary and did not have a master's degree. To him, the title of "Doctor" was the ultimate praise, and one which he richly deserved based on his "outstanding achievements." It took a long time and a lot of lobbying, but it worked. He was bestowed with an honorary Doctor of Letters degree. The next thing anyone knew he was wearing doctoral robes while preaching and insisted on being called by the title of Doctor as if he had earned the degree and title. To him, of course, he had.

Uniqueness

It is generally not good politics to proclaim one's own uniqueness loudly or often, particularly when one is a pastor. However, there is another way of doing it that people often do not see through. The narcissist will claim that his church and the ministries within it are better than others or even are unique. In this way, he builds a sense of pride among the congregants that masks his own pride. It also tends to justify isolating the church from other churches. After all, other churches have nothing to offer if we are unique. Instead, they should come to us to see how we do things. One pastor proclaimed often that other churches were coming to him to see how he did what he did, in an effort to duplicate it. He also claimed that he was besieged by young pastors coming to him for advice and his mentoring in their budding ministries. All of which was both interesting and contradictory as he deliberately cut off any attempts at inter-church cooperation and generally stayed behind the buffering wall of the executive pastor if he deemed the people unimportant. Unfortunately, he could not name any of the churches or pastors who were coming to him. The reason was simple enough: they did not exist. In fact, his church had a reputation in the community as being shallow, standoffish, and prideful.

Uniqueness can take many forms. It may be music, a ministry, a curriculum, or a program, even well after the honors have faded into nothing. One pastor repeatedly told his congregation about how they, with his inspirational leading, had won a national Sunday school attendance contest some thirty years before. The key is that uniqueness, to be real, must be different from what others are doing or must achieve outside acclamation, but the reality is that uniqueness is rarely purely the product of that pastor; in most cases, it is borrowed or hijacked from a more famous pastor and church, and then modified. As soon as it is modified, it can be claimed as unique. Uniqueness being a necessity to the narcissist pastor, one of the markers some have noticed is sudden course changes toward and away from new programs, where things are always changing, or a proclamation that the church is starting a new tradition—that is quietly abandoned after a few weeks. This constant churning will eventually produce something that works, which is its purpose. The failures will never be acknowledged—only success is worthy of a place in our memories and church histories. As a result, churches create narratives about themselves that can be a mixture of fact, fantasy, and outright fiction. We will explore this in chapter 8.

The narcissist pastor may talk quite a lot about how everything must be done perfectly, from newsletters to bulletins, yet their newsletters and bulletins tend to be wordy, poorly written, tacky, and even gaudy—as if they are caught up in the color combinations of the 1970s. If that is not the case, then it is likely that printing projects are rarely done on time because they are continually being revised in order to get the wording "just right."

Control

I have mentioned that the narcissist pastor must be in control of everything all the time, but let's go a bit deeper. Under the narcissist pastor, no one else in the church can make anything but the most routine decision, and sometimes absolutely no one can spend money on anything, not even parts for the lawn mower, without his approval. In addition, his control of the money is not subject to review or challenge. This comes out when the pastor suspends whatever financial control may be in place as unnecessary, or he may simply ignore them.

In more than one situation the pastor simply refused to give any accounting of how he spent the pastor's discretionary fund because it was at his discretion and therefore beyond any accountability.

In one incident, increasing belligerence about his use of the pastor's benevolence fund (he gave his sister several thousand dollars) was one of the major reasons the pastor was eventually fired—at which point he started a new church, took a third of the congregation and the church records with him, and held all of the church records hostage to force a large payment in return for his resignation. He then sued the church for improper termination. The church countersued for taking the church records and called the police to prosecute him for theft. I was flown halfway across the country to mediate the case. I was not encouraged when the lawyers for both sides said this case would never settle short of a full trial.

We met on the neutral ground of the town library. Three of the elders represented the church, and the former pastor appeared with his wife and a silent observer in tow. It took me about thirty minutes to realize that this was about pride and not money. Even though the pastor had almost demolished the church financially and had taken a third of the congregation with him when he left, he believed that the church owed him several months' worth of wages and an apology for how badly he had been treated. In listening to him present his case, it became apparent that the only thing truly at stake in this lawsuit was his pride. Ever the narcissist, he had not considered that his lawsuit had forced the church to hire an attorney, which had depleted its last financial resources. For some reason he believed the church's attorney would do the work free of charge, even though his lawyer expected to be paid up front.

After listening to the arguments and counterarguments for about an hour, I split them apart and met with each group separately. The narcissistic pastor was genuinely shocked when told that the money was gone because the church hired a lawyer to defend against his lawsuit. What did he really want, I asked? An apology for firing him and a written and public proclamation of all the "wonderful things I did for that congregation." He refused to admit that the congregation had shrunk under his ministry, let alone that he was the cause. Recognizing a narcissist at work, I was able to negotiate a tepid letter of commendation for him, at which time he dropped the lawsuit and returned all of the church records, and the church dropped its lawsuit and criminal charges against him.

The narcissist must not only control his world; he must also control everyone in it. This is true of the narcissist pastor as well. An example of this is control of church board meetings. First, he may attempt to appoint the members of the board directly or will try to maintain veto power over the recommendations of a nominations committee. This vastly increases his ability to operate without constraints, as he will never choose anyone who he believes might oppose him. He will then do everything possible to control the agenda of elder's meetings by forcing his or her own agenda.

Another effective means of control is intimidation. The narcissist is a master of intimidation, particularly of the church staff. This is done through the carefully unpredictable application of narcissistic rage.

Rage

Most narcissist pastors have learned the social skill of not exploding in public and many will not confront someone who criticizes them immediately, but do not mistake the lack of immediate response for acceptance. It is an attempt to tamp down shame, humiliation, and rage into something they can control like a well-trained sniper controls his breathing and fires the killing bullet between heartbeats. It may even seem that they have accepted your critique and are even thankful for it. Instead, their rage simmers in the background until the pressure becomes too great and they explode over seemingly meaningless slights. One of the issues of working with a narcissist is that you never know when the explosion will come, only that it will. Consequently, the people who work for him or her are always walking on eggshells and never certain of the reaction they will get. They know that rage will come back to them; the only question is when.

Their rage when it does come out is amazing to behold but terrifying and bewildering to experience. "This rage resides mostly within, a private, inner experience that nevertheless dominates all behavior from its internal hiding place. Only occasionally does the rage burst forth into open, violent, vindictive, and revengeful attacks on those whose real or imagined slights create immense suffering for the protagonist."[11] They will squirm and scream to place the blame on someone else. Often, they will have a scapegoat on whom to place every sin and mistake, and then sacrifice to preserve their own aura of competence and perfection. Perhaps the fastest (and most humiliating) way to staunch the vitriolic flow when you are on the receiving end is to quickly claim the blame and plead for mercy. In doing so you give the narcissist what he needs: blamelessness and the power to forgive.

11. Ornstein, "Chronic Rage from Underground," 138.

However, do not believe that you are forgiven in the sense that the offense is wiped from the slate; it isn't—the slate of sins only gets longer. They never really forgive, and they never forget. The clinical literature is very clear: they do not even know what it means to forgive others or to seek forgiveness through apology. Your self-abasement serves to fulfill their need to be more powerful. They do not have equals.

Humor and Emotional Masking

The narcissist more often than not has a poorly developed sense of humor and may lack a sense of humor altogether. About the only time you will see a true narcissist in a belly laugh is when he is laughing at the plight of someone else and is simply overjoyed that it's not him. Their attempts at humor from the pulpit are usually awkward and fall flat, getting only a polite chuckle when what they crave is roaring laughter. One narcissist pastor told how he was hunting deer in the Adirondacks. He fired a shot and thought he had scored a kill, but the deer disappeared. He stepped over a log—right onto the wounded buck, which reared up and tried to run. Straddled across the buck's back, the pastor pulled out his hunting knife and cut the deer's throat, and held on until it bled out and died, leaving him covered in gore.

He thought this story was hilarious, but many in his congregation were sickened, to which he was oblivious. Too, the narcissist pastor will almost never try to tell a joke in private; he knows humor is expected as a necessary part of social life, but he rarely can differentiate between what is funny and what is simply dull. He has tried it and the results were far from positive; thus, he does not tell jokes. The closest he may come to telling a joke in private is through sarcasm, which he understands as humor while everyone else feels it as a splash of acid in the eyes. Sam Vaknin describes it this way:

> A narcissist rarely engages in self-directed, self-deprecating humour. If he does, he expects to be contradicted, rebuked and rebuffed by his listeners ('Come on, you are actually quite handsome!'), or to be commended or admired for his courage or for his wit and intellectual acerbity ('I envy your ability to laugh at yourself!'). As everything else in a narcissist's life, his sense of humour is deployed in the interminable pursuit of Narcissistic Supply.
>
> I am completely different when I lack Narcissistic Supply or when in search of sources of such supply. Humor is always an integral part of my charm offensive. But, when Narcissistic Supply is deficient, it is never self-directed. Moreover, when

deprived of supply, I react with hurt and rage when I am the butt of jokes and humorous utterances. I counter-attack ferociously and make a complete arse of myself.[12]

While the overt narcissist must be in the center of every gathering and actively seeks the presence of those who admire him, the covert narcissist often uses the masking device of appearing to be in deep self-concentration that says to others that he is caught up in solving profound problems, and should not be interrupted. If you do interrupt, expect to be met with at least irritation. The deep-thought gambit is a great way to avoid having to interact with other people, particularly if they are having a good time.

Social Life

Another notable marker of the narcissist pastor is their strange social lives. As Kyle Vandeven writes, "The pathology of Narcissistic Personality Disorder is very complicated. Suffice it to say, many people with NPD are extremely adept in social situations, but this behavior is almost always an affectation. They are . . . social chameleons."[13]

Studies have shown a majority of clergy are introverted in nature, meaning that they are uncomfortable in social situations and in fact find them to be emotionally taxing and physically draining.[14] The problem, of course, is that the church is a center of social life for many of its members, who expect the pastor to be an active and enthusiastic participant. Pastors are routinely invited to dinner at the homes of members and to social events within the church. For the introverted narcissist pastor, socializing for more than a few minutes is agony. He is aware of his lack of social ease but is unable to do anything about it. In one case, the pastor never accepted a dinner invitation at someone's home but would always meet them at an expensive restaurant and expect them to pay (see Entitlement below). By meeting at a restaurant, he gained public visibility while minimizing the possibility of his hosts criticizing him in public and was able to leave when it was most convenient for him. He also terrorized his staff and had all the other attributes of NPD. This went on for fourteen years until he was given an ultimatum: retire or face formal charges before the entire congregation. Unable or unwilling to face the shame of formal charges, he retired.

12. Vaknin, "The Self-Deprecating Narcissist."

13. Vandeven, "Are Narcissist Always Extroverts?"

14. Francis et al., "Psychological Type."

Another narcissist pastor would not attend any social events at his own church, not even the frequent banquets and receptions. He justified this with the claim of his shyness and his terrible workload that simply did not leave time for such things. He was notable primarily by his absence.

By contrast, the extroverted narcissist pastor needs to be included in everything and will do whatever is necessary to become the center of attention. In this way, she maintains control of the gathering, which dampens any inclinations of people to complain or criticize. It is even possible (I've seen it happen) that she will call everyone together for an impromptu sermon regarding something "the Lord has just laid on my heart." This makes her the controlling force and spiritual guru even in a social setting. The only worthwhile way to have fun is to be admired and the center of attention!

The extroverted narcissist pastor in a social setting is a thing to behold. She moves from group to group but always gravitates to the group where the most powerful and important people are. That way she is always associating with people she considers to be in her own class of brilliance and importance. She then gradually takes the spotlight by speaking authoritatively on the topic or changes the topic to meet her own needs. When the group disintegrates, she is immediately off to the next group. If she feels that the new group is beneath her she will abruptly move on. It is not unusual for her to walk away in mid-sentence when she spots someone of greater importance than the person she is speaking to (notice that I did not say "speaking with" as that implies equal give and take, which the narcissist can tolerate only up to a point).

Entitlement

Before one can explore narcissistic entitlement, it is important to place a baseline for socially normal entitlement. Dr. Susan Krauss Whitbourne defines it this way: "People whose entitlement is in the normal range have high self-esteem based on actions that were truly laudatory. They expect to win not because they think that all others should bow down to their greatness, but because they typically do win. Normal entitlement, we might further argue, applies to specific areas of abilities. You may expect to win at chess because you usually do but have no such illusions of grandeur about beating your favorite cousin in a friendly game of pool. The entitled narcissist doesn't make these distinctions but instead thinks every enterprise should end in success."[15]

15. Whitbourne, "Revisiting the Psychology of Narcissistic Entitlement."

Narcissists believe that they are entitled to everything they want, but that is a difficult proposition in the church. Hence, they develop covers for their sense of entitlement. They may demand that their salaries and benefits be kept secret, and then mandate an exorbitant amount. They may turn in falsified expense reports or place personal expenditures on a church credit card. One of the better legal ways of hiding income in the United States for pastors is in the housing stipend. She may only be paying $15,000 per year in mortgage interest and principal and another $5,000 on property taxes, but demand a housing allowance of $40,000, which is an additional tax-free income of $20,000. The secret to understanding this phenomenon is this: they must always win, and this is just another way of winning.

Caution is always advised in what you might expect in return for gifts to a narcissist. There may be effusive praise when you offer the gift, but the gift may well be discarded because it is "cheap" or because you, the gift giver, no longer have enough status with the receiver. One man returned from South Africa with a hand-carved Zulu war mask and presented it to his pastor as a peace offering to heal a rift that had developed. The pastor looked at it, looked at the giver, then threw the mask aside and walked away.

Narcissists believe they are entitled to friendships no matter how poorly they treat others and cannot understand why they find themselves isolated. They believe that the humiliation they hand out so generously is normal and acceptable behavior for them to others, but never others to them. When others do not act in ways the narcissist believes they should, the narcissist reacts with rage and paranoia. Yes, he knows he is being paranoid, but he operates under the mantra of "Just because you're paranoid doesn't mean they're not out to get you!" He sees paranoia as reasonable self-protection in a world where everyone is jealous and envious of him and his obvious gifts and will do what they must to tear him down.

Staff Relations

Under a narcissist, the church staff is expected always to toe the company line, praise their leader, and fend off any incoming criticism while at the same time always maintaining a stance of humble obedience and being, as one narcissist pastor called them, "loyal little soldiers all in a row." The social context is one of unquestioning servitude in exchange for friendly relations. These expectations may never be verbalized but they are always operating and woe to whomever ignores them or even slightly violates their terms. A staff member is never allowed to be placed in a position where the pastor sees him as potential competition. To survive in this environment, the staff members often gush and grovel when in his presence. In one instance, a female pastor babbled at a weekly staff meeting that her narcissistic pastor's most recent sermon was "the most amaaaaazing sermon I have ever heard!" The problem was that she said that at almost every weekly staff meeting. Why? Only praise was acceptable, and she knew there would be a severe price to be paid if she made any form of critique. She was terrified of him but needed her job.

The narcissist pastor operates in ways that confuse the staff as a means of maintaining absolute control. He is predictable in his unpredictability, and those who truly know him automatically take an emotional temperature check when he enters a room. They will relax a bit if he is in a good mood, but they are also aware that his mood can change in the span of one heartbeat from seemingly satisfied to viper-venomous. This keeps everyone on guard but emotionally unstable as they never know quite what to expect. Again, this is intentional and part of his larger strategy to maintain control by eliminating threats: they cannot plot against him if they are constantly confused and demoralized, but he still expects perfect obedience.

The narcissist pastor tends to take one of two routes when making assignments. She will give general, even nebulous, directions and then expect the work to be performed exactly to the unexpressed picture she has in her head. Conversely, directions will be so minute and precise that doing the work is simply a means of filling in the blanks. However, even following precise directions precisely is no guarantee that the work will meet with approval. It is not uncommon for the narcissist to simply disown the entire project with a "that's not what I wanted" dismissal. Don't assume that checking in with her and giving periodic progress reports will do the trick. They won't because this is not about generating a product; it is about power and control of others.

As noted earlier, the narcissist sees rage as a normal emotion and has no compunctions about releasing it on his staff, even over the smallest of errors or missteps. Fear of the boss is one of the most effective means he has to maintain control. Being subjected to this amazing torrent of rage is disorienting, confusing, frightening, and disheartening. People who have been through it would rather drink from a firehose at full blast.

More than anything else, narcissists expect unwavering—and unquestioning—loyalty from those who work for them, whether it is a part-time secretary or a huge staff. The penalty if she believes you are disloyal is rage and isolation to get you to resign on your own, which is what happened to David. Her goal is to get rid of you and this is so she can say you left voluntarily. Having to fire someone is too much a reflection on themselves, e.g., they were unable to coach the person into acceptable work. Of course, those at the pinnacle of power do not hesitate to use the power of termination. Just don't expect them to feel bad about what they are doing. They enjoy it.

Manipulation

Being able to manipulate people is to control them, and the narcissist, whether pastor or not, is a manipulator without peer. Her radar is attuned with laser focus on your weaknesses, hopes, fears, dreams, and so on. She is so good at it that you likely will have no idea it is happening until you are pulled in so deeply that you wonder how to get out.

The narcissist begins learning how to read and manipulate others as a child and works to improve and perfect her most effective techniques as she gets older. Narcissists can be winsome and a joy to be around, but it is often an act to encourage you to lower your guard and reveal a more intimate portrait of yourself. It has a purpose. While most of us interact to communicate and form relationships, the narcissist interacts to make an impression. She studies your face and body language for reactions to what she is saying and files those reactions away for later use, neatly catalogued with the behavior that caused it. If the reaction is not what she wanted or expected, she will change her approach instantly and try a new tactic. Eventually she will know much more about your weaknesses than you do. The ability to read, if not understand or experience, another's emotions is frequently mistaken for empathy or caring, "but it could also translate into more effective manipulation for certain individuals, such as those high in exploitativeness. . . . Exploitative people may be especially attuned to vulnerability in others in order to find people who are easy to take advantage of and prey on, and who may not be in a position to fight back."[16]

For example, you are meeting alone with your new pastor who asks you, "What's your greatest hope in life?" It's a normal kind of question when getting to know a pastor and you answer honestly. He then asks, "What is holding you back?" You name financial issues, time constraints, perhaps a fear of failure. He then asks, "What's your family like?" You tell him about how your son is an "A" student in college, but your daughter has been having some emotional issues that you are worried about, and your husband seems more and more distant . . . Are you getting the picture? The healthy pastor will keep all of this in confidence and work to find ways to help you. To the narcissist you have volunteered a complete arsenal to be used in gaining control over you. He will collect more and more information over time under the guise of caring for you and your problems. Eventually he will know

16. Konrath et al., "The Relationship Between Narcissistic Exploitativeness," 139.

the locations of all of your fear and insecurity buttons and exactly when to push them.

The tactics of manipulation include:

- Positive Reinforcement: Praise, flattery, adoration, attention, affection, gifts, superficial sympathy (crocodile tears), superficial charm, recognition, and appreciation. These are the various baits designed to pull you in.

- Intermittent positive reinforcement: There is a sudden change in the atmosphere. Where once the praise was constant, it is now erratic. This tactic is designed to create a cloud of uncertainty, anxiety, and confusion, and it works very well. Where once you were comfortable in the relationship and acted in the belief that it was reciprocal, you are suddenly filled with doubt and anxiety. The most common feeling is, "What did I do?" If confronted, the narcissist will deny that you did anything wrong because it's the truth. This is an intentional tactic to increase power and control over you. When it works, you are pulled in even deeper.

- Indirect aggressive abuse: This is a not-so-subtle means of psychological abuse that creates a deeper sense of confusion and wondering what you have done to deserve it. Under the guise of teaching or mentoring, he will tear you down and insult you, all the while appearing to care deeply about you. You are pulled in even deeper if you fall for it. What this illustrates is that he is now comfortable enough in his control of you that he can start turning you into his next bodyguard or scapegoat.

- Blaming the victim: He will blame you for the abuse he is heaping on you. This tactic is a powerful means of putting the victim—you— on the defensive while simultaneously masking his aggressive intent towards you. His goal is to prevent you from asking difficult questions and to drive you deeper into confusion, with the hoped-for outcome often being that you will worship him even more. We could call this the "you made me hurt you" syndrome.

- The use of ambiguous language: This is done to insinuate things and get a negative emotional response from you. After all, he knows your weaknesses and this is one way of using them against you. His defense is plausible deniability, that is, the words are ambiguous enough to where he can respond to an accusation with, "I never said that. I would never say anything like that. What I meant was . . ." Conversely, it is designed get you to do something that he dares not state clearly and with which he cannot be connected.

- Empty words: The narcissist, like the sociopath, can turn on the charm and tell you exactly what you want to hear: "You are amazing." "I don't know of anyone else who can do this." "You're the only one who can . . ." These are empty words. The narcissist uses them when he wants something from you or is trying to win you over because he sees you as a powerful threat. What is clear in this behavior is that he wants something from you. He knows that praise is a potent motivator and controller because it is among the primary things driving him.

- Denying or invalidating reality: Reality is very fluid to the narcissist and can be changed on a whim—but only by him! It really does not much matter how many witnessed something, he will deny it with all sincerity if that is beneficial to him.

- Minimizing: One rather well-known narcissist pastor was finally cornered about things he had been saying that had no basis in reality. In plain language, he was lying. When called on it she said, "I don't lie! I sometimes exaggerate a bit, but I don't lie!" And she believed it because what she said was her truth of the moment, subject to instant change without reason or explanation.

- Withholding: One of the more confusing tactics to continue control over someone is to emotionally withdraw and refuse to acknowledge their existence as punishment for sins real and imagined—and for the narcissist, the imagined sin is real. Since he was never "there" emotionally to begin with and there is no emotion to withdraw, he feels absolutely no remorse.

- Lying: Narcissists lie with absolute sincerity, and even lie when there is absolutely no reason to. They are excellent liars but they lie so much that eventually they begin getting the details of the various lies mixed up and intertwined or the details change with each telling. The phrase, "Tell the truth; there's less to remember" is lost on them.

- Lies of omission: It has been said that the most effective lies are those containing mostly truth with fiction replacing truth at crucial points. The goal of lying can also be accomplished though lies of omission where the truth is told without critical information. This is an elusive form of lying where an important part of truth is left out if it contradicts what he wants others to believe. Very often, the story is then rewoven around what it is he wants the story to be, which is then presented as the whole truth.

- Denial: He denies doing something that was witnessed by others and calls into question the truthfulness of those who are challenging him on it. This is an especially frustrating tactic where you know you heard him say something or saw him do something but when you confront him, he simply denies it. This is a variation on the "Bart Simpson defense": I wasn't there, I didn't do it, and you can't prove it.

- Projecting the Blame: Nothing bad is ever a narcissist's fault, and he will always find some crafty way to find a scapegoat. In this way, he projects his own sins on to others as he cannot tolerate the possibility of having to confess, let alone repent, from wrongdoing. On the flip side of this tactic, he will claim the glory for all successes no matter who actually did the work. He may acknowledge that others did the work at the outset, but eventually the success story will be rewoven around him as the primary figure.

- Turning the Tables: The goal is to make you look like the abuser. When all else fails, he wants you to explode in anger, which then justifies his next stance, which is that he can't deal with you because you get violently angry. This is one place where their manipulative abilities are particularly useful. If narcissists can goad you into an angry outburst they feel genuinely attacked, victimized, and abused, which justifies their judgment against you.

- Nonverbal attacks: The narcissist has an arsenal of nonverbal ways of attacking and diminishing others, particularly when in the company of those he wishes to impress. He will roll his eyes in contempt, shake his head while offering a low, snickering laugh, and in general let you and others know of his contempt in ways that he can claim were misunderstood when challenged.

As you can see, all of these interact with each other as a theme with many variations.

It's difficult for most people to believe that a pastor could or would use these tactics. Let me assure you: narcissist pastors do, and they will continue to until they are stopped. I've seen it and experienced it, and perhaps you have as well. A church staff working with these conditions will be bludgeoned and demoralized—but is always expected to rally around and protect him with their lives and reputations if necessary. As one pastor noted earlier said, staff are expected to be "good little soldiers, all in a row."

It is also difficult to understand how almost everyone can be manipulated and fooled by a narcissist pastor, but that is the case. What follows is an email from a licensed psychologist with some identifying markers changed to protect identity.

Mariana

Your paper could have been written about my pastor.

Since I am a psychologist, my pastor, Mariana, identified me early on as a person worthy of her association. For a time, I was flattered, and did not correctly interpret her motives. She began sharing confidential information with me about members of the congregation and their personal problems. I should have stopped it right away, but I was flattered that she saw me as being on a par with her. About a year ago, I calmly requested that she stop repeating to me things that had been shared with her in confidence by other congregants. I was surprised by her sudden shift to an angry and defensive stance, and was berated for the better part of an hour.

This is when the scales fell from my eyes and I realized the extent of her narcissism. I, a trained and licensed psychologist, had been pulled into her web and was now about to pay the price of resistance. Over the ensuing months I have been demonized and made into a scapegoat, with Mariana stating that the entire problem is me and I have been (accused of) inciting other congregants to turn against her.

I have been pressured by her continued verbal abuse to resign my position as an Elder. Because there is a member of the Women's group that, despite frequent reminders about confidentiality, will repeat every word said during meetings to the pastor, I have had to remove myself from the prayer and fellowship of women I care about. My Covenant Group has a written confidentiality statement, but there is also someone there who reports everything we say to the pastor. Therefore, I had to leave that loved group as well, leaving me with no one in the church I could trust. After the pastor hounded the associate pastor into resigning, due to her jealousy of his popularity, I realized I had no pastor there and have been unable to attend worship in many months. Recently, after being made unwelcome in the church and its ministries, I was removed from active membership despite my written request to stay.

I am not alone, and there are others who have gone to the Presbytery for assistance. I think it's possible that help will be coming soon, but the pastor has hurt many people and a large segment of our congregation has left the church. Others, not surprisingly, are devoted supporters and staunch defenders.

I have seen many books and articles about how pastors are hounded out of their vocation by "evil" congregations. One of my favorite titles is "When Sheep Attack." While I understand the biblical metaphor, many pastors do want their congregations to behave like sheep, uncomplaining and unquestioningly following the pastor wherever s/he wants to go.

I believe Machiavelli is right: Power corrupts, and absolute power corrupts absolutely. We put our pastors on a pedestal and then are upset when their egos grow to intolerable dimensions. Pastors often have no peers, no one to whom they are accountable, and no friends outside the congregation. Few churches have requirements that their clergy meet with other clergy regularly for peer supervision, have supervisors or mentors who monitor them closely, or encourage pastors to develop relationships outside their own church. I am not sure how many seminaries teach the ethics of the pastorate or how to prevent their own power from being their downfall. (My [former] pastor vigorously defends her unethical practices as being holy and necessary.)

4

Unmasked

Masks camouflage the faces of both good and evil;
keep hidden what is a truth and what is a lie.

—Patti Roberts, *The Angels Are Here*

It is one thing to describe everything in the abstract, but it is something altogether more meaningful when placed into the context of real life. How do all of these come together? The following are just a few of the stories that I have collected.

THE PURITAN PRINCE

One case from history stands out as the narcissism of this minister may have been the cause of calamity for his town and congregation. It is Stacy Schiff's description of Puritan minister Samuel Parris:

> Few of them dealt as severely with their congregants as did Parris. He could be tedious, mulish, sulky. In possession of standards, he liked for things to be done properly. He applied

great energy to small matters; he had the proclivity for tidiness that creates a shamble. When the wife of tailor Ezekiel Cheever went into labor in early 1690, Cheever impulsively borrowed a horse from his neighbor's stable without permission, presumably to summon a midwife. Resolving the matter fell to Parris, who required three meetings to do so. He demanded a public apology. Cheever readily submitted one. Parris deemed the effort "mincing"; he ordered the new father to repent again in the meetinghouse the following week. He was the type of person who believed he alone could do the job adequately and afterward complained that no one had helped. He could be petty.

Parris tried to cram a great deal into a sermon; he could belabor, and exhaust, a point. He knew he often fell short but did not like to concede [that] . . . The pewter tankards on the communion table were an eyesore. Could they not be replaced? (Wealthier congregations had silver communion pieces.) To the parsonage he brought a number of items rare in Salem village: his own silver tankard, a writing desk, and a mirror. He boasted a coat of arms, a rarity among Massachusetts ministers. He quickly began lobbying for ownership of the parsonage and its land. The request was not inappropriate, but it was premature; towns made such grants to their ministers after long time service. The villagers demurred.

Less than a year after his ordination, Parris compiled a numbered list of complaints. Neither the house nor the fence and pasture nor the salary nor the firewood supply met with his approval. His fence was rotten and on the verge of collapse. Brush over-ran two-thirds of the pasture. He could not subsist on an unpaid salary. Firewood he left for last. It was now the end of October. Without wood, he warned his congregants, they would hear no further Scripture. "I cannot preach without study. I cannot study without fire. I cannot live quietly without study."

To his petition Parris affixed a line in his signature brand of high-handed self-pity: "Let me add if you continue contentious, your contention will remove me either to the grave, or some other place." He understood that his predecessors had been treated kindlier. Nor were his predecessors as sensitive to the cold as was he, after nearly a decade in the tropics.

The villagers met repeatedly to discuss their minister's predicament; as early as the fall of 1690 a movement was afoot to dismiss him. The committee to collect his salary voted later in 1691 not to do so.[1]

---

1. Schiff, *The Witches*, 39–40.

Parris was the minister in Salem, Massachusetts. From this sparse narrative we can see the elements of toxic narcissism in him. His home life was no less dictatorial and must have been very difficult for his wife and children. It seems the pressure on them was so great that, in 1692, his two daughters were the first young girls to accuse various Salem men and women of witchcraft, which eventually led to the Salem witch trials and the hanging executions of nineteen people, including the village's ex-minister, George Burroughs. One, Giles Correy, refused to answer any questions and consequently was pressed to death by placing large stones on his chest, and his wife hanged. At least four and possibly as many as thirteen died in prison.

In other words, the phenomenon of toxic narcissism in the clergy is not a new issue; rather, it is newly recognized.

As is the case throughout this book, in what follows the names and identifiable details have been changed to protect both the guilty and the innocent.

ROCKY

Rocky had been a trucking company owner in the Atlanta area for many years before switching careers and going into ministry. He now was the pastor of two small churches roughly thirty miles apart in a rural area, and it wasn't working well. I first learned of him when the council of one of his two churches asked to meet with me. They were confused and disheartened. Rocky had been there for only two years, but the congregation was shrinking rapidly. There were complaints about his sermons being too long and too pointed, complaints about his personality and the way he treated people, and people were voting with their feet. Neither church was quite at the level where it could employ him full time; it was obvious that the split assignment was part of the problem, but how big a part I did not know.

The members of the church governing board unloaded their stories on me in a closed session one winter evening. Rocky had a domineering manner, did not listen to suggestions, became angry at criticism, was extremely controlling, and was demanding more money . . . All of this had a familiar ring, but with a twist. He demanded the entire month of August off to go kayaking along the Inside Passage of British Columbia's west coast. He claimed it was for his spiritual renewal as he traveled alone with only what he could carry in his kayak, while eating the fish and crabs that he caught along the way. The problem was that the churches needed to be in contact with him at least occasionally and had passed a policy that no more than two consecutive weeks could be taken as vacation. He first challenged their authority in changing the policy, claiming that it constituted a change in working conditions and could not be done without his written agreement. When it became obvious this line of reasoning was not working, Rocky simply stated that he would use sick leave for the second two weeks. He then demanded more sick leave.

Rocky asked to meet with me privately a few days later, and I agreed as I was planning on interviewing him anyway. Interviewing everyone involved in a church conflict is part of my standard operating procedure.

Rocky was fairly tall with an athletic build. He walked in with the assurance of a professional athlete and proceeded to make himself at home, but not fully. Even though he appeared to be assured and comfortable, his eyes betrayed his wariness. He knew that I had been called in to solve a problem and that he was at the center, and so he was a bit afraid of me as I had power that could negatively or positively affect him.

Pastor Rocky spent the next half-hour fervently trying to convince me that the only way he could function was if his yearly kayak trip was done in four consecutive weeks. This was an interesting argument as it was not a long-standing practice; he had done it exactly twice in his life. He was unwilling to place any restrictions on it or to be available at any point to anyone other than his wife who remained at home with their young children. He claimed that he was entitled to continue his kayaking practice because the churches had allowed it during his first two years and that it was now a condition of employment. He had additional complaints and demands, which he laid out in detail, and then asked me if I would negotiate a new, more complete employment contract for him with the church. When I said that I could not do that, he asked if I would be his counselor and mentor. I explained to him that I had been retained by his council and that entering a counseling/mentoring relationship would be a conflict of interest. I did, however, refer him to a friend who is a Christian therapist.

I met again with the council, told them my findings and their options, and then listened. They said that they knew what they had to do to protect the church, but they were afraid Rocky would sue them and were clearly intimidated by that possibility. Instead, they did nothing. He is still there as of this writing and the congregation is still shrinking. One parishioner said, "Here's a pastor who displays a complete misunderstanding of Christian tolerance and who split a congregation in the process to form an intolerant, bigoted church and then refused to baptize my granddaughter. Can you imagine withholding the one sacrament that Christianity is founded on—ordained by Christ? How petty can you get?" It is only a question of time before he leaves or the church dies.

The Ghost

In another situation, three church elders contacted me in a conference call and said they did not know what to do. Timothy, their pastor of seventeen years, was rigid and unwilling to change, the entire paid staff (associate pastor, business manager, teen pastor, organist, etc.) was ready to quit because of his unpredictable and dictatorial ways, and could I do something?

I began by individually interviewing the entire staff, and a pattern emerged.

They described a man who is generally kind and gracious when with several others but who would "ream you out when no one else was around." They said he could "put on a good face" but turn instantly to rage when things went wrong. In fact, several used the term "Jekyll and Hyde" in describing Pastor Timothy. He had a long-standing pattern of paranoia and had been convinced for several years that people were plotting behind his back to undercut and get rid of him—which was now becoming reality. They described a work atmosphere of unpredictable and abusive anger. Some of the women were physically afraid of him even though he had not actually threatened or attempted violence—his presence and demeanor when angry were enough to intimidate the best of them.

A couple of the staff referred to Pastor Timothy as "the Ghost." When I asked what that meant, they said that Timothy was at the church at all hours of the day and late into the night. You might see him standing in the shadows as he moved silently about the building or sense his presence but not actually see him. The women refused to work alone at night because of his quiet and eerie presence. Or, they would leave in the evening only to find that papers on their desks had been moved during the night.

They stated that Timothy could never be wrong and lashed out at others unpredictably, blaming them for any mistake or failure. In one instance where he was clearly in the wrong and could not escape it, this was his apology: "I'm willing to be the martyr. I will accept your apology." As in so many other cases, they described him as manipulative, shallow, vengeful, and vindictive.

Timothy had never married and worked at the church from 6 AM until late at night but had remarkably little product for all the time he put in. The church was his life and he refused all social invitations. His preaching was dry and intellectual and his attempts at humor generally fell flat.

His demeanor with his parishioners was better than with his staff but had been deteriorating for some time. He was cold and unemotional as he worked with bereaved family members or others in emotional crisis, and the people took notice. Over the course of the years, the congregation simply grew older and smaller until the average age was sixty-five years. Younger families came a time or two, but then disappeared. The church was dying.

The associate pastor, Zachary, was in the worst place. He had come from Texas only eighteen months before with his young family, expecting opportunities to expand, grow, and be innovative. Instead, Pastor Timothy dictated what Scripture he would preach from on the rare occasion he was allowed to preach, wrote the script to his sermons, was highly critical of his theology, education, and personal dedication, undercut him, and in general made life miserable. Zachary now doubted his call to ministry and was ready to quit even though he did not have another job lined up. He was willing to risk living in their van with his wife and two young children rather than stay with Pastor Tim.

In sum, every staff member truly was ready to walk out the door and never look back.

Then I met with Pastor Tim. Living not too far away, he insisted on coming to my office. He was in his mid-sixties, tall and thin with graying hair and a condescending air about him. He tried to project a patrician air, but his clothes were outdated and threadbare in places. He examined my office and was particularly intrigued by my books on church conflict, psychology—and narcissism. He chose one on maintaining healthy boundaries by a famous Christian author and proclaimed it to be an excellent book, so I thought I would start with a light discussion on boundary issues. It was quickly obvious that he knew about the book, but not what it was about. He really had little concept of what personal boundaries are or how important they are to relationships.

He proclaimed how happy he was that I had been retained to work with his church. He had researched me, he said, and was amazed that someone of my incredible gifts, talents, and education not only lived so close by but also was now working with him and his church! He was certain that there was nothing wrong beyond some very minor staff issues. In fact, Pastor Tim claimed that part of the problem was that he was suffering from burnout due to the long hours and stress of his ministry, particularly since Pastor Zachary had proven to be such a disappointment. Would I please be his counselor? He just sensed God's presence with me and was certain that I could help him rejuvenate and again be the amazing minister he was in his early years. I referred him to the same therapist I had sent Rocky to, and shortly thereafter received an email asking me to please stop sending narcissists!

Pastor Tim denied ever raising his voice in anger but had no explanation of why anyone, let alone everyone, would want to quit, and he seemed genuinely surprised that some of the women were afraid of him. He said he was so loving and warm to "those people" but they were not loyal to him and took every opportunity to undercut him and his ministry. That, of course, was why the congregation was shrinking; it certainly was not his fault!

Hiring Pastor Zachary was his biggest mistake, he said. Pastor Zach had presented himself so well in the interview and had such glowing reports from his previous congregation that they fairly expected him to walk on water. Sadly, that was not the case. Pastor Zach was not only lazy, he was incompetent. He was meeting with parishioners at Starbucks when he should have been hard at work in his office to correct his deficiencies. Not only that, Zach was insubordinate. Pastor Tim had given him explicit instructions about what Scripture text to use for a special service, and Zachary had used not only different texts but had also allowed the organist and choir directors to change the music that Pastor Tim had specified! It was abundantly clear, Tim said, that Zachary would have to go.

Tim claimed that his bachelorhood was his gift to God so that he could devote all of his time to serving the precious flock that he been entrusted to him. He refused social invitations because he was generally too tired and was shy, but the main reason was that he did not want anyone to become jealous because he had gone to someone else's home for dinner. He simply changed the subject when I pointed out that he could have gone to everyone's house multiple times during his seventeen years there.

Pastor Tim then seemed to grow weary and sad. When I asked what he was experiencing, he said in a totally different voice that he was just burned out from all the work and lack of support. He then said that he had left his previous church for similar reasons. He simply could not understand why people could treat him so badly after everything he had sacrificed for them. He then said something both telltale and startling: "They only crucified Jesus once. This is the second crucifixion for me."

I met with the full council and laid out their options. Surprisingly, they said that they knew what they had to do in order to protect the church—they had just needed someone to tell them what they already knew. They met with Pastor Tim and told him that he had two options: he could voluntarily retire, or they would file formal charges against him with the congregation and demand he be dismissed. Pastor Tim retired rather than face the shame of formal charges.

I worked with the council and the new Senior Pastor (Zachary) for about three years. They have redefined themselves and the church, attendance has stabilized and is beginning to grow with young families coming in and a rejuvenated youth program.

I SPEAK FOR GOD!

Pastor Mike is a no-nonsense, in-your-face evangelist. He is a powerful and charismatic preacher and the third senior pastor in a church that has grown steadily since it was founded twenty-five years ago. Pastor Mike's sermon style is peppered with stories and illustrations that are relevant and timely. The church recently moved to a new multi-million-dollar facility where it will have room to expand. Even though the building is behind several commercial buildings, there is no sign by the road to indicate its presence. Pastor Mike sees his ministry as so powerful and the church such a draw that there is no need for a sign—God himself will bring the people to him.

Pastor Mike is certain that he is anointed by God to be the pastor of this growing church. As such, he and he alone is in charge. The boards of elders and deacons are to do his bidding without question. His personality is so powerful that the elders and deacons have acquiesced. The few who did not or questioned this authority were told to leave.

He speaks with great and convincing authority, throwing Bible verses into the conversation right and left, but without any regard to their context—what is important is that the out-of-context verses support his position. He has been known to rephrase Bible verses to more strongly emphasize his point.

Pastor Mike has little formal theological training. He has never attended a Bible college or seminary, nor does his denomination require it. All Mike needed to do was convince denominational leaders that he was "called and anointed." He believes and argues that the Holy Spirit comes over him to interpret the Bible and that he does not need any outside resources, not even a basic understanding of the underlying Hebrew, Aramaic, and Koiné Greek languages.

Pastor Mike is not alone in ministry but is a team with his wife, Marlene. While he is the "first among equals," Marlene's authority in the church is also largely unfettered. They officially are described as co-pastors. Marlene is of the same mind as Mike: she is anointed and fully filled with the Holy Spirit, and so needs no formal biblical education. When she speaks authoritatively, it is the Holy Spirit directly speaking through her.

Together Mike and Marlene are a formidable pair. Both are extroverts who must always be at the center of attention. They try to accept every social invitation, but as a means of keeping tabs on what people are saying within the congregation and to quickly stamp out any resistance or even questions, while keeping themselves and their authority at the center.

They are ruthless. Rather than meeting doubts or questions with curiosity and love, they immediately confront the individual and accuse him or her of heresy from which he or she must repent immediately. They have been known to release their narcissistic rage from the pulpit on people, naming the individual and verbally and emotionally tearing him or her to shreds. Rather than anyone coming to his or her side, the accused are shunned. Anyone offering comfort is next on the target list, accused of being "soft on sin." Gentle restoration as required in Galatians 6:1–2 through spiritually mature congregants and pastors is not even a consideration. You must be harboring secret sin if you are spiritually wounded. The wounded are spiritually shot on the battlefield.

In fact, their church is not a hospital for sinners at all. Sinners are not welcome. This congregation is only for those who have found "victory in Jesus" and toe the company line—which is whatever Pastor Mike says it is, and any changes from previous statements are revelations from God or are simply denied. Members are encouraged to shed outside friendships and focus their energies on growing the church.

Pastor Mike is large and athletic, and in his mid-forties. His rage is barely contained. In fact, he feels so sure of himself and his own righteousness that he has been known to physically corner people who he thinks are disagreeing with him and threaten to break every bone in their bodies. He then tells them to leave and never come back, and that he will sue them for slander and libel if they ever say anything derogatory about him, his wife, or their church (yes, they believe that the church belongs to them). In fact, they will force out the entire family of an individual who crosses them.

The congregation, which numbers several hundred, has taken on cult-like characteristics. The members live in fear of Pastor Mike's wrath and tend to follow his every whim. They provide him with a new car every year, a lavish home, and large salary, justifying it on the basis that the church is growing and the only reason is Pastors Mike and Marlene. They shun anyone who has left the church, regardless of the reasons for leaving. They accept Mike's teachings, even though many are not actually biblical, and believe that they are hearing directly from the Holy Spirit when either Mike or Marlene is preaching.

There is talk in the community of the cruel and confusing nature of Mike and Marlene's approach to people. Like so many other narcissists they will verbally shred someone to the verge of tears and collapse, and then demand a hug while saying, "You know, everything I said was in love and a spirit of godly correction. Your resistance is going against God, not me!" While both bridle at the community murmuring, they dismiss it as satanic slander and place the blame for what they have done on none other than God as they were merely acting on his behalf. Meanwhile the church grows due to their combined charisma while the number of devastated individuals and families also increases.

Some of the elders and deacons told others how intimidated both boards were by Mike, which got back to Mike. He called a special combined board meeting and in a screaming rage demanded to know who had said these things and that he would break their necks. He then demanded to know who was afraid of him. No one dared answer.

JACQUELINE

The email was unsettling. An associate pastor wrote that there was a major conflict in his church that the senior pastor refused to address. The board of elders had asked him to contact me after locating me in an Internet search. I wrote back and asked a lot of questions, which is my normal method. The contact for the board of elders could only tell me that there was a serious rift between the boards of elders and deacons, that it involved strong personalities, finances were an issue, and the senior pastor was oddly silent. It wasn't a huge church by Texas standards but it was growing rapidly and they were having to deal with multiple major issues at the same time, such as financing the new auditorium, finding enough qualified Sunday school teachers, enlarging the parking lots, replacing the recently resigned worship and music ministers, and other issues that are part of rapid church growth. I was intrigued and a few weeks later flew to Houston and then drove the seventy-five miles to where the church was located.

As always, my first stop was to see the lead pastor, pay my respects, and learn as much as I could about the people and the problems.

Pastor Jacqueline did not seem overly happy to see me. While she smiled and told me how relieved she was that I was finally there, her eyes were wary and betrayed her discomfort. She said that she had been the lead pastor for eight years. During that time, the congregation had more than doubled in size as a new subdivision of upscale homes that almost surrounded the church itself was built. She said that they had an overabundance of blessings and admitted to being stressed but added that she could handle it. My job was to figure out who was stoking the flames of conflict and bring the elders and deacons back together. She claimed that she had an excellent working relationship with both boards and could not understand why they were fighting. She also said that they were adults and she expected them to work it out without her intervening.

My practice is to interview everyone I can find from every level in the hierarchy, from janitor to senior pastor. Pastor Jackie, as she preferred to be called, offered me an office so I could conduct private interviews with board members, the associate pastors, and lay leaders. She also gave me an interview schedule that ran into the evening and through the following day. The first interview was in about an hour.

I spent the intervening time gleaning as much as I could from the surroundings. The church housed a burgeoning preschool that obviously needed more space. The carpets were worn but clean. The auditorium (not "sanctuary") would seat around 500 people in stackable chairs. The entire building looked tired and in need of a facelift.

In all I conducted eighteen interviews, each lasting thirty to forty minutes, with short breaks in between. In going back to the original interview notes, the issues became apparent. Issues are often symptoms of the problem and finding the sources of conflict means gaining an accurate understanding of what the issues represent.

The board of elders had the usual officers: chair, vice chair, treasurer, and secretary. The board chair was a nice, older gentlemen who was also extremely frustrated. He said the board was left to fend for itself and was not united in vision or purpose. Pastor Jackie insisted that the elders act autonomously, meaning she provided little if any leadership. She would ask the board to approve this or that, but the board had never received any training in its legal purposes, fiduciary responsibilities, nor had it discerned a clear role for itself. The strongest personalities were controlling the agenda and direction, but the two strongest personalities did not like each other so there was a constant sense of tension whenever the board met. As a result, board meetings tended to be short and superficial.

There were conflicts between some elders and deacons as well. The deacons saw the power vacuum caused by the elder board's dysfunction and moved to fill the void. The elder board refused to give any power beyond facility oversight to the deacons. The deacons were determined to fulfill the roles of both boards if they could. An elder who tended to fall asleep during meetings did not help matters. Pastor Jackie's only response had been, "Fix this." Underneath all of this were other currents, including strong feelings of resentment at who was recently appointed to the position of preschool director (the wives of an elder and a deacon had applied for the position, with the elder's wife being appointed). There were accusations of unfairness and not following protocols in the interview and hiring process. There were also accusations of dishonesty and demands for repentance from both sides, which only drove them further apart.

Their conflict communication skills were not only ineffective, they tended to make things worse. The strongest personalities tended to be blunt, and one deacon saw himself as both champion of causes and a martyr

when the others did not agree. I was told that the issues themselves could
be resolved; what was blocking resolution were attitudes of disrespect and
black-and-white thinking with no middle ground for compromise.

The preschool was seen as being out of control as it had taken over the
entire Sunday school wing and the adult groups were no longer able to use
the rooms on Sunday mornings. The financial practices of the preschool
were not in accord with best practices and there were insinuations of money
disappearing and fraud, but no clear accusations. The bookkeeper resigned
due to the lack of cash controls. There had been accusations of embezzle-
ment of more than $20,000, but no formal investigation. The deacon mak-
ing the accusations was asked to offer proof or step down but refused both
requests.

While these conditions might seem hopeless to many, my experience
led me to believe the conflicts were at a low enough level of intensity that
I could facilitate a resolution. People had said and done things that were
hurtful, but that is the normal way of conflict. Trust had been broken but
could be rebuilt.

There was one major obstacle: Pastor Jackie. She was described as being aloof to it all. She did not engage in the elder meetings and did not
attend deacon meetings. She spent most of her time in her office and rarely
did any outside visitation unless it was to a prominent member. Her preaching was passionate, but her preparation was lacking. She had said multiple
times that a staff member was causing all the dissent but refused to offer a
name. Most disturbingly, the interviews revealed that she was pitting elders
and deacons against each other by feeding different information to each
one, but neither the elders or deacons realized it.

I always try to interview the lead pastor last and this situation was no
different. My alarm bells were ringing within ten minutes.

She said the church had had ten pastors in its first ten years, but she
brought stability out of the chaos. She saw the elder and deacon boards as
being largely nonfunctional but necessary if only because the church bylaws required that they exist. She would rather just get rid of them entirely
to simplify her life. That way, she could simply dictate "what the Lord is
telling me to do." She said that she had total control over the budget and
spending—"and that is as it should be. In the early church the apostles controlled the money, and I am a modern-day apostle. We are just following
biblical precedent."

She had no interest in mingling with congregants and was even less interested in the sick. "That's what I have associates for," she said. She insisted
that she had posted office hours and people should come to her during those
times, and those times only. It did not matter to her that her hours were in

the middle of the workday and most people could not meet during those times. Again, "That's what I have associates for."

She was upset because the elder and deacon boards had agreed that members to both boards would be elected. She almost demanded that the right to appoint whom she wanted to be returned to her. Since the first election a year ago, the new board members were trying to make far too many changes; they were not people she would have appointed. As a result, she was writing a new church constitution and bylaws that would return all "ecclesiastical power" to her. After all, there was nothing biblical about elections!

During the interview, Pastor Jackie was losing energy fast and it was obvious. She looked worn out and a bit haggard. I asked when she had last taken a full two or more weeks of vacation. "Never," she said. "I take a day here and a day there, but things will fall apart if I'm not here. Jeremy [one of the associate pastors] would have a field day." This suddenly got even more interesting as Jeremy was the associate who first contacted me.

I commented that she looked tired. The floodgates opened. "I am more than tired; I am exhausted, and nobody cares! People go behind my back all the time and leave me out of the loop so I don't know what's going on. Some are trying to sabotage me, especially Jeremy—I can't trust him as far as I can throw him with a broken arm! He's been building his power base and one of these days it's all going to come down to a showdown between him and me! And I WILL WIN!" Her tone was more than determined; it was vicious.

I had scheduled the following day, a Saturday, to be a facilitated intervention with both boards and all pastors present. I thought Jackie might cancel it, but instead she was openly in favor, or so it seemed.

We started at 9:00 Saturday morning in a comfortable meeting room. Both boards and the pastors were there, as well as two or three influential members of the congregation. We gradually worked our way into the issues, but the issues were not my focal point. I was far more interested in having each one express their emotions from the conflict and the physical, spiritual, and emotional effects each was experiencing. I wanted them to truly understand how deeply they had hurt each other, the pain they had caused, and the toll it was taking on them. This technique effectively bypasses the argument stage and further escalation. Slowly, they began to engage and open up to each other. Ever so slowly they began to grasp how badly they had hurt each other and how much they mourned these broken relationships. Pastor Jackie was sitting apart and conspicuous by her nonparticipation.

By midafternoon we had reached the point where I can do nothing but turn it over to the Holy Spirit to convict each of their sins, encourage them to openly confess what they had thought, said, and done, and seek forgiveness. It was totally quiet when Pastor Jackie almost yelled, "Robert, are you willing to submit to my authority?!" Silence. She did it again. Robert said that this was not the time or place for this confrontation. Pastor Jackie was clearly furious but said nothing.

Another few minutes of silence. Then an elder stood up, addressed a deacon, and said, "My brother, I have sinned against you. Will you please forgive me?" The two men embraced, crying. Then others stood and did the same. Within a few minutes all the elders, deacons, and pastors were confessing their sins, seeking forgiveness, and embracing in reconciliation. All but Pastor Jackie, that is. She stormed out of the room, muttering, "This is bullshit!"

I tried to catch her, but she pushed past me in open anger. I tried calling her that evening and before I left for the airport the following morning. She did not answer. About a week later I submitted my written report and recommendations to the board of elders, as the board was my employer. One of the things I recommended was that Pastor Jackie be granted a one-year, fully paid sabbatical. A few weeks later I received an email from Associate Pastor Jeremy. Pastor Jackie had trumped up charges against him and he had resigned. She had also intercepted the report and destroyed it without the board members ever seeing it.

What is truly remarkable in all of these stories is the absolute inability of the pastors to experience empathy for others or even begin to imagine what life is like to those they abuse. Their power and control is paramount. They could not understand that they were at the center of the problem. They simply did not care about the difficulties others experienced or how their inability to empathize or to forgive authentically caused lasting damage. Perhaps the most damning case against them is that they truly believe that how they take out their rage on others by humiliating, belittling, and emotionally raping them is completely normal and acceptable for themselves but never for others. And then they want a hug.

I could go on as the variations are endless, but I believe I have given you a baseline to understand and identify the narcissistic pastor.

5

The Narcissist as Leader

Thus, in a middle course between these heights and depths, they drifted through life rather than lived, the prey of aimless days and sterile memories, like wandering shadows that could have acquired substance only by consenting to root themselves in the solid earth of their distress.

—Albert Camus, *The Plague*

Camus captures the essence of narcissist pastors. They are the prey of aimless days and sterile memories, always seeking to replace the emptiness within with something substantial, but unable to do it.

One of the few narratives published about serving in ministry under a narcissist is by Adam Harbinson, who served as an associate pastor under a man with raging NPD. After a considerable period of healing, he wrote about his experiences. In describing his own pain-filled exodus, he offers this observation: "A narcissistic obsession with themselves as God's anointed leaders of the work of the Lord has replaced the earlier selfless commitment to the Lord of the work."[1] His words are beautifully phrased and surgically

1. Harbinson, *Savage Shepherds*, 99.

accurate. It is our expectation that our pastors will *do* the work of the Lord rather than *be* Lord of the work. The narcissist insists that he is the Lord of the work and all others should serve him.

I did not find any narratives about identifying and protecting oneself or a congregation against the narcissist pastor. In researching the peer-reviewed published literature from a variety of disciplines, I found the same dearth of data. What I did locate indicated that, while the majority of pastors have strong narcissistic tendencies, they also manage to channel those tendencies into positive directions. We might call them "healthy narcissists." They have the same needs for praise and recognition but are not consumed by them nor are their relationships with others or with their churches toxic. As I wrote in the introduction, I am not overly concerned with the "healthy" narcissists who comprise most pastors. My focus is on those who I would say have *predatory* or *malignant* narcissism, which is a disease as toxic as it sounds. They do incalculable damage.

High levels of leader narcissism have been shown to be detrimental to the organization by demoralizing those who work under the narcissist. The higher the levels of leader narcissism, the higher the levels of employee negative emotions such as malicious envy, which leads to jealousy among employees and even sabotage of each others' work, with a resultant lowering of employee productivity in both quantity and quality.[2] Overt narcissists as a group are highly aggressive in meeting their needs for power, admiration, and so on. However, there are differences in their focus based on gender. High aggression males "were more influenced by leadership and authority aspects of narcissism and females were more influenced by self-absorption/self-admiration aspects of narcissism." While both genders identified with being helpers, defined as "either as a help-seeker or defender," and both were positively tied to exploitativeness. In other words, they use the mantle of helping people to exploit them.[3] But there are also differences. In comparing men and women narcissists in the role of CEO (which is the role of pastor in most cases), women were found to be more ethical than their male counterparts, were more inclined to follow rules and policies, and were more committed to concepts of fairness and transparency than men. "Importantly, when women CEOs display narcissistic personality traits, women are less likely to put their organizations at risk compared to men."[4] Perhaps women represent a kinder, gentler form of narcissism.

---

2. Braun et al., "Leader Narcissism Predicts Malicious Envy," 738.

3. Gumpel, Wiesenthal, and Soderberg, "Narcissism, Perceived Social Status," 138.

4. Ingersoll et al., "Power, Status and Expectations," 14.

One of the first indications of the possible scope of the problem was a study on narcissism in Korean Christian seminary students, who exhibited higher levels of narcissism than any other personality trait.[5] This presents a problem as the Korean Presbyterian Church constitutes 75 percent of Korean Christian churches in the United States.[6] While many pastors are perceived as living on a pedestal above everyone else, Korean pastors find themselves climbing onto it with the impossible cultural expectation that they be the perfect pastor, without blemish or flaw. That reality may discourage healthy candidates from seeking ministry while encouraging the unhealthy (who think they already are perfect) by providing what they need most: praise, power, and control, which technically is termed "narcissistic supply."

The primary studies on narcissism in the clergy were done in the Netherlands and Poland by Dutch researcher, Assistant Professor of Psychology Hessel Zondag of the University of Tilburg in The Netherlands. Zondag, who recently retired, specializes in the psychology of religion. He has developed four classifications into which pastors tend to fall. The first group consists of those he says have a natural orientation that causes them to see religion as a way of life where they may live out their piety and convictions. The second group encompasses those who seek to maintain a balance between faith and doubts; they tend not to be totally convinced of doctrinal teaching and often accept tentative answers to major theological problems. Those in the third group rely on others to help them shape and understand their faith. The fourth group is the one that concerns us most: narcissists who "turn to religion for support, safety and social security."[7] Put a bit differently, those in the pastorate, like most professions, cover a wide spectrum of mental health from perfectly healthy to abysmally sick. In later work, Zondag discovered that a large majority of pastors had strong narcissistic tendencies but were able to channel their drives into positive outlets in ministry.[8]

We want our pastors to be bold and even audacious leaders, but leaders with a heart of compassion, which is empathy in action. A pastor without empathy, without the ability to feel and authentically reflect the pain and grief of others, is a contradiction in terms. Zondag's work on empathy and narcissism examined the relational nature of the pastorate, focusing on the development of a healthy pastoral relationship. As previously discussed,

5. Pan, "Pastoral Counseling of Korean Clergy," 251.

6. Hammond, "Second Generation Korean American Presbyterians."

7. Zondag, "Involved, Loyal, Alienated, and Detached," 314–15.

8. Zondag, "Unconditional Giving and Unconditional Taking," 431.

empathy is defined as being able to experience the full range of feelings in others, from the heights of joy to the depths of despair and the quiet pain of suffering, but without being caught up in it. Those who possess this empathetic ability to understand someone else's suffering seem to have a heightened capacity to imagine different outcomes, to imagine the desires and needs of the other, and to thus understand their motives. When this happens, they are able to lead the suffering parishioner quietly through the fog of confusion to a brighter future.

Interestingly, Zondag uncovered a strong connection between the ability to empathize and personal stress: those who scored high on compassionate perspective and the ability to see a brighter future had low personal distress—their ability to understand the pain of others normalized their own painful experiences. Narcissists, on the other hand, seek peace of mind through admiration and praise, and cannot relate to the pain of anyone other than themselves, and even then they do their best to block it from any personal awareness. As stated earlier (and which possibly cannot be overstated), those with NPD have a blank spot where empathy should be, making it nearly impossible for them to understand life from a perspective other than their own and making authentic sympathetic connections with others impossible. They simply have little to no idea of the inner workings of someone else's emotions, nor do they particularly care. Unfortunately, true narcissists, in not having the ability to emotionally connect, never find peace of mind. Their lives live out the entirety of Jeremiah 6: disaster, battle, fear, shame, humiliation, rage . . . and thus they live out the words of Jeremiah in proclaiming peace when they have found none (Jer 6:14). However, the acting ability of the narcissist must not be underestimated or misread. They are consummate chameleons, able to change their colors effortlessly as they mimic the background of whatever situation they may be in, and that includes their ability to appear compassionate. Covert narcissists in particular can mimic compassion for extended periods, but overt narcissists tire of it quickly and are able to mirror empathy only in short swatches. In a certain sense they are the mirror images of empathetic people, and we must never forget that the mirror image is thin, fragile, and reversed, as neither type actually experiences compassion for other people. We expect and demand compassion in our clergy, of course, but what Zondag did not expect were the high rates of both overt and covert narcissism that he uncovered among the pastors he studied.

It is common for pastors to preach about self-esteem, but how they preach about it also depends on their theological beliefs about humility. This is one place where the narcissistic pastor cannot remain hidden, even though he or she will place great effort into the attempt. Regardless of whether he or she sees self-esteem as a positive quality (you are made in the very spiritual image of God Almighty), or a negative (repent from your prideful ways or burn forever), the narcissist pastor will find a way to insert himself into the sermon in a positive way. It may be a statement about how good it is to have self-esteem and how wonderful he feels at knowing that he is a child of God, or it could be subtler in softly proclaiming his own humility, which is in itself a contradiction—he's proud of his humility. The narcissists' self-esteem is built on recognition of their good works by others, but it is always a mask covering feelings of failure and shame.

Donald Hands and Wayne Fehr, in their *Spiritual Wholeness for Clergy*, studied spiritual wholeness and they describe narcissism without naming it. They concluded that many pastors seek to earn self-esteem through their good works yet "no amount of admiration and successful ministry to others manages to fill the gaping void within."[9] To counter this tendency, Hands and Fehr suggest that pastors rigorously pursue a pattern of three disciplines to maintain emotional, spiritual, and relational health: spiritual renewal, rest-taking, and developing personal support systems. Narcissistic responses to these patterns are interesting. Some insist on taking extended leaves and others never take any form of vacation at all because they are thoroughly convinced that the church cannot function without them or they fear a coup d'état in their absence—or both. Spiritual renewal for covert narcissists is generally done in more passive ways such as reading, perhaps in the mountains or by a lake, while overt narcissists are more apt to choose physical activity in the outdoors. Either way, they are least likely to create intentional personal support systems—the prospect of having other people know you as you really are being too threatening even to consider.

Pedophile priests have plagued the Roman Catholic Church. One might expect the narcissist, with his lack of boundaries, might also constitute a high percentage of sexual predators, but that does not appear to be the case. As others have noted, religious narcissists tend to be puritanical, which finds an outlet in tightly controlled and very private relationships with other adults. There are aberrations, of course, but the sexual predation of children is not a high narcissistic priority.[10] The writers did note, however, that pastors who self-reported their sexual misconduct moved more frequently from parish to parish, left a string of victims, and sometimes destroyed congregations.[11]

---

9. Hands and Fehr, *Spiritual Wholeness for Clergy*, 67.
10. Francis and Baldo, "Narcissistic Measures of Lutheran Clergy," 86, 92.
11. Francis and Baldo, "Narcissistic Measures of Lutheran Clergy," 92.

A DIFFERENT BRANCH OF THE FAMILY TREE?

Ministry is a calling and it is my observation that in many ways it tends to attract men and women who are generally perceived to be a bit different from the rest of us. Thus, it would not be a surprise to learn that our churches tend to expect that pastors come from a slightly off-centered branch of the human race, making eccentric behaviors acceptable where in other positions these behaviors might be criticized or even punished. For example, the Menninger Foundation, which has a long history of treating mentally ill clergy, released some interesting findings. Samuel Bradshaw, on reporting the findings, wrote, "ministry offers another source of help to the severely disabled man by its closeness to sanctioned figures suitable for overidealization or omnipotent identification. These are divine figures the minister is to interpret and, in a way respect. Any acts of contempt towards those figures due to unconscious envy of their superiority are unlikely to cause a reaction from God or the minister's environment, and identification as such as 'the man of God' are acceptable role statements."[12]

The front-line preaching pastor is where the action is and where sufficient amounts of narcissistic supply such as praise can be found; hence, the narcissists tend to gravitate to pulpits rather than to administrative desk jobs, although they can be found there as well. Bradshaw went on to suggest that the "hellfire and brimstone preacher" has often had a grudgingly accepted place within North American Protestant churches and that this is a façade behind which many narcissists hide, and from which they can safely express narcissistic rage and be praised and paid for it. While their rage, fear, envy, and shame are readily accessible, their lack of connection to their other emotions tends to make them aloofly obscure in the pulpit when engaged in the more normal modes of preaching—not much warmth or humor but they are dedicated, conscientious—and puritanical. Thus, a narcissist would be able to survive and for a time thrive as a church pastor because of this greater level of tolerance in the church for peculiar personalities.

A narcissist often has surface gifts of leadership and therefore naturally gravitate to and actively seek leadership positions. To be sure, extreme narcissists are absolutely convinced that they are the only people who can resolve a situation or solve a problem up to and including the highest political offices. They have no need to be charming or empathetic when they are comfortable and in control of their situation. However, all of that changes the moment he or she feels threatened. The ultimate threat is rejection such as that found in forced unemployment, which brings them into a desperate

12. Bradshaw, "Ministers in Trouble," 234–36.

situation. They have lost control, their gifts have been unfairly rejected, and they see themselves as misunderstood and unappreciated victims. I have observed that the more desperate they see their situation as being, the more charming, persuasive, and manipulative they can be with anyone they perceive might be able to help them, and the more bombastic and threatening they are to those who oppose them. The most common reason a narcissist pastor will be seeking a new job is that his behavior is causing him problems, he is personally threatened by resistance and seeks relief through a change of scenery, or he has been fired.

The job interview is their perfect stage: they will turn up their charm wattage to its highest level, all the time reading the reactions of the interviewers and adjusting accordingly to maximize their effectiveness. Being nonempathetic, though, they do not read body language overly well without having the time to study it in conjunction with statements and behaviors. This can cause some interesting and awkward responses to questions and opposition or resistance to pointed queries about past or present problems. We will revisit this phenomenon later when discussing ways of protecting the church.

Power is the narcissists' aphrodisiac, for it means control of those who could otherwise bring harm. As a result, they actively seek positions of power. In doing so they exude confidence and competence, though their confidence is a sham and their competence often lies more in mediocrity than in excellence. In response, and as compensation, they will surround themselves with visible symbols and artifacts of their success and importance so that others will automatically be impressed and acquiesce.

I once worked with a high-ranking executive who had a million-dollar smile, a great handshake, perfectly tailored clothes, and a vanity wall in his office covered from floor to ceiling with awards, certificates, and pictures of him with "important people." This was how he reassured himself of his own importance and how he sought to impress others. Unfortunately, he was glaringly incompetent, once promising the same position to five different people. He went on to become CEO in another company; within three years, he had almost bankrupted it, and was fired. He went into consulting work. He had risen in position because of his initial impression, good looks, and narcissistic charm but was unable to compensate for his lack of ability. Some might argue that this is the infamous "Peter Principle" at work, where people rise to the level of their incompetence, which implies that they have levels of competence. That is not always the case with narcissists as they tend to be somewhat incompetent throughout; they manage to rise on the power of a high-wattage personality and intentional deceit. Where an incompetent worker can often be taught competency, the narcissist tends to move from semi-competency to incompetency.

While narcissists love to win, they just as often do not do the preparation that is necessary for winning. One result of this is that they often start projects that they never complete. In fact, they tend to "churn" projects by starting multiple ventures that compete with each other until one wins outright and the others are ignored into oblivion. As a result, the church hiring a narcissist as pastor can expect a flurry of new and exciting projects that gradually are abandoned and replaced by others. This project-intense environment justifies their claims of terrible workloads but also drains the church of resources that cannot be recouped; for all their activity, there is little produced. Then they move on to the latest revelation God has given them and the project that will come from it. One pastor changed the surface direction of the church every year with his annual "vision casting." According to him, God gave him a new and different vision and theme to follow every year. One year it was the "year of the child," then it was "the year of kindness," followed by the "year of the dove," then the "breakthrough year," and so on year after year. Nothing visible changed, nor did his sermons suddenly become wider or deeper. The only legacy was the annual engraved granite slab commemorating that year's theme, and those who supported it financially. The church grounds was studded with these self-memorials.

Entitlement is one of the most common expressions of narcissism. The narcissist expects to win simply because he competes. For many narcissists, the sermon is considered to be performance art, a time to show off his intellectual and spiritual prowess. He expects his sermons will be accepted as "world class" simply because they are his, advertising them with bombast such as, "This amazing sermon series from Pastor Phil is guaranteed to change your life in every way—and then some!" The rule of mediocrity prevails here as well regardless of their intellectual capabilities. This includes their sermons. The narcissist pastor would much rather ignore the routine and mundane work of carefully researching and constructing his sermon or building something that will last in favor of more exciting—and thus more interesting—endeavors. Even when they do spend considerable time in sermon preparation, their inability to read their audience and their belief in their own oratorical dexterity makes them tone deaf to how they sound to others.

An early indicator of mediocrity and entitlement translates to their grades in college and is a possible indicator to others that something is not as it seems. For example, narcissistic college students, who believe they can do it all better than anyone else but with less effort, actually tend to earn poorer grades over time than do their less narcissistic and harder working peers.[13] After all, they feel entitled to good grades without having to earn them like everyone else. Moreover, they are generally unable to assess their own personalities accurately and persist in maintaining lofty views of their own abilities even though they tend to be mediocre students and later, mediocre producers. One student at a small Christian college demanded to know why the paper he turned in did not receive an "A" grade. He became quite upset when told that it was at best "C" work. He then exclaimed "But I have to get an 'A' in this class!" He truly thought that this line of reasoning should result in an excellent grade, even though his work was far below the excellent level where he thought it was. In these situations, overconfidence backfires largely because "narcissists are lousy at taking criticism and learning from mistakes" and "lack motivation to improve."[14] From the narcissist viewpoint, they do not need to improve; we need to appreciate and reward them more for their greatness.

Narcissists generally do not excel in creating long-term growth in an organization, be it a secular corporation, nonprofit institution, or a church. In fact, they generally are detrimental to organizational growth and stability. A study by management guru Jim Collins showed that, while some companies headed by narcissistic leaders made short-term gains, the leaders with the fewest narcissistic personality characteristics consistently produced the steadiest growth. Collins notes that the best companies are managed by those who have a high mixture of ethics and entrepreneurship and can work in a culture of discipline,[15] which the narcissist rarely can do. While narcissists often think they possess entrepreneurial ability, they are not generally effective in creating the teams necessary for long-term success, nor do they have the self-discipline that long-term growth requires. The reality is that they lack the discipline to learn from their mistakes and prefer to keep the glory for themselves rather than allow highly functional teams to emerge.[16] Other researchers have said that narcissists in business tend to be "ethically challenged" as empathetic and narcissistic personality traits are significant predictors of ethical decision-making. Their lack of empathy often leads them to take the path of least resistance on ethical issues and ultimately into an moral quagmire.[17]

Narcissists gravitate towards institutions where they can wield power over others, such as business, academia, law, military, medicine, and the

13. Twenge and Campbell, *The Narcissism Epidemic*, 42.

14. Twenge and Campbell, *The Narcissism Epidemic*, 42.

15. Collins, *Good to Great*, 122.

16. Twenge and Campbell, *The Narcissism Epidemic*, 45.

17. Brown et al., "Ethics and Personality"; Fritz, *The Path of Least Resistance*.

ministry.[18] Each of these fields offers prestige and power. In medicine and the military, there are hierarchies of structure in which the narcissist can climb, and each rung on the ladder upward means increasing power of life and death over more and more people, as well as additional power over resources. It makes sense, then, that narcissists would seek out power positions as clergy. Being charismatic, full of energy and ideas, and able to persuade others, they find their needed praise and adulation in the ministry. Where else might one be able to tell hundreds of people how to live their lives on a weekly basis, find themselves trusted to help with all manner of emotionally traumatic circumstances, have people bare their souls and most intimate secrets to them, and then be invited to dinner as an honored guest?

Narcissists in general and narcissist pastors in particular tend to be ethically challenged. It's not that they don't know what the ethical solution is, it's that they believe they are not bound by such mundane ideas as ethics. The connection comes from their religiosity, which is external and not an integral part of their lives—it is not internalized.[19] "Christian ministers with low levels of [internalized religiosity] were more likely to exercise poor ethical judgment, thereby jeopardizing their own reputation along with the reputations of their ministry and the body of Christ as a whole."[20] Their religious exterior serves as mask behind which they hide and an entry point for what they want most: power and glory.

In our increasingly entitlement-driven society, David Augsburger notes that narcissism is but one of multiple factors along with individualism, isolation, a value-free society, decentered faith, superficial reconciliation, and confused authority that come into play with problematic clergy. He advocates for these narcissistic clergy to place themselves in accountability relationships by which they may be taught what "personhood in community means."[21] The problem with Augsburger's theory is that narcissists rarely recognize themselves, are not willing to seek help when they do, refuse accountability, and there are few proven and effective treatment models.

That is not to say there is no hope at all.

As noted previously, the narcissist generally will not seek treatment for their primary narcissism but may be open the treatment for the results of their frustrations and fears that take the form of depression and burnout. These could prove to be an entry point; the challenge for the therapist is in

---

18. Amernic and Craig, "Accounting as a Facilitator"; Clark, Lechon, and Taylor, "Beyond the Big Five"; Bradshaw, "Ministers in Trouble."

19. Cooper, Pullig, and Dickens, "Effects of Narcissism and Religiosity," 42.

20. Cooper, Pullig, and Dickens, "Effects of Narcissism and Religiosity," 47.

21. Augsburger, "The Private Lives of Public Leaders," 23–24.

establishing a trusting relationship when the narcissist rarely trusts anyone. "These patients are acutely hypersensitive to slights (though they may appear otherwise) and cover their vulnerability with illusions about their importance, and at times with condescension and rage. . . . Yet the patient will not be able to explore his interpersonal distortions or the relational dynamics in the transference unless he feels understood by a therapist who sees beneath the distancing persona."[22] The psychologist Steven Sandage reports that keeping narcissists in treatment for the long-term is difficult, but that he has seen some success if a trusting long-term treatment relationship can be established.[23]

Healthy narcissists and their unhealthy peers can be found in every profession. A certain amount of narcissism is necessary for anyone to stand before a crowd of people and proclaim, "Let me lead you." Or, "Let me cut you open to fix what is wrong." Those who manage to channel their narcissistic desires into positive streams of actions, behaviors, and decisions that are beneficial to those they lead are much more likely to be successful long-term leaders. They are shepherds who do not like lamb stew, and we need more of them.

22. Bennett, "Attachment Theory," 53.
23. Sandage, email to Puls.

6

The Toll

Our stories always contain average, ordinary people.
They are the most unsuspecting victims of all.

—D. J. Weaver

Over the course of the last few years I have been contacted by hundreds of people who felt compelled to share their stories of emotional and spiritual devastation at the hands of a narcissist pastor. So far, I have described extreme narcissism in detail as it relates to pastors and their churches, but I have maintained a bit of distance from the bloodied trenches where the victims lie. To more fully understand the human toll, we must meet them and read their stories.

The stories that follow are used by permission. They have been lightly edited to preserve the privacy of the writers. Some stories flow easily while others are somewhat disjointed as the writers try to make sense of what happened and how it has affected their lives as well as the lives of their closest family members. I'm going to start with the first story I received. It broke my heart.

PHILIP

Dear Dr. Puls,

My name is Philip. Since you have your email address readily available on your website, I figured I'd send you an email to share with you our journey. We hadn't come across your work until my mother heard you speak at the recent AACC [American Association of Christian Counselors] conference in Nashville. She bought the CD audio and gave it to my wife and I saying, "You need to listen to this!" We have been researching resources on the issue of narcissism, manipulation, covert aggression, and spiritual abuse since November 2009.

Currently I'm in my final year of seminary. My wife and I are in our mid-30s with three young children. To be honest, after our experience we have some serious trepidation about ordination and service in the church. The reason is that we spent 5 1/2 years under a covert-aggressive senior pastor while I served in full time youth ministry from 2007–2012. We realized what we were up against in 2009, and we managed to barely survive his assaults, traps, sermons aimed at us (damning me to hell in one of them), and many other devious tactics. The guy could weaponize a compliment in such a way that everyone in the room would think he was praising me, but only he and I knew he was slighting me.

My wife and I prayed and waited for the Lord to lead us out, and he did by calling us to seminary. We left on good terms (so we thought), but in August 2015 the elders held a congregational meeting after a third staff member (I was the second of 3 to leave in 3 years). The elders (at the behest of the senior pastor) proceeded to tell disparaging half-truth stories about the 3 of us to prove that the senior pastor is not the problem, but that they had 3 really bad employees and each left for their own reasons. They rewrote history to protect the senior pastor and scapegoat the 3 of us in order to "bring about much necessary healing to the flock." When this news reached us, it all but paralyzed us inwardly and we felt as though we had never left. We realized that time hadn't healed our wounds, and that we needed help.

Needless to say, three and a half years later we still struggle with PTSD (occasional nightmares, general lack of trust in people, somewhat antisocial), and we are wondering how we can put the trauma behind us so it doesn't negatively interfere with our pursuit of ministry. We certainly appreciate God giving us greater wisdom and discernment in that we can sniff out a potential manipulator a mile away. That gift is not somewhat of a curse because I naturally and instinctively stay out from under the thumb of insecure flatterers who can tell I'm on to them, which of course draws their negative attention toward me. Yet I'd never give up the school of hard knock education we received by God's providential hand.

However, with all this said, we really need to heal more thoroughly, and though we have sought marriage counseling, pastoral/professor counseling, and even abuse counseling, none of these people seem to fully grasp the type of suffering we went through, and therefore have a difficult time empathizing with the depth of injury that remains within our souls.

We need help.

GEORGE

I know this is a long shot, but my wife and I would really appreciate speaking with you.

My name is George. I just resigned my elder position at church. I have been confused, I have been yelled at, I have witnessed a demand for total control of all decisions, money, etc. I have never been apologized to, yet I have been mocked regarding an incident of my own repentance. I have wept at the loss of my hopes and dreams at this church. My heart breaks for God's children who are being hurt.

I have no idea where to turn or what to do next. I am considering reaching out to the denomination about reconciliation services, but I'm not comfortable entering in without someone present who is familiar with "the fool," "the wolf" and NPD.

Thank you so much for what you do and shedding light on what is happening in so many churches.

(A few months later):

Hi Darrell, I also have a brief follow-up regarding Pastor Anne. Last year around this time she left the denomination and went to a UCC Church. Recently a friend was at a dinner where she happened to be seated next to someone who is a member of the congregation at Anne's new church. After making this discovery, they quickly shared information and stories about how Anne behaved at the old church, and how she is behaving at the new church. Here are the particulars. Same behaviors, almost unbelievable that she would start in right away with her agenda at a new church!

- She made them sign a 3-year agreement at the start of her position there
- She is rarely on site, yet she is full time
- She is trying to change everything at once
- The newsletter regularly features her
- Her sermons are carefully worded to draw attention to her achievements and glorify herself
- People are starting to leave
- She has fired two staff members and has advertised for new worship leader and secretary positions

MARCY

I actually didn't know what narcissism actually meant until I began searching words to describe my husband/pastor. I searched emotional abuse and narcissism kept coming up to the top. Once I read and researched narcissism, I have pretty much diagnosed him somewhere on the narcissism scale.

We've been married almost 23 years and I feel that his behavior is worse now than in the early years, although there has been abuse in one form or another since the beginning of our relationship.

We have been in ministry since we married. In the past 10 years, after moving back to Oklahoma from the mission field, my husband will teach a good, solid Sunday morning message, minister to others, show "love" to those in the church and get home and turn into another person; yelling, demanding, isolated, non-communicative, controlling, calling me names on occasion, insulting me, etc. Over time, I felt like he was and is living a double life.

Our adult children serve in the church we pastor and all of us feel trapped. They want to serve the Lord, but their father is very critical of their ministry some of the time. Mixed signals. Love and criticism. Acceptance and rejection. Loving, then anger outbursts. He will shoot them an angry look from behind the pulpit if they play a wrong note while they play during worship.

I have left him three different times in the past 10 years. I have tried to set boundaries with him and his behavior. I feel trapped now because I worry about the people in our church who love us and who are loyal to us. If I leave, I feel certain he will be "the victim" and I will be the one "who has gone off the deep end" or who has "flipped out" and has abandoned the family. I have gone to our "elders" and the leadership of our denomination, but they do not know how to handle our situation. After his talk with lead pastors, my husband said he felt victimized. He couldn't even admit to me what he had done wrong and why I had to go and tell them what was happening in our marriage. I reminded him that I would not have told anyone anything if he hadn't abused me!

I am now trying to figure out what to do and say to our church family if I was to leave my husband for good. I am really trusting in the Lord for my husband, children and my marriage. It is a very lonely marriage. For him and for me. We are currently at a point where we rarely talk to one another and he criticizes my every move because I can't read his mind, basically.

During our marriage, I've experienced physical, emotional, financial and spiritual abuse.

Why am I even still with him???

Thank you for listening.

BETHANY

Hi Darrell, my name is Bethany. I'm 22 years old I'm from Florida. Like a lot of young women, me and my mother's relationship has been rocky and over time I thought it was because I wasn't being the most obedient teenager, but as time went and I matured and tried to right my wrongs things never seemed to change. No matter what I did it just didn't matter. After awhile I prayed about it because my relationship with God had become stronger. He then began to reveal things to me, and I began to research narcissism and it began to come together, but who was I to diagnose anyone when I have issues myself? Well, mom is also a pastor, and something never sits right with me when I'm in church like it seems like we really all playing church like everyone is my mom's dolls and the church is her doll house. Now I've prayed and read and drove myself crazy really trying to figure out if this is what I think it is. My life has been totally manipulated and I can't stand by and watch people's faith be manipulated either. Please help!!!!

MARCUS

Nearly three years ago I walked away from a church I had been a part of for nearly 12 years. I served in almost every ministry in that church over those years. It wasn't until the last couple of years there that I experienced some very troubling behavior from the Senior Pastor. I also saw things happening very subversively as I took on more leadership roles in the church. I had no idea what was happening or why. I later came to realize this pastor might have malignant narcissism.

Needless to say, I have been trying to find help to deal with the scars of what had happened to me as I stepped into leadership there. To make things worse, this pastor is well known in the area I live in. I'm not sure why I haven't been able completely get over the hurt I experienced. I have forgiven him, but I still struggle with anger towards myself and others.

I'd love to get some counsel, but struggle with who to talk with. Not many Christian leaders know much about NPD. When I read your article, I thought maybe you might know some ways I can get some help putting what happened truly behind me.

JESSICA

My name is Jessica. I just finished reading your article about so many pastors "suffering" from NPD. My ex-husband (senior pastor) was one of them.

Today would've actually been our 28th wedding anniversary. He's always been arrogant, but so smart. I just thought he had a reason to expect others to admire and respect him. About seven years ago, there was a significant shift. I now know that was when he began having an affair with a co-worker. Our girls were hitting the teenage years and he lost a lot of interest (Daddy was no longer the hero). Our marriage relationship declined. I was lonely and depressed. I begged for time with him, but he always said I was asking for too much. He spent less and less time with his family. He was always "working." He also had a target on our Worship Pastor's back. He brought the WP before the elders many times with many accusations. The Worship Pastor ended up resigning. In a terrible turn of events, the most caring of all the pastors, our worship pastor died suddenly after a fall. If you can believe it, my husband had poisoned the elders to such depths that they left his wife and family to grieve on their own. I'm still so embarrassed by my ex-husband's actions.

Fast forward to 2018. I knew something wasn't right. I now know my ex was using covert narcissistic moves such as gaslighting, crazy making, projection and blaming. I thought I was losing my mind. He had turned friends against me by telling them I had Borderline Personality Disorder, and all the while accusing me of ruining his reputation. Over the last several years I had asked a handful of church leaders for help (seven times). Finally, I went before the elder board and begged for help with my marriage. I was finally heard. They approached my husband and soon after, he (in a narcissist rage) resigned. My fault, of course.

The last straw was on August 15. My ex would never share his phone passcode with me. At one point when it was unlocked, I added my thumbprint in order to gain access. My worst fears were found that night. He was having another affair and already pursuing the next (another staff member). His current affair was with the director of the church's preschool. I was devastated.

I immediately filed for divorce. Through some manipulation (his gift) and tricks, he walked away with all our money and left me with a large car payment, bills, and our oldest daughter's college tuition. We had to sell the house and my daughter had to change schools. He continues to berate the girls to see him, but they will not. They are old enough to make that decision themselves. Meanwhile, he emails them and myself to say what a terrible mother I am for sabotaging his relationship with the kids and how my denial of my "mental illness" is immature and sick. I truly cannot believe this is the man I once loved (and unfortunately still do to be honest). He has destroyed our family, our marriage, and turned the church on its side. I desperately want to hate him.

I really didn't mean to write a book. Sorry. I guess telling my story is a little therapeutic. I've read tons of articles and have seen too many similar stories. Is there any help out there for pastors' wives that are being emotionally and psychologically abused by their narcissistic husbands/pastors? It's too late for me. My girls and I are moving on, trusting in the Lord's plan and timing. We are going to counseling and trying to heal. But what about all the others? I'm not sure how or if God will use my story one day, but I'd really be interested if you know of a ministry that is a safe haven for these silently suffering women.

Thank you so much for your article and for letting me tell my story.

RICHARD

My name is Richard. I am a graduate computer scientist, as well as a former military officer. I have recently come out of a toxic "Christian" cult/ministry. The main so-called "elder" is a classical overt narcissist (persecutor). As a co-conspirator, he has a "prophetess" supporting his abuse—she is a covert narcissist. There are other co-conspirators too as well as the other roles as outlined in Steve Arterburn's book *Toxic Faith*.

I came across your article "Let Us Prey . . ." from December of 2017 in the AACC when doing a search about NPD pastors and toxic faith systems.

I (and others) have witnessed the infidelity of this married "elder" and his prophetess (who was married but is now in the process of a divorce by her husband because of her infidelity with the "elder"). The elder has been estranged from his wife for many years; we only hear one side of the story regarding this separation and are forbidden to talk to her. Because I confronted this elder about this affair, he has proceeded with a vast smear campaign against me to the local congregation and is threatening to go larger in the public realm. He is careful not to mention his allegations against me outside the local core group as he knows it would be documented evidence for libel, slander and defamation charges (I have talked with legal council about this). The local congregation still does not know about his affair as I confronted him with only one other person present. He has been scrambling to cover up this scandal and smear me as the outcast so nobody will receive my witness. After he would not confess/repent per the scripture, I left this ministry. I started searching for answers as to what happened to me and why I was drawn into this cult. Arterburn's book (*Healing Is a Choice*) was recommended to me. I and another outcast have learned a lot and want to do something about this type of abuse. I am not the first person he has smeared as a result of leaving this "ministry."

This narc-elder and his co-conspirators are leading many into deception and heresies keeping them locked in a prison through fear, intimidation and other cult-like techniques. Talking with other abuse victims and outcasts who have left this cult, we have determined this group is on a dangerous trajectory whereby people's physical lives are at risk (i.e., Jonestown, a 7-day fast without food OR water). My heart breaks for my dear friends who are still trapped in this ministry and are not allowed to hear from anyone who has left. They are imprisoned.

My wife died and I was blamed for "not having enough faith." She did not heal and did not rise from the dead because of my lack of faith. It was my fault that she died! I was so confused that I was not making rational decisions. No more than 5 minutes after she died, I get a phone call from "the elder." His first words were, I am sorry. Then he proceeds to tell me not to start looking for another wife, then he asks me if I believe God can raise Marci from the dead. I of course say, God can do anything. So, he said don't let the doctors do anything with her body, wait until we have our prayer meeting in the morning, and we will decide what the Lord wants to do then. So, I find myself, sitting 5 feet away from my wife's body, waiting on David's prayer group to get a word from the Lord on what to do. Needless to say, after a couple of hours I called him back and told him to just pray over the phone because I was so distraught and I needed to make funeral arrangements. I had no sleep for the past 5 days, but it was all about raising my wife from the dead, so he could be affirmed to others who had been questioning him on why she died in the first place since they were believing for her healing. His objective was to blame me, the widower, for everything. Lack of faith, allowing Pharmacia to kill her and lack of faith for a resurrection. It was the most horrendous and traumatic ordeal I have ever been through; and it was starting to destroy my soul and my mind.

Months later I talked with a psychiatrist who told me I had C-PTSD [Complex Post-Traumatic Stress Disorder] as a result of this traumatic abuse. It wasn't until this last time that I came out of the cult that I started searching for answers as to why my thinking and behavior was not my typical self.

After this abuse, I had memory problems, I would make irrational decisions that I would have never made, could not trust others, didn't sleep and other effects of this abuse. Here is the kicker . . . even months after I buried her, he was still telling me and others in his group that my wife would rise from the dead when the man-child anointing would fall on the Church. So, when I needed my so-called Pastor and church support group to help me through the grieving process I was instead blamed for her death due to lack of faith, blamed for her lack of resurrection back to life, due to my lack of faith, AND then told, "Don't worry, Marci will knock on your door next week when the anointing is supposed to fall."

The psychiatrist told me that because of this abuse, my mind was playing the death, funeral and other horrors of this ordeal over and over again in my head 24/7 non-stop. I could not get closure, so my mind started to shut down in certain areas as a defense mechanism. I could not move forward and properly grieve for her since my "Pastor" kept telling me my wife would be back in a few days. It never happened, of course.

It's an abuse that I can't quantify, only to tell you that the doctor told me she was surprised I was still alive and had not died myself. There's so much more bizarreness but I spare you this. Suffice to say, this pattern of abuse happened to others in the group for various reasons. As such, I too plan to write a book about my ordeals, and recovery from this narcissistic psychopath.

ROBERTO

I read your article and other articles on narcissist pastors with great interest. The subject is close to my heart. My girlfriend and I serve as worship leaders in a Church, and in addition, my girlfriend is also the church secretary, and works very closely with the pastor on any number of administrative items.

I am quite familiar with the personality disorder. I was married for 18 years, went through a divorce, and then the first woman I met and began a relationship with, turned out to have this disorder (it took me about a year to figure it out). I also worked for a male supervisor who had it, though his was more overt. Needless to say, these two people caused a great deal of stress in my life. Eventually I left both the job and the relationship. I met my girlfriend and discovered that she too had been with a guy who had the same disorder, and now, here we are serving together in a church with a pastor who has it. We both know the signs very well. Our pastor is one of these people.

For almost everyone in this small congregation (the church went through a split about 8 years ago) her strange behavior has been noticed but not correctly identified. Thus, although they know something is "off," they don't know how to deal with it. Over the last few years this pastor has done tremendous damage to the congregation and has effectively crippled the church from being able to serve and work together with any sense of purpose and mission.

The denomination and lay leadership, with a couple of pointers, have recently come to understand the true nature of the problem, and are trying to figure out how to deal with it.

Thank you for listening.

DENNIS

Hello Dr. Puls. My name is Dennis, and my wife just forwarded your article on Narcissistic Pastors to me and like her, it made me nauseous because it hit so close to home. I recently in the last year encountered a situation where I and another staff member were let go from a church, and everything was covered up by the lead pastor who was abusive in several ways. He manipulated the entire process to make sure his tracks were clean. The deacons were aware of his behavior and yet did nothing. I had been a worship pastor for 11 years and was hired by a former pastor whom I had a very healthy ministry relationship with . . . we worked together for over a decade. However, he resigned and moved away & the church hired a new pastor and from the time he arrived, it was 6 years of hell. I endured it because I felt I needed to, and being the provider for my family, I felt it was something I would have to just endure. Where else could I go? Of course, it ended with my being forced to resign and I was notified a week after my 49th birthday and the church was never aware of what happened behind the scenes. I had a great relationship with my team of volunteers, and had a successful ministry, but everything I did was scrutinized, and criticized . . . often in front of other staff. I was constantly harassed about my age. This pastor was clever at dividing people and would make people pick sides . . . all behind the scenes. It left me feeling hopeless, too old, flushed and blaming myself.

Over the last year, I and my family have been healing but it's taking time. Sometimes I can't sleep, sometimes I have anger, hatred and then sometimes I'm driven to tears. It's a very long story that I have wanted to share but out of fear, I've not really come forward with my story. I would like to have a chance to talk with you sometime. I just haven't known where to turn to seek help. It's been a horrible experience and one I never wish to experience again.

This pastor is a lead pastor of a large church in the Dallas area. They've had a lot of staff departures, and new staff hires. It seems like a revolving door. In addition, several attendees and members have left. He's been there 7 years and the church really hasn't grown much past the 3,000 mark. There are a few staff there that are not being treated well, but no one will speak up.

After reading your article, I saw where you encouraged anyone facing this type of situation to reach out so at the suggestion from my wife, I've decided to email you.

I apologize for the length of this email, but I am hoping what I have to share makes some sense.

(Later email.)

Hello Darrell. So good to hear from you. I'm excited to hear that you are revising the book to include personal stories.

Over the last several months my biggest frustration has been having no voice, and no one who would ever believe me. Some of the other people who were mistreated by this pastor, and those who experienced firsthand, have just moved on quietly and don't wanna talk about it. One of our former pastors from what I've heard no longer attends church anymore.

People just don't wanna talk about it.

But for me and my wife we know personally what we experienced.

That pastor has now surrounded himself with his dream team and new unsuspecting people continue to come to that church because he surrounds himself with young and attractive people and gives them a leadership role . . . they will remain as long as they adhere to his way. Because it's a large church the district never did anything & my guess is because of the finances it brings in . . . who knows. Several of the leaders knew what was going on quietly just watched and did nothing.

All this to say . . .

Over the last two years I have often thought, "I wish someday I could share my story in hopes that it will help somebody else." While I completely understand that you cannot guarantee using my story, I will be prayerful about it and if God feels it could help somebody else, then that's what I desire.

MARYANN

Hi Darrell! I came across your article and wanted to reach out. My family (and about 20 other families) have recently left our church. I have uncovered multiple stories of emotional abuse by the head pastor and his wife. We brought up our concerns with them and some other staff at the church in a meeting yesterday. Their response was stunning. No emotion, no ownership, not even an ounce of at least feigned concern. I have been long convinced the wife has a personality disorder (I am a licensed therapist) who seems to run the show. Literally their very best friends and everyone in their "Life Group" has left the church. There is an isolated accountability structure there, so any grievances taken to elders are dismissed as gossip and explained away.

Not really sure why I'm writing to you other than to say I am trying to expose this issue but feel helpless. This was the response of my pastor after sharing the issues I brought up in the meeting (stories of close friends and my own experiences): "If you gave me time I am convinced that you would walk away from our conversation convinced that all of those things are not true." There was no posture of humility or even feeling concerned or alarmed that 40 members (and more in the pipeline) have had negative experiences with them—some which include extreme control and verbal abuse—and have left.

Anyway, just wanted to share that I valued your article and am just praying these issues will be exposed.

JANELLE

Hello Darrell. I found your information by doing a Google search on "can a minister be a narcissist?" I am reaching out because my boyfriend is an ordained minister whom I believe to be a narcissist or have strong narcissistic characteristics. I'm so confused. He's not currently active in a local church but places a lot of blame on our relationship as the reason why he cannot be active. He does regularly attend church, but he isn't active in the pulpit or any auxiliaries. Here recently he's been putting a lot of emphasis on us getting married but since his mask has come off, I am very hesitant.

The part that I would like insight on is how a person can go so low at times (privately with me) but claims to be filled with the Holy Spirit and knows the Word so well. He speaks against premarital intercourse but has wanted it since the very beginning. I was willing because of my attraction to him and believing early on he would eventually be my husband. And he said the Word warned against us having a sexual "lifestyle" which we weren't going to do but is eventually what happened.

The sex isn't my biggest concern. It's moreso character. The character he has shown to me doesn't add up to the person he initially presented to me and absolutely doesn't match the person he presents to the world. With me, he's a drinker, gambler, manipulator, with a lot of rage inside. He's had a LOT of legitimate life circumstances that have happened which is how I was able to give him a lot of passes early on. But now I see him for who he's been with me, don't really know who he really is.

According to him he will get back to "himself" soon since "the storm is clearing."

If possible, I'd just like insight into this. I know we all fall short and have our individual issues, but it seems off that a person can exhibit darkness and light in the same breath. Consistently. Sometimes with seemingly no remorse.

ELLEN

I do not send this email lightly. The church where my husband and I currently serve is experiencing internal conflict like I have not experienced before.

To give you some background, for point of reference, my husband and I are both PKs and have served in full time ministry most of our lives. I have a bachelor's degree in psychology and a master's degree in business. For some time now I have noticed cyclical and patterned behavior from the lead pastor which align most closely with the clinical definition of Histrionic Personality Disorder. However, after reading an article on Narcissistic Personality Disorder in Orthodox pastors and finding your article and story, I'm not sure he isn't more closely aligned with a covert NPD. In any case, I am not certified in clinical diagnosis nor do I have a masters or doctorate degree in it and have been praying for some time that a third-party intervention with more education, wisdom and insight would be provided. I came across your contact info this morning and wanted to reach out.

In the past two months (beginning in June of this year), 6 staff members have left or have been asked to leave. Of these 6, only 1 has continued forward in ministry. The others have taken jobs coaching, working at Lowe's, selling cars and welding.

Several of these staff members approached the Leadership Board (we operate under a modified version of elder governance, all board members are hand picked by the lead pastor) this past April, giving them a long list of concerning behavior consistently displayed by the LP (lead pastor), including deceit, manipulation, inappropriate comments, patterns of angry outbursts, triangulation, gaslighting and so on. My husband and I were not part of this group, but because my husband is an XP (executive pastor), one of the board members called him to ask about specific instances of these behaviors. My husband shared several firsthand examples with him.

The board called the LP in to address these behaviors, and then all fell silent. In the coming weeks, the lead pastor called staff members into his office, one by one, and used bullying tactics (including tears, misuse of Scripture, passive-aggression, anger, etc.) clearly stating that the board realized their "wrong-doing" and have repented for confronting him, and that no one should ever approach the board without telling him first.

In July, the lead pastor had the HR director teach a staff seminar on "biblical conflict resolution" which he wrote—but said was coming directly from her. This further sealed and clarified the cultural reality of eggshells and silence.

To be honest, it seems bleak. This is a very small town and this church is the largest and most influential. The LP is charismatic and charming. There is zero accountability and no recourse for those who have been wounded.

My husband and I have only been here for a year and 10 months. When we went through the interview process there were a number of red flags, but we put a fleece out, telling Jesus that we would go wherever He leads. To our surprise, He confirmed the fleece that we were to move here. We did. It has, without question, been the most difficult few years in ministry I've ever walked through. We've fasted and prayed through this time and feel clear release to go when God opens the door. We are seeking, in the meantime, to be honoring in the best ways we know how. Our hearts are heavy and grieved over what is occurring and would love any counsel you would be willing to offer.

JERRY

I have been struggling since 2006 with a pattern of spiritual abuse, lying, and intimidation by my pastor (now my former pastor). I was told to leave the first church by a Certified Biblical Counselor from another church for my spiritual, mental, and physical well-being. The denominational hierarchy will not sustain my appeals or communications even though they are written and composed precisely per the Regulations of denomination. The church leaders are bending the Church Order to protect the pastors!

While at the second church, the Certified Biblical Counselor assisted several members with presenting the courses to the Adult Sunday School. We did so under the oversight of the Elders. I was humbled and grateful to be a part of this process as the facilitator to begin the organization process for the two

Peacemaking courses. However, when I desired to biblically reconcile with the former elders from my previous church, the Consistory of the second church placed a "gag order" on me ordering me not to communicate with the former or present office bearers of the first church. How can this be?

Using Peacemaking Principles, I have met twice with my former pastor. After much time spent in two personal meetings and several email exchanges, he has admitted some sorrow and remorse—although with a far away look in his eyes—for his past actions but is unwilling to address "specific" sins and apologize specifically for the numerous inappropriate actions he has taken against me in the past. He is no longer willing to communicate with me to resolve the conflict. His former elders have not been willing to address any specific wrongdoing as well. Since January 2018, my former pastor, in addition to his pastorate, was elected by his fellow board members to be the President of the Board of Trustees of a seminary!

I have symptoms of PTSD and many times wake up in the middle of the night and have difficulty getting back to sleep. The arthritis in my hands, cervical, and lumbar region has gotten worse periodically since 2011. I experience Pre-Ventricular Contractions (PVCs) occasionally. I am a tired-retired physician and have been a confessing member of the Reformed faith since childhood.

I am attaching a summary of my recent experiences with this former dear pastor. We were good friends prior to 2011. Soon thereafter, when I challenged him on the unacceptable oversight of a missionary our church was supporting—who admittedly was an alcohol abuser—my pastor then decided to place me under discipline "on his own." He soon convinced the elders to submit to his wishes and placed me into Step One of church discipline without any personal visits by him or the elders prior to discipline. Doing so is contrary to denominational policy, which allows members to appeal their grievances to the elders, the Classis, and the Synod—if need be. They took that right for "fairness and justice" away from me. The pastor would compose all the abusive letters and would have the elders sign them. I have retained on my personal computer numerous documents (unloving, harsh, and misleading Consistory letters sent to me) which verify the pastor and elders are failing to follow the Church Order which they had agreed to submit to when the congregation joined the denomination.

I sincerely believe they are committing perjury (lying under oath) by failing to honor the vows they have signed on to in the presence of Christ and His church. I have read Rev. Jeff Van Vonderen's book *The Subtle Power of Spiritual Abuse*—an excellent book which has assisted me greatly in understanding the abuse and exploitation my family and I have had to endure.

Now . . . my wife and I have left the denomination where we were members for some 17 years.

However, I wish to assist those many families who are ready to leave the church who are presently (or have been in the recent past) experiencing the abusive behavior of certain pope-like pastors and their elders.

Other church members have experienced similar situations with their pastors. In my case the elders submitted to the wishes of the authoritative pastor. The ruling elders' task is to oversee the teaching elder (pastor). My former pastor was extremely authoritative, influential, and well respected by his elders and the pastors of other nearby churches as well. I served as an elder for one "three-year term" with him.

I hardly dare to ask you the following: What is your opinion of pursuing legal action to halt the progression of this disease process as it continues to destroy the lives of many church members and their vulnerable families?

TRACE

We moved about year ago to help out with this parachurch ministry because we felt like God was leading us to do so. Very quickly there were some unhealthy things that the wife was doing to my wife. She tried to address [this] with her, but it quickly became something really big for them. Now they have distanced themselves from us and said they were too busy to meet (they constantly use "too busy" to control things we realize). We are being shut out of that ministry and had to leave the church that we were both going to because it was just too unhealthy and painful. So much subtle unhealthy things happening. We originally thought it was just the wife and the husband (ministry leader) was just covering it up so they don't lose supporters, but now we realize he is the worst and most deceptive of the two because he is so charismatic. The pastor and wife are totally strung along by them especially the wife because she is such an empath and the couple is loosely affiliated with a ministry they look up to so the couple has been able to convince them of their spiritual superiority. The pastor seems to see some things but does not recognize, or probably even know how to deal with toxic narcissism. The husband (ministry leader) spends much time on Facebook flattering others and posting all his good deeds to promote his ministry but he also is using this as a weapon against us it feels. Both husband and wife have been using their networks to find out who we associate with so that they can spend focused time with them to win them over to them and shut us out which has worked with quite a few it seems. We have felt really alone in all this and don't even know who to talk to because not many understand or know how to deal with something like this.

Is it worth trying to expose this all? This family moves every three years or so "for ministry" and now that makes sense. They are trying to stay put here so they probably see us as a liability to those plans if we were to expose them, but at the same time it does seem like they are looking at some possible moves to leech off other ministries. We had worked with them 10 years ago and that ministry fell apart. I originally thought it was the leader's issues that caused it, but now I see it was this family. The husband came in there like Absalom and turned everyone to him which caused major insecurities with the leaders of the ministry that they where "helping." I'm imagining he has done this at other places as well and he is doing the same thing here with the parachurch ministry as well as the church that we all were going to.

My wife now realizes that they are very similar to her parents who have similar issues, but not nearly as severe as this couple. She really wants to make sure she is fully healed so she doesn't attract this. I didn't have such unhealthy parents but also don't want this to be repeated. I think we have learned a considerable amount about this and see the warning signs that we did not before but still want outside help to ensure this doesn't happen again.

We also need help with how to deal with the "crazy making" and ways that it feels like they are trying to shut us out. We are afraid that when they find out what church we are going to that he will try to connect and flatter the leaders there as well to try to shut us out there as well.

Also, now all the sudden after 8 months of ignoring us, they want to meet with us "to do the right thing." It seems obvious that they just want to do it so that they can say that they met with us and use anything that we say against us. We don't really want to meet at this point because we feel that if they really were caring and concerned they wouldn't have shut us out, or be doing all the negative things they are doing towards us and they would want to make restitution instead of just having one meeting because all the sudden they have a "little" free time but they will be really busy again soon. I also just don't even know what to say at this point because I really don't believe anything we could say would make a difference because they are so hardened.

DARCY

Hello, my name is Darcy and I would like to share my story with you. I have been in a relationship with a pastor for a few years. I am 50 years old, mother of three grown children, and a widow. About a year after my husband died, I met Rob on an online dating site. He is 58 years old, a retired HS teacher/coach and part time pastor for many years. I say part time because it is a very small church with a congregation of maybe 30 people. Apparently, he had been with a larger church but that was before I had met him.

We hit it off the moment we met. We seemed to have so much in common, still do, it was the closest thing to love at first sight that I had ever experienced. I was lonely, widow[ed] and my youngest child had recently moved out. His wife had died several years ago and he also was very lonely. Everything felt so right. We saw each other daily, I started attending his church. He told me I was the first woman since his wife that he had really dated. He told me he was in love with me and wanted to get married. I was in love with him, still am. This all happened so quickly, but it felt so right. Couple months after we met I retired from my job, I hadn't planned to do that yet, but I had enough years in to start drawing my pension and I thought I could help him with his elderly parents. He was their sole caretaker and they were still living in their home, but needing assistance. Mostly I wanted more time to be with him and he had said we would have more time available to travel and enjoy life together. He was such a blessing to me; I didn't know how I could have been so lucky. When I was sick he was a Godsend, so attentive to me. Well, by our third month together, I noticed a change in him. Getting tired of the act? He seemed to pull away somewhat and I noticed several "likes and hearts" by a particular woman on his Facebook account. The name rang a bell as I had come across it on an envelope and gift package that I had recently seen while helping him clean his car out in my garage. About this same time, I consulted with an ex co-worker who happened to live in the same town as Rob. (I live 40 miles from him and did not really know many people in common.) The co-worker told me she didn't know Rob personally but that she knew of him, and that he was very respected, involved in the community, announcer for the HS baseball games, good Christian etc., etc. but that she was sure he was engaged to a woman from out of state. I was certain there was a mistake. Rob had mentioned an old college friend he corresponded with a few times last year through FB but that it did not turn into anything, and besides she had a boyfriend. I asked Rich about the friend on FB and he denied any close relationship with her, just an old college pal. My gut told me something felt off though. I inquired some more and heard the same story from a reliable source that my daughter knew. The tote with the trash and things from his car was still in my garage so I looked through it and found an old cellphone he must have tossed in there. Reluctant to do it but in a terrible sick panic, I charged the phone and scrolled his call log and text msgs. There was the FB friend, 100s of text messages right up until February (he started seeing me in April). They were planning to get married, in fact in June. She was already married and had filed for divorce in May. I discovered through courts online that she had withdrawn the divorce papers from her husband of 30 years shortly after filing. Not only were there msgs to this married woman, but also to another woman that sounds like it could have been more than friends. I was devastated, but so in love with him. I called him and told him I had found his old phone and looked at it. He immediately went into a rage, screaming at me, told me he never wanted to see me again and that he was going to get a restraining order against me.

I was absolutely beside myself, I wanted to die. This perfect man that I was head over heels for. The man I had told all of my friends and family about. After a couple days my pain and shock grew to anger and humiliation. I started texting him as he would not answer his phone. He told me the relationship with her was over and if I would have just asked him about it he could have explained. Blaming her, he told me it started out as friends, that she had looked him up on Facebook a year ago. She was having marital problems and he told me he was counseling her. He said he tried his best to keep them together but that her husband was a real loser, abused her etc. He said they started dating but only saw each other a few times. He claimed he was not serious about marrying her. He said she went back to her husband and it was over. He said in the beginning he felt sorry for her, and that she sucked him into the relationship—he was the victim because of his caring heart. He was angry and blamed her for the whole deal. He said he was so embarrassed about being dumped that he never told anyone that he was no longer seeing her. He apologized to me (one of the few times) and bombarded me with love and promises. He seemed so sincere, I finally forgave him and against that feeling in my gut, went back to him. In hindsight I should have ran and never looked back, but I was lonely, the kids all grown and moved away, and I had retired from my job and just didn't have the human contact that I used to. I was so in love with him. This was the first situation with Rob. I hate to admit it but there have been countless more. Not necessarily other women but many other things. Lies that I have caught him in. Not following through on things, not returning calls. Just basically disregarding my feelings on so many things. And each time I approach him, it's the same scenario. Starts out with over the top rage, then cuts me off, breaks contact, refuses to talk on the phone, will only text or email then twist the story and blames me. I often wear out and apologize for his transgressions. He hates conflict, extremely defensive over even minor issues. We have been on and off again more times than I can count. I took anti-depressant[s] for a time because he thought I needed to. He said his wife was on them for their entire marriage of 9 years before she died of cancer. Of course, he said it was due to problems she had with her grown sons. They refused to come see her and they kept her grandchildren from her. (I suspect due to him.) He always told me that he and his wife were the perfect couple, he said they were "the couple" in town, always together, fantastic marriage and seldom conflict. The mythical perfect marriage. I have never talked to anyone who knew her. She was from out of town and no family in the area. He had no contact with her sons or other family members. He said they were a bunch of low life leeches. He spent two years in court with them after her death over her will. Anyway, I used to feel bad and think it was me that caused some of the strife in our relationship, because he said he and his wife got along great. I am beginning to doubt they had a great marriage; I suspect she was very passive. He told me that her ex-husband was verbally abusive. In fact, he counseled her when they used to work together.

I don't know many people that Rich knows, he claims he has many friends but in our whole time together I have only met a few. Most of the friends he mentions are attorneys, doctors and bankers, name-dropper, powerful people. He knows lots and lots of people, but I suspect not on an intimate basis. He said he and his wife were very private people, didn't want anyone knowing their business. In town he seems to be kind of a big shot. He is on many boards and clubs. He has an office with walls literally covered with community awards, pictures of him with various celebrities from his days of radio broadcasting, and autographed pics [of] ballplayers and politicians that he has gathered through the years. He likes to talk about how he should have run for state legislature because he had so many people tell him he would be good at it and because he knows he would have won. However, he likes to throw in there that he knew if he did there would be no time for "us." He is a fantastic public speaker, one of the best. His church sermons are very good, although I don't understand how he does it because very little prep work goes into them. The church is very small; mostly retired people attend. There have been issues and some people will quit coming for awhile. He always says they got their nose out of joint or something. The church is not in the town he lives so none of them know his personal life. In fact, he has never preached in his own town. I used to attend his church, I loved to listen to him, but there was a problem and now I no longer go. Several months ago, I found out he was talking to the married woman from out of state again. We got into it over that I was very angry. I threatened to contact this woman's husband and tell his church people. Of course, I didn't but I think he thought I would because the following Sunday when I showed up to church he looked very nervous. I saw him privately talking to a couple of the congregation before the service. He held a very short service and bypassed the "sharing" time altogether. We broke up again, but like the other times we got back together. I do feel bad that none of them have stayed in touch but I suspect that he told them I was crazy or something. The reason I say that is because one of the women there told me she heard his old girlfriend (the married out of state woman) was psycho. Rob claims he is quitting the pastor job soon and just doing volunteer work with the Graham organization. He said we can pick another church and attend together.

I am pretty sure I am about to the end of my rope. Rich's last angry outburst happened a few days ago. He had been staying at my house these past couple weeks because his father died, and he said he was just too depressed to stay alone at his house. He still talks of marriage, but I don't think I can ever go through with it. It was early in the morning and I sensed something was wrong, so I asked him if things were ok. Well, I should have stopped at that, but I didn't, and I said it again, and that's all it took. He flew into a rage. I finally asked him to take his things and leave. He grabs his things, jumped in his car, slid on the ice with the car and plowed through my wooden fence as he left. It's been 4 days now and after a bunch of text msgs blaming me for kicking him out, playing the victim and projecting (he projects all the time), now he is telling me how much he loves me, what a mistake I am making, sending Bible verses about forgiveness etc etc.

You know the thing is, I feel sorry for him. For all of his showboating and name-dropping, I think he feels very insecure. He confessed to me at one of his low moments that he was bullied as a child. He says he has feelings of insecurity and has suffered from depression. I don't doubt that. He is unwilling to go to counseling, though. I suggested couples counseling and he refused, said that was dumb as he knows all about counseling, he has done tons of marriage counseling. I know what I need to do—never see him again. I almost am there. It's so discouraging because on the surface he is a great guy. There is a loneliness to us though because it really is all about him. I think I may be the only one who sees the dark side. He has no children, which is a blessing.

His biggest issue with me is that I don't believe in him because his words with me don't always match his actions. He complains that I have short-term memory loss and I forget how problems we have had really transpired. He says I should just trust his heart. I just pray I have the strength to not go back.

7

The Spiritual Life
of the Narcissist Pastor

God is everything the narcissist ever wants to be:
omnipotent, omniscient, omnipresent,
admired, much discussed, and awe inspiring.

—Sam Vaknin, *Malignant Self Love*

THE CONFLICT BETWEEN SPIRITUALITY
AND NARCISSISM

If the predatory narcissist pastor is severely compromised in the ability to relate to other people, to feel for them, and to be the shepherd rather than the wolf, and if he or she sees God as a primary rival rather than as their main support, what kind of a spiritual life does he or she have? Can anyone who sees God as a rival rather than a refuge even have an authentic spiritual life? It would seem at first blush that approaching the God you fear and are competing against to help and sustain you would be a dreadfully shame-based enterprise that would lead only to failure.

Spirituality and spiritual practice are integral parts of the personal search for significance and provide a buffer against the narcissist's need to manipulate and control others. However, it would also naturally produce a tension between his drives for narcissistic supply and the ethics of Christian belief that stand in opposition. Does the narcissist pastor see the personal aspects of spirituality in Bible study, meditation, and prayer as confirming his worthlessness or even as personally threatening, and thus not engage in them except superficially? This would explain in part why their sermons are often described as shallow and repetitive. Convinced of his own superiority, the narcissist pastor may sermonize rhapsodically to the bemusement and frustration of his listeners, or she may wander off into intellectual and philosophical quagmires to their boredom and confusion; she has no built-in measurement system to tell her when to stop or how she is being received. Conversely, it was possible that they would be deeply immersed in these disciplines in the attempt to fill the void within in a sort of desperate spirituality. I did not—and do not—know for certain but some trends have appeared. "Emptiness, self-alienation, guilt, and shame—these are the profound feelings from which the narcissist runs. Behind the perfect persona lies a tremendous sense of failure and a terror that one is, in essence, unlovable. Here is the abyss of the soul."[1]

They key to understanding the pseudo-spiritual life of the narcissist is understanding their spirituality. People who report a deep religious experience tend to internalize it and incorporate it into their daily lives. Their religiosity becomes part of them, inseparable from who they are. Narcissist spirituality tends to be external, an experience observed but separate from them. The difference cannot be discounted. For those who have internalized it, their religiosity is part of their daily lives. It influences and guides them through the temptations and pitfalls of daily living. It brings comfort in difficult times and inspiration for challenging tasks. It is an internal compass that leads steadily homeward. The narcissist has an opposite experience. Whatever religiosity he or she may have is separate from them. It is something to be used when necessary and appropriate, but its connection is superficial and easily disregarded. It is a tool, and nothing more.[2] In other words, it is a compass without a magnetic north.

---

1. Halligan, "Narcissism, Spiritual Pride, and Original Sin," 310.
2. Cooper, Pullig, and Dickens, "Effects of Narcissism and Religiosity," 47.

SPIRITUAL PRACTICES

I think we all have an image in our minds of how a pastor spends the day. We imagine them in prayer, Bible study, and serious research for their next sermon. We see them going to visit the sick and the dying, counseling the confused and lost, comforting the afflicted (and perhaps afflicting the comfortable?). It is a long list. Too often, though, the pressures of the day squeeze out the spiritual disciplines. After observing pastors closely for many years, one writer notes five distinct reasons why pastors may not practice the ancient spiritual disciplines:

1. They were never taught how to do spiritual disciplines. Most were told to do the disciplines but not taught how.

2. They equate ministry activity with spiritual disciplines. After all, they read the Bible in preparation for sermons and teaching. They pray when others ask them to pray; they often take the lead in praying at events. Surely these activities suffice.

3. They've lost a sense of desperation for God. Think about it—it's easy to forget how desperately you need God.

4. They sometimes struggle with discipline in general. Too many pastors eat too poorly, exercise too little, get too little rest, and spend too much time wasting their time.

5. They're not always the best time managers (see 4 above).[3]

Forgiveness

I've touched on forgiveness and narcissism, but I want to go deeper because forgiveness is at the very core of all Christian belief. Without forgiveness through the cross, Christianity is just another hollow religion requiring people to go through the motions in the hope of something better after they die.

Jesus did not ask his followers to forgive; he commanded it. Unfortunately, we often have difficulty forgiving or just plain refuse to do it for any number of mythical "reasons." Perhaps the primary argument against forgiving is the claim that the perpetrator gets away with it, there is no justice, and the victim continues to suffer. The argument sounds logical, but it is totally false. The one who benefits is the forgiver, for in forgiving we break

3. Lawless, "8 Reasons Pastors Struggle."

the chains of imposed power that bind us to the perpetrator, thus setting ourselves free. Jesus knew that and wants us to live in freedom, not bondage. I will deal with this in greater detail later.

What may be more difficult than forgiving is seeking forgiveness. We shy away from it because it is so risky. We must admit to what we have done without any defense, ask for forgiveness, and then make ourselves open to whatever "justice" our victim may insist upon. There are no guarantees in seeking forgiveness, and we fear the humiliation of rejection.

Christian clergy cannot ignore the many instances where Jesus made it clear that forgiving is mandatory, not optional. He not only spoke of it, he practiced it. "One of the most celebrated forgiveness texts is Jesus' prayer from the cross, 'Father, forgive them; for they do not know what they are doing' (Luke 23:34). This is often cited as the quintessential moment of unconditional Christian forgiveness and held up as a model that believers should seek to emulate."[4] We know these things and the question to our pastor, "How can I forgive this?" is a common one. Even the most attuned pastors may have to admit that they get to a certain point and then must say "Leave the rest up to God."

In order to forgive you I must first feel empathy for you, meaning I must understand who you are beyond what you have done, and see you as separate from the offense. But you will not find the word *empathy* is Scripture. Why? Because empathy is just a feeling, but when experienced with love towards the offender it becomes compassion, which leaves you little choice but to act to alleviate suffering. In fact, in every instance where Scripture says Jesus was moved to compassion, he took decisive action to heal whatever wound was before him.

Since we see our pastors as being above us in spirituality, we expect them to be paragons of forgiveness. Many are and many are not, but that is only because they are as human as anyone else and struggle with the same issues. But what of the narcissist pastors, many of whom are intensely "religious" but without empathy or compassion? Should not their religiosity make it easier to forgive or to seek forgiveness? Well, maybe. While early studies showed that deeply religious people do forgive more easily than those with shallower religious commitment, the studies did not connect the role of religion to their abilities to forgive.[5] Later studies examined the differences on forgiving and seeking forgiveness of internalized and externalized religiosity. The religiosity of the narcissist tends to be external, sort of a coat he wears, and not part of who he is. Internalized religiosity promotes

4. Mayo, "What Does the Bible Really Say About Forgiveness?"
5. Sandage et al., "Seeking Forgiveness," 28.

forgiveness, while externalized religiosity inhibits or prevents both forgiveness and seeking forgiveness. "Unwillingness to forgive is associated with narcissistic behavior and accordingly indicates a lack of willingness to be obedient to Christian tenets of unlimited forgiveness toward those who commit transgressions."[6] Since the narcissist is never wrong, seeking forgiveness borders on the inconceivable.

Narcissism and grace are not only incompatible, they are opposites that cannot be reconciled. Mercy and justice, however, are part of a healing dance as proclaimed in Psalm 85:10, "Love and faithfulness meet together; righteousness and peace kiss each other." Narcissism repels grace.[7] We already know that the narcissist's religiosity is a shame-driven enterprise and one where "he believes that he believes" . . . but does not truly believe. In fact, increased narcissism significantly predicts decreased forgiveness-seeking and granting. The narcissist's lack of empathy cripples the ability for forgiveness in either direction. In other words, the narcissist pastor must preach it and teach it but cannot practice it, leaving both preaching and teaching empty.

Self-Forgiveness

We increasingly hear of pastors preaching self-forgiveness, borrowing the concept from therapy. Since the narcissist pastor cannot—or will not—seek forgiveness from God or anyone else, it is likely she may try to practice "self-forgiveness" and even encourage it in others as a means of releasing her internal shame. There are major problems here, however.

> Self-forgiveness is a misleading and inaccurate concept for understanding the condition to which it is applied. Besides the fact that traditional religion provides no rationale for self-forgiveness, four specific criticisms are presented.
>
> 1. Self-forgiveness requires splitting the self, creating various problems. It requires splitting oneself into two beings, one of which forgives the other.
>
> 2. It involves a conflict of interest between the self that judges and the self that is judged.
>
> 3. Through its extreme emphasis on the self, it promotes narcissism and appeals to narcissists. If I can forgive myself, then

---

6. Cooper, Pullig, and Dickens, "Effects of Narcissism and Religiosity," 47.

7. Burijon, "Narcissism and Grace Inherent Incompatibility."

I have no need to seek out those I have hurt and ask their
forgiveness.

4. Research indicates that interpersonal forgiveness or intraper-
sonal forgiveness involve different psychological processes.[8]

Self-forgiveness is completely self-centered and declares that the individual has no obligation to those he has hurt, while seeking forgiveness
seeks to heal the victim as well as release the offender. Since the narcissist
believes himself to be so broken that not even God can fix him, the only
solace he may find is in the false safety of self-forgiveness.

Prayer

Prayer is one of the most ancient of spiritual disciplines and has been practiced for thousands of years. It is the primary form of humans seeking God.
It is also the most common form of religious activity as it does not depend
on a specific time, place, or persons. "Praying is a religious act that links up
well with the preference for doing things one's own way. People can pray
anywhere they like (at the dining table, in a church, on the beach, in bed);
whenever they like (in the morning the afternoon, the evening or the middle
of the night); in any form they like (formulaic prayer, personally composed
prayer); and whichever way they like (kneeling down, standing up, walking slowly, lying down."[9] There is a general image of clergy as ordained and
set aside "holy ones" engaging daily in extensive prayer and Bible study.
However, and as was noted earlier, previous studies have indicated that narcissist pastors are less inclined to pray, to thoroughly prepare their sermons
(except for style rather than content), or engage in spiritual disciplines.

There is a belief that guilt drives people to prayer, but that is not the
case for the narcissist. "The current findings . . . are consistent with the notion that feelings of guilt do not motivate those high in narcissism to seek
God or engage in spiritual activities in general," nor does shame motivate
prayer.[10] Since the narcissist's spirituality is external there is little to no connection with guilt (which he does not feel) or shame (which he does feel),
and he is never wrong so he does not need forgiveness. During the 2016
election season a US candidate for president was asked if he had ever asked
God for forgiveness. His answer was, no, I have never done anything I need
forgiveness for.

8. Vitz and Meade, "Self-forgiveness in Psychology and Psychotherapy."

9. Zondag and van Uden, "My Special Prayer," 9.

10. Simpson et al., "Interpersonal Transgressions," 202.

Prayer tends to be a private thing. Jesus said, "When you pray, you are not to be like the hypocrites; for they love to stand and pray in the synagogues and on the street corners so that they may be seen by men. Truly I say to you, they have their reward in full. But you, when you pray, go into your inner room, close your door and pray to your Father who is in secret, and your Father who sees what is done in secret will reward you" (Matt 6:5–6). We seek out private places to be alone and pray, but there are indications that narcissists can pray anywhere, anytime, for any reason, and in front of anyone. Why? It places the spotlight squarely on them.

Bible Study and Sermon Preparation

We expect that our pastors would be engaged in a disciplined and daily study of Scripture. We are wrong. In one study, slightly more than half stated that their Scripture study was on a regular basis, but almost as many claimed that their Scripture study was "hit and miss." Other studies conclude that pastors in general do not engage in prayer or Bible study at the rates that their parishioners might expect. According to one source, "70% of pastors only study God's Word when preparing a message."[11]

The sermon is the weekly high point for pastors. It is where they can proclaim the Word of God as they interpret it and receive high praise for their efforts. Sermon preparation is vital to the life of worship in that the sermon is often the only chance the pastor will be able to communicate with his parishioners in any given week. Therefore, it would seem reasonable to expect a great deal of time spent in sermon preparation as poor or sloppy preparation leads to poor and sloppy sermons.

There is some evidence that suggests covert narcissists spend the least amount of time in sermon preparation. Only about half report spending any time at all alone in sermon preparation while slightly less than half seem to "wing it," that is, to improvise on the spot while starting with a favorite Bible passage or reading from another source. This is not overly surprising, though; every narcissist believes himself to be above average and the narcissist preacher is no exception. This is backed by research data: "They don't just believe that they are good, they KNOW it, even though their parishioners complain that the sermons are too long, too boring, too pedantic, and too much about themselves."[12] The highly respected Barna Group researched how pastors viewed their skills in a wide range of areas through self-appraisals. While not searching specifically for rates of narcissism, the

11. Urban Ministry Institute, "Interesting Statistics About Pastors."
12. Barna Group, "Pastors Rate Themselves Highly."

Wow!

researchers did set off some alarms by showing how highly these pastors
viewed themselves in 2002—90 percent scored themselves as above average
in preaching and teaching! This finding confirms Zondag's observations in
The Netherlands and Poland that up to 80 percent of all pastors score high
in narcissism.[13]

TABLE 2: PASTOR SELF-APPRAISALS

How good are you at:	Excellent %	Good %	Average %	Not too good %	Poor %
Preaching/teaching	31	59	9	*	1
Encouraging people	24	61	13	1	*
Pastoring/shepherding	21	61	16	*	*
Leadership	16	57	25	2	*
Motivating people around a vision	15	53	28	3	7
Discipling/mentoring people	12	52	32	2	*
Evangelism	10	50	36	3	1
Counseling	9	45	38	4	2
Administration/ management	14	39	35	7	4
Developing ministry strategy	10	43	41	3	1
Fundraising	6	25	37	14	9
				* Denotes less than ½ of 1%	

Barna Group 2002 (Printed by permission)

Even when confronted with dissatisfaction and suggestions for im-
provement, the narcissist will generally reject both outright. Case in point:
"The head of the vestry pulled him aside and sheepishly told him that his
sermons tended to focus too much on himself. He also said that other
congregants were put off by his use of personal anecdotes. The head of the
vestry quickly clarified that this was not his own view—he was simply passing on what others had said. [Pastor Jones] vehemently disagreed, believing
that what he preached in his sermons was of vital importance and that his

---

13. Zondag, van Halen, and Wojtkowiak, "Overt and Covert Narcissism in Poland
and the Netherlands."

interpretation of theology was divinely inspired. He summarized his view by emphasizing to the head of the vestry, 'I KNOW I am a good preacher!'"[14]

There is also some evidence that overt narcissists may spend as much or even more time in sermon preparation than their "normal" peers. This is despite their belief that they are superior to everyone else, which would logically lead to a perceived need for less time in preparation. I see two possibilities here, and they are connected. One is that they see God as a rival and believe themselves to be competing with God. The second is that they see the sermon as performance art, and they need to practice their delivery much the same as a musician practices before every performance. The sermon, then, is their opportunity to prove their own superiority. That does not necessarily equate to higher quality sermons, however.

14. Crisp-Han, Gabbard, and Martinez, "Professional Boundary Violations in the Clergy," 8. Emphasis in original.

8

The Narcissist Pastor
as Spouse and Parent

I would drown in the ocean every morning just by stepping out of bed.

—Casey Renee Kiser

Having already described the thinking and behaviors of toxic narcissism, we can move directly to how they play out in relationships as intimate as marriage and parenting. In general, any toxic narcissist is a terrible spouse and parent, but you get an altogether different mix when the narcissist is a pastor who must also lead a double life as a caring shepherd.

A large majority of narcissist pastors are male, but there are female narcissists as well. The problems faced by the families of male and female narcissist pastors are very similar.

The narcissist, being self-preoccupied and living in a different reality, assumes that everyone is like him: a rival and potential threat. To the narcissist pastor, God is the ultimate rival, leaving the narcissist in both fear of God's wrath being turned upon him, and in awe that God has such power. The covert narcissist desperately wants God's blessing and lives in deep shame at his desire to diminish God and ascend himself. In his favor is his ability to mimic humility and caring. The overt narcissist, however, can preach powerfully, know Scripture well, and entrance others with his charisma, but is much more up front in promoting himself as the authoritative leader, all the while undercutting God and praising himself.

Such overt hostility is not tolerable in a pastor, of course, leaving him or her to more subtle devices to attain dominance and eventual supremacy. This presents an unrelenting paradoxical tension for the narcissist who understands God as a rival to be vanquished rather than an overpowering love to be served. The result is the narcissist pastor equates his sermon to a performance where God is the supposed object but he or she, the pastor, is the true object of affection. This creates a pseudo-intimacy between pastor and congregation and the belief in the narcissist that he or she is relating to others.[1]

Given their compelling and even pathological drives for glory and power, the narcissist pastor faces several layers of unresolvable paradoxes: 1) Protestant Christianity expects them to be an exemplary spouse (Eph 5:25; Col 3:19) and parent (Eph 6:4; Col 3:21; Luke 11:11–12, etc.); 2) they are expected to be faithful and monogamous; 3) Scripture requires that spouses be honored and protected (1 Pet 3:7); 4) they are to train their children in the way they should go (Prov 22:6), and 5) they are to treat their children with kindness and respect (Eph 6:4).

Now add the expressed and unexpressed expectations placed on pastors by their churches. Thomas Rainer questioned hundreds of church members on what they wanted most in their pastor. Here are the top 10 responses with the counterpoint of a narcissist pastor:

1. *Love of congregation.* "If we know that our pastor loves us, everything else falls in place. If he doesn't, nothing else matters." The narcissist pastor loves the attention, power, and control granted a pastor—but not the congregation or the people within it. He is a chameleon and expert in the art of camouflage and will steadfastly profess his love of all, even though he holds the congregation in contempt.

2. *Effective preaching.* "I don't have any expectation that my preacher be one of the best in the world, I just want to know that he has spent time in the Word each week to teach us effectively and consistently." Extraverted narcissist pastors tend to see preaching as performance art with themselves as the focus and spend considerable time in preparation.

---

1. Pinsky et al., *The Mirror Effect*, 105.

Covert narcissists have a few favorite verses and themes and tend not to prepare much if at all.

3. *Strong character.* "No pastor is perfect, but I do want a pastor whose character is above reproach on moral, family, and financial issues." The narcissist pastor believes that the rules of conduct regarding morals, family, and finances do not apply to him. However, he will do his best to keep his illicit, and even illegal, activities out of view.

4. *Good work ethic.* "I don't want either a workaholic pastor or a lazy pastor. Unfortunately, our last two pastors have been obviously lazy." The narcissist pastor claims long hours of arduous work but has little to show for it. It seems that the narcissist pastor does as little as possible while claiming as much as possible.

5. *Casts a vision.* "Our church has so much possibility; I want to hear what we will do to make a difference in our community and the world." The narcissist pastor is full of wonderful ideas that are usually not his own. He tends to "churn" projects until something works and may claim that the church is so amazing that others are copying what they do—which is the first step in creating a narcissist church.

6. *Demonstrates healthy leadership.* "Most of the pastors in my church have demonstrated a good balance; they have been strong leaders but not dictators." The narcissist pastor violates all boundaries and may be inspirational to the congregation but will single out and attack (scapegoat) anyone he sees as a threat, and his staff will live in fear. As I've noted, one hired and then drove out twenty-one associates before being forced into retirement.

7. *Joyous.* "Our current pastor is a man of joy. His joy and enthusiasm are contagious. I love him for that!" The narcissist pastor does not know or understand joy, laughs only at the expense of others, and tends not to understand humor. It is rare to see more than a flash of a smile.

8. *Does not yield to critics.* "I know that every pastor serving today has his critics. And I know it's tough to deal with them. I just want these pastors to know that we supporters are in the majority. Please don't let the minority critics dictate how you lead and serve." We learn from critics. An old proverb says, "Listen to your enemies, for God is speaking." The narcissist pastor does not tolerate or allow criticism, but instead attacks and belittles critics and will try to drive them out. That is how he maintains a "critic-free zone."

9. *Transparent.* "Every pastor that I have had has been open and transparent about the church and the direction we are headed. It sure has made our church healthier." The narcissist pastor will proclaim transparency but not practice it, particularly in financial and personnel matters. In one church, an elder was dismissed after he asked to see a budget.

10. *Models evangelism.* "Our pastor is passionate about sharing the gospel. His heart and attitude are contagious." The narcissist pastor is passionate about promoting himself.[2]

Humility is perhaps one of the most desired and assumed personality traits in pastors but is rarer than most believe. Grandiose narcissism eclipses humility no matter how hard it is projected, while covert narcissism carries with it a false humility where the narcissist puts himself down in self-deprecating ways in the expectation of being corrected with praise. "Despite its centrality to Christianity and its complex theological background, there is a dearth of empirical research on the prevalence of humility among clergy. This is particularly surprising given that existing research suggests that humility may be relevant to clergy's individual well-being and the well-being of the institutions they lead."[3]

The narcissist pastor, being pathologically dishonest, fears exposure as a fraud, finds most of these traits impossible and may only be able to do two of them: cast visions (he lives within a fantasy of unlimited power and ability) and not yield to critics. Narcissist pastors tend to be vision casters extraordinaire in the fervent hope that something will work. This leads to "churning," which is the practice of introducing multiple new things in a short time span, most of which will quietly disappear. Having little actual imagination, they tend to copy what others have done and then claim it as their own. And, since they believe they are always right, they rarely yield to critics, instead disparaging them as ignorant fools or worse.

Finally, the narcissist pastor may engage in a "secret life" where he is free to do those things prohibited by his church, marriage vows, his own puritanical conscience, and society. This may include drug use, sexual perversion, frequent infidelities, and even drug and sexual addictions. These serve as emotional pressure relief valves for pent-up feelings of entitlement, rage, and unmet needs.

2. All quotes in this passage are from Rainer, "The Top Ten Things."

3. Ruffing et al., "Humility and Narcissism in Clergy."

FAMILY DYNAMICS

The expectations of our pastors may not always be fair or even known, but they are real. One of these silent expectations is that of the pastor's "perfect family." He knows that he must pass successfully as a caring, dedicated, and called man of God, spouse, and parent. It begins with "the seduction." The seduction is intentional and carefully executed with the sole intent of pulling the victim into an "intimate" relationship totally controlled by the narcissist.

Narcissistic men are highly predictable in their "narcissistic love patterns," states Associate Editor of *Gestalt Review* Elinor Greenberg. She has observed that the same patterns are reproduced "over and over again with different women," but with the same dysfunctional results. The pattern she terms as the most problematic is "the Romantic." His pattern is one of showering his targeted victim with gifts, praise, appreciation, and of being together in a fantasy of the perfect couple in the perfect marriage, until she succumbs.[4]

Love-Bombing

The romantic seduction is usually defined by "love-bombing."

According to Darlene Lancer in a 2018 article in *Psychology Today*, "Getting hit by a love bomb feels glorious. The lavish attention and affection seem to answer our prayers. We've found Mr. or Ms. Right—our soul mate—unsuspecting that we've been targeted by a narcissist." The bomber lavishes gifts, money, and praise on the target. You might hear, "You are the most amazing woman I have ever met! How can I be so lucky as to have you with me?" And so on. The bomber initially idealizes his target: she is perfect in every way. He may propose marriage within a few weeks of meeting. Swept off her feet, she agrees. It is the worst decision she will ever make, as many women have told me.

He believes that he is in love with the woman he pursues but is in reality in love with the idea of being in love, which is not love at all. We already know that the true narcissist is incapable of the empathy necessary for love, is unable to form strong and healthy attachments, and as a result is unable to love another in the conventional sense. Noticing her flaws, he magnifies them and abruptly loses interest, and often becomes verbally and even physically abusive. What was a dream turns into a nightmare. "It's a traumatic shock to our heart. We feel duped, betrayed, and abandoned. We're confused and try to make sense of the nightmare that was once a dream.

4. Greenberg, "Narcissistic Love Patterns."

What we thought was real was, in fact, a mirage. We search for answers, doubt, and blame ourselves, often losing trust in ourselves and the opposite sex."[5]

What is happening: Narcissists idealize prospective partners to augment their own lack of self-esteem. Their thinking is, "If I can win over the admiration of this very attractive person, then I must be worthy."[6] It does not take long before the novelty of enacting the perfect loving couple wears off and he begins to see you more realistically. He has started to see things about you that do not exactly fit his fantasies of perfect love. He is also getting slightly bored. He has run through his repertoire of romantic gestures and now that it is time to seal the deal and either move in with you or propose; otherwise, he wants out of the relationship. The sudden change from apparent devotion to derision is confusing at best. Many times, the marriage partner will discover that they have been discarded for another love interest or that they've been cheated on from the very beginning. It is devastating and many cling to the memories of good times in the hope the love-bomber will return. Others blame themselves and try to be perfect to regain his attention. Many go into denial and refuse to believe that things could have gone so wrong so quickly, but eventually they are left with the harsh reality of manipulation and rejection.

Greenberg writes, "If you have ever been wildly and passionately in love with a narcissist who left you crying and wondering what happened, you may have asked yourself: 'Did he really love me at all? Does he ever think of me? Will he come back to me?' Narcissists idealize their romantic partners at first, but when imperfections become apparent, they develop feelings of contempt."[7] No, he did not really love you. Yes, he remembers you for the pleasure he found in victimizing you. He might come back, but only to relive his conquest and perhaps try for more.

If the deal is sealed, narcissists do not make warm, caring partners. When they realize their spouse is not perfect, their attitudes quickly change from warm and cuddly to cold and prickly. Narcissists believe that they have greater alternatives for romantic partners than non-narcissists, and this leads them to be less committed to their relationships.[8] The higher their narcissism the greater their vindictiveness, domineering, and controlling approaches to others, and intrusiveness in their relationships.[9] Resist-

---

5. Lancer, "All You Should Know About Narcissistic Love Bombing."
6. Lancer, "All You Should Know About Narcissistic Love Bombing."
7. Greenberg, "Narcissistic Love Patterns."
8. Campbell and Foster, "Narcissism and Commitment in Romantic Relationships."
9. Ogrodniczuk et al., "Interpersonal Problems Associated with Narcissism."

ing them is often met with shame-based rage and attacks on the loyalty, character, integrity, and fidelity of their partners—all of which are reflections of the narcissist's own faults. Though he will preach fidelity on Sunday mornings it is always a shock for his partner to learn the truth: monogamy is not characteristic of narcissistic sexuality.

The spouse of a narcissist is tolerated only if she caters to his needs in a soul-deadening instance of codependency. In trying to survive, the spouse either leaves or loses her sense of self in what psychologist Martin Seligman first described as "learned helplessness." Nothing the spouse does is good enough and they are often belittled and psychologically undermined so much that they eventually give up. The spouse of the narcissist is always walking on eggshells, fearful of saying or doing something that the narcissist does not approve. She knows the rage that will explode if she does and she lives in terror of it. It is common to see the spouse shrink almost into oblivion when the couple is together, as the narcissist will tell her what she thinks, believes, and says, and further instruct her on how to behave. Somewhere along the line she loses the ability to see herself in a healthy relationship, and thus finds it excruciatingly difficult to leave. In a real sense it becomes a master-slave relationship where the only way to survive is to accommodate the master's every whim. What is worse, the narcissist pastor uses Scripture to justify it: he is the head of the woman and she is to submit to him in every way. Somehow, it seems unlikely that the Apostle Paul meant this type of submission when he wrote the letter to the church at Ephesus (Eph 5:21–33).

Why do they turn on their partners so vehemently? You aren't who they thought you were. This explanation shucks off all blame. It is your fault that things did not work out, not their inability to stay committed. Now that the narcissist knows you well enough to see your flaws (and in a narcissist's mind, to be flawed is to be worthless) there is no point in staying with you. The truth is that they were never actually in love with you; what they were in love with was the idea of being part of a perfect couple that everyone envied.

The covert/shy narcissist seems benign to those outside the relationship, but it often is far from benevolent. The covert/introverted/shy narcissist has been closely tied to physical assault and sexual coercion.[10] "[F]or men, covert narcissism significantly correlated with physical assault and sexual narcissism significantly correlated with their partner's sexual coercion." This is confirmed by many of the women who have contacted me.

---

10. Ryan, Weikel, and Sprechini, "Gender Differences in Narcissism and Courtship Violence," 807.

The covert narcissist is hypersensitive to his own physical aggression in romantic relationships and his added hypersensitivity to criticism. He knows he should not do it, he knows it is wrong, but it is his way of expressing rage without screaming and yelling. In other words, he feels compelled to satisfy his sexual fantasies whether his partner agrees or not.

Covert and grandiose narcissists are often seen as opposite sides of the same coin, but in fact flow along different spectrums of severity. Put simply, extraverted narcissists don't care if you like them, while introverted narcissists are deeply hurt by your dislike. Likewise, the more extraverted the narcissist the more likely they are to behave badly in public, and feelings of thwarted entitlement lead to expressions of anger towards God and refusal to forgive others.[11] Both of these, entitlement and God-as-rival, are an abomination in Christian clergy.

The narcissist pastor, then, must maintain a duality of living. At church and before the congregation, he must project an image encompassing leadership, charisma, scholarship, deep empathy, and humility. This façade breaks apart at home, where he can be sexually aggressive, demeaning, demanding, self-focused, arrogant, and nonempathetic. Since toxic narcissism is shame-based, marital sexuality is a battle between shame and intimacy, with shame usually winning. "Shedding one's shame over nakedness and gently overcoming the partner's shame are important tasks here. Fears regarding the real and imaginary blemishes of one's body have to be put aside. For this, genuine self-regard and trust in the partner's goodness is needed. The narcissist lacks both and is therefore uncomfortable with foreplay . . . The narcissist shows a proclivity to disregard the partner's needs, lacks tenderness, and tends to move too quickly toward the next step."[12] In other words the narcissist spouse is sexually obnoxious and frustrating to his partner.

Pastors are typically not paid on a level with similarly educated peers in other professions. Their unfulfilled belief in entitlement often leads to frustration and rage. Interestingly,

> vulnerable narcissism is even more strongly associated to high levels of entitlement rage than grandiose narcissism. Covert or vulnerable narcissists report that they become more upset or angry when they do not receive what they think they deserve. Thus, vulnerable narcissists are much more sensitive to judgments of outcome fairness, ruminating over the outcomes they did not get but believe they deserved. This creates a paradox in vulnerable narcissism that does not exist in grandiose

---

11. Exline et al., "Narcissistic Entitlement as a Barrier to Forgiveness," 196.

12. Akhtar, "Love, Sex, and Marriage," 188.

narcissism. Vulnerable narcissists' entitlement leads them to think deep down that 'I deserve more!' but then they doubt this sentiment, consequently turning to other individuals for assistance with self-regulation and approval. As a result, these characteristics create the perfect storm.[13]

The most convenient and available targets for that rage are the spouse and children.

The results can be devastating to the victims. The spouse may not dare say or do anything to contradict the narcissist for fear of emotional and physical revenge and even violence. In fact, the narcissist spouse may answer questions directed to the non-narcissist spouse as a means of control. It is almost as if the partner has been absorbed by the narcissist and now plays the part of supportive puppet. In one case, I was with a narcissist pastor and his wife. No matter how many questions I asked of the wife, the narcissist answered for her, tightly gripping her hand as a warning to remain silent. It appeared that she had lost her sense of self in this warped relationship.

Others have contacted me to relate their stories of victimization at the hands of their narcissist pastor husbands. They report severe psychological abuse through gaslighting,

> which is a form of psychological abuse in which narcissists systematically undermine other people's mental state by leading them to question their perceptions of reality. Narcissists use lies and false information to erode their victims' belief in their own judgment and, ultimately, their sanity. Common gaslighting techniques come in the form of denying and projecting: After an abusive incident, narcissists refuse responsibility, blame the abused, or outright deny that the abuse took place. They may say things like, "You're too sensitive," "You're crazy," "That's not what happened," "Why can't you let anything go," or "You made me do it." The term *gaslighting* comes from the 1944 Hollywood film *Gaslight*, where the husband intentionally set upon a course of behavior designed to make his wife believe she was going insane.[14]

13. Freis et al., "Shame, Rage," 878.
14. Hall, "Narcissism 101."

The Risk to Children

The children are at particular risk. Seth Meyers writes in *Psychology Today*, "Young children of narcissists learn early in life that everything they do is a reflection on the parent to the point that the child must fit into the personality and behavioral mold intended for them. These children bear tremendous anxiety from a young age as they must continually push aside their own personality in order to please the parent and provide the mirror image the parent so desperately needs. If these children fail to comply with the narcissist's wishes or try to set their own goals for their life—God, forbid—the children will be overtly punished, frozen out or avoided for a period of time—hours, days or even weeks depending on the perceived transgression in the eyes of the narcissistic parent."[15]

Now add in the pressures of being a "preacher's kid" and the unexpressed expectations of the congregation along with the duality of private and public life under a narcissist parent. Is it any wonder that these children are almost forced into a variety of dysfunctional behaviors and mental disturbances? "Research studies indicate that certain personality disorders, notably Antisocial Personality Disorder and Borderline and Narcissistic personality disorders in parents show relationships to both parental behavior and ensuing childhood problems."[16] There may be a "golden child" singled out unfairly for favoritism, such as special privileges, more attention, high regard, exemption from discipline, and exemption from certain chores and responsibilities. Such favoritism is typically at the direct expense of a disfavored scapegoated child and pits the children against each other. The golden child can do no wrong while the scapegoat can do no right.

Narcissist parents tend to produce narcissist children, as the children adapt to their environment to survive by reflecting or being subsumed by the narcissist parent. Efrain Bleiburg writes in the *American Journal of Psychotherapy*, "In pathological narcissism, by contrast, youngsters crystallize their reliance on an omnipotent sense of self, refuse to acknowledge their shortcomings and vulnerabilities, project onto others disowned self-experiences, and demand public affirmation of their illusory power."[17]

Surprisingly, there is very little specific research on the effects of a narcissist pastor-parent on the psychological health of the child or the pressures of being a "preacher's kid" in the first place. However, when taking

---

15. Meyers, "Narcissistic Parents' Psychological Effect on Their Children."

16. Dutton, Denny-Keys, and Sells, "Parental Personality Disorder and Its Effects on Children," 268.

17. Bleiberg, "Normal and Pathological Narcissism," 30.

into account the research on the formation of narcissism in the family and the behaviors of narcissists towards their children, it would seem that the combination of a narcissist pastor-parent coupled with the duality of church and home life, and with the added expectations of congregations of pastoral children, there would be a strong potential to produce significant psychological trauma in those children.

Origins of Narcissistic Pathology in Children

Over the course of several years, therapist Karen Kernberg observed several ways in which a child became a narcissist while still a child, rather than following the usual pattern of narcissism resulting from psychological trauma in late childhood or early adolescence.

From her clinical experience, those children with the greatest risk of becoming narcissists were 1) the child of narcissistic parents, 2) the adopted child, 3) the child of successful parents (particularly if the child lacks similar ability), 4) the overindulged or wealthy child, and 5) the child of divorce.

According to Kernberg, narcissistic parents may over-idealize their children and insulate them from disappointment or criticism. By not experiencing the normal pratfalls and failures of childhood, the child can easily conclude that they are, in fact, superior to others and above criticism and failure. She gives this illustration:

> One couple, convinced that their 5-year-old was a genius, removed him from consecutive schools they deemed incompetent and mediocre because he was not receiving teachers' praise. They dismissed the school's concerns about the child's aggressive behavior as irrelevant and justified his poor adjustment as boredom.

> When they received a report that the child tested as having average intelligence, they complained to the head of the psychiatric hospital about the incompetence of the evaluator.[18]

Adoptive parents may be so grateful to finally have a child after years of trying that they may try to counter the rejection the child is likely to feel on learning of her adoptive status by emphasizing how they are more special than biological children because they were chosen, especially if biological siblings are part of the family. One of Kernberg's child patients announced that if he had not been adopted by his current parents, another set of parents

18. Kernberg, "The Cracked Mirror," 149–50.

would have adopted him because he knew that there were so many parents in line that would have been eager to have him.

Children of the wealthy, or who have been overindulged, may be raised in an environment where entitlement and control of others is accepted and reinforced. Wealthy parents may also be invested in protecting the child from disappointment and accommodate to his wishes. These children may expect to have the best and internalize the devaluation of more common lifestyles. Kernberg's child reported that a fellow camper at an overnight summer camp complained that the bathrooms were not made with marble floors and walls and that he would not return to camp again. Deferential treatment of the child because of his connections can further fuel grandiosity.

Consider the case of Ethan Couch, whose trial for killing four people while driving drunk sparked widespread conversations about the privilege of being raised wealthy. Mr. Couch became known as the "affluenza teen" after a psychologist suggested during his trial that growing up with money might have left him with psychological afflictions, namely, he was too rich to tell right from wrong. He attracted further attention when he and his mother, Tonya Couch, fled to Mexico in an effort to evade possible jail time.[19]

Children of successful parents may be hobbled by an expectation that they should naturally be as talented as the parents without effort because they were born from brilliance. Meeting such expectations is difficult to impossible if the child has less ability or has any deficits that affect success. Narcissistic pathology serves as a compensation for a sense of inadequacy that is too painful to acknowledge. The son of a famous basketball player failed to be accepted in his school basketball team and responded with severe tantrums and devaluation of the coach.

Children of divorce are particularly susceptible if the parents convey that they are prized possessions that are vied for. Each parent in an attempt to curry favor with the child may be at risk for not providing critical feedback and refusing to indulge the child with material goods or excessive privileges. In turn, some children of divorce develop a sense of self-importance, entitlement, and devaluation of the parent who does not offer immediate gratification or flexible limits.[20]

19. Daniel, "Ethan Couch," *New York Times,* April 2, 2018.
20. Kernberg, "Narcissistic Personality Disorder in Childhood."

DIVORCING THE NARCISSIST

Divorce is always difficult, but it is much more difficult with a narcissist. In the worst scenario, the wife files for divorce against the narcissist husband and her life becomes more of a living hell than it already was. Why? In divorcing him she broke the rule. The rule is that only the narcissist can file for divorce. Only the narcissist is allowed to reject their partner because that partner is deeply flawed. The narcissist, being superior, may not be rejected. Divorcing him (or her) is rejection of the worst kind and results in unrelenting rage fueled by humiliation. He will fight everything even if he goes broke in the process. It is not unusual, though, to find he has taken all of the assets, leaving her with nothing. He then goes after the house, the car, the children, and anything else he can think of just to punish her for rejecting him.

It does not get any better after divorce. According to Erin Leonard in *Psychology Today*, "Marrying and divorcing a narcissist is rough, but co-parenting with a narcissist is almost impossible. The demands, attacks, threats, and attempts to inflict guilt are so skillful, they rattle a parent, sabotaging his or her mental health.

"However, awareness of the narcissist's dysfunctional tactics protects the parent struggling in this situation. Once these relational patterns are identified, it is easier to co-parent with a narcissist."[21]

1. *Know and understand his game plan.* It includes general nastiness, resistance, and character assassination. Knowing what to expect prepares you to a certain extent and makes them easier to ignore. Ignoring them is the only defense tactic that actually works. "Otherwise, when a narcissist blindsides you, it feels like an emotional slap in the face, which evokes a knee jerk reaction. This is the narcissist's goal. They want to elicit an emotional response, so they can accuse you of being, 'out of control.'"[22]

2. *Be aware of triangulation.* The narcissist will try to convince others to go against you, and particularly will try to convince the children to turn on you by making you the "bad guy" in all of this.

3. *Be ready for threats and guilt-trips.* Place healthy boundaries between you. If necessary, communicate only by email or through your attorneys. His intent is always to keep you off balance, confused, and second-guessing yourself.

21. Leonard, "Co-Parenting with a Narcissist."
22. Leonard, "Co-Parenting with a Narcissist."

4. *Be aware of the narcissist's tendency to play favorites and to divide the children into hostile camps.*

5. *Be totally present emotionally for the children and encourage them to express their emotions.*

"Remember: Believe in yourself, parent with empathy, and stay calm. Narcissists will often eventually trip over their own ego."[23]

---

23. Leonard, "Co-Parenting with a Narcissist."

9

The Narcissistic Church

Hate is the complement of fear and narcissists like being feared. It imbues them with an intoxicating sensation of omnipotence.

—Sam Vaknin, *Malignant Self Love*

These are times of uncertainty and unease. To many it seems that the world is edging ever closer to the brink of something they cannot quite comprehend or explain, but which has created a feeling in some that we are closer to the abyss than ever before. In the Middle East and Europe, radical groups such as ISIS and the now-underground Islamic State actively commit atrocities in order to hasten the apocalypse. Meanwhile, the institutional church is hemorrhaging supporters every day while people claim more and more that they are spiritual, but not religious. Without the security of a spiritual anchor, they are looking for something they cannot define, drifting with the wind and the currents. They are spiritual refugees seeking answers that satisfy, and many are not finding them in the more traditional forms of church and worship.

Some churches are drifting as well without a vision of what God is calling them to be, not realizing that, while their anchor is down and even on the bottom, it has not dug in and they are slowly going with the wind and tide. Eventually they sense the drift but don't know what to do about it, particularly if their current pastor is not really a leader but himself a follower. When he or she leaves (voluntarily or not), it is common practice for churches to search for someone with vitality, vision, energy, and a charismatic presence. Since that is what the search team members are looking for, they will zero in on the applicants who seem to best represent those qualities. It is fertile ground for the narcissist.

THE SEARCH PROCESS

The search process has a way of bringing the narcissist out in everyone, but some have no sense of subtlety at all. In one case, there were more than 200 applications for the senior pastor position for a large congregation. Each application had to be examined and winnowed, an exhausting process. Interestingly, several of the applicants wrote in their cover letter something along the following lines: "I know without a doubt that God has called me to Rivers Edge Church. I have prayed about it and waited upon the Lord, and he has told me that this is where I am meant to be. Together we will take the church to a higher level." Two claimed to have "placed a fleece before the Lord" a lá Gideon, and the fleece was dry in spite of rainy weather (or something like that). Well, it is unlikely that God called several to the same position, but it was a great way of identifying narcissists through their senses of entitlement and grandiosity. Fortunately, the selection committee was very aware of narcissist pastors and what to look for—they had just come out from many years under one. They eventually recruited a pastor who was healthy and happy where he was.

Uncertain people and drifting churches that want to be more than they are is a recipe for exploitation and disaster. It is under these conditions that charismatic, narcissistic leaders tend to arise as they offer innovative solutions to the problems faced by their followers[1] and in the desires of the people find the opportunity to remake the church in their own images[2] rather than the image of God. They tend to be dominant, charming, and narcissistic men, although there are women as well. Their followers see them as extraordinary and gifted leaders and tend to resonate to the visions they cast. Followers, in responding to the message and vision, become advocates willing to make personal sacrifices to advance the cause, which they find meaningful. And so they begin the process of creating either an

1. Sosik, Chun, and Zhu, "Hang On to Your Ego," 65.
2. Brown, "Narcissism, Identity, and Legitimacy," 656.

empowering or a narcissistic church culture. As the paths the leaders take diverge, they take their followers with them. Three researchers offer this observation: "When the leaders use their charisma to meet the needs of the followers as they work towards a moral collective cause, they display *socialized charismatic leadership* by empowering followers and promoting their independent thinking and personal development. In contrast, when leaders use their charisma to satisfy their selfish needs for personal power and self-aggrandizement, they display *personalized charismatic leadership* that exploits followers."[3]

THE CHARISMA TRAP

The key to understanding how the positive and negative directions take root is found in the visions the overt and covert charismatic leaders offer. The well-crafted vision pulls you in. As excitement builds, people begin to commit. Once a sufficient number of people have committed to the vision, it begins to take root. Once the vision takes root and begins growing, the unhealthy narcissistic leader finds more and more room for self-aggrandizement, whereas the healthy leader empowers the people and diminishes himself much the same as John the Baptist did when recognizing the ascending Christ (John 3:30).

The differences are not as obvious as one might suppose, even to a trained observer from the outside. From the inside, it becomes even more difficult to tell in which direction the leader is going. If the narcissistic leader is charismatic enough or is able to sustain the excitement long enough, his followers will place him on an ever-higher pedestal and commit even more, which begins the process of creating an internal group narrative that will take hold as a legitimate truth story, and which encourages the pastor to become even more overtly narcissistic.

Eventually, the new narrative becomes a commonly held—and believed—history of humble beginnings, overcoming barriers, and spectacular success. The narcissist will believe it, proclaim it, and act on it even if it is largely a self-aggrandizing myth. One pastor liked to tell over and over the story of how he started this tiny church in "the ugliest little building in the world," and how God led him in growing the church to its present multi-building, twenty-two-acre campus. It was all true, but in his telling it was all about what he did to make it so; he told the story for his own glory.

Jennifer Dyer writes in the *Journal of Religion and Health*,

---

3. Sosik, Chun, and Zhu, "Hang On to Your Ego," 67. Emphasis in the original.

> For many Evangelicals and other Christians, the idealized self-object takes the form of a pastor, speaker, or leader. An idealized self-object is a person for whom the patient has deep respect and wishes to emulate. The Evangelical subculture has allowed for the emergence of many leaders, as celebrities, playing roles as artists, authors, pastors, and speakers. Some are even actors. The fans among these celebrities treasure their words and message. The commercialization of Evangelicalism through publishing, recording, and parachurch organizations that create spaces for festivals, concerts, and conferences further aids in constructing celebrity for these Evangelical leaders.[4]

This process has the capacity to kick-start a circle of reciprocity between the narcissist pastor and his church that enhances and exaggerates both church and pastor while creating unhealthy relationships throughout.

We have all seen cults led by such men as David Koresh and Jim Jones, men so strong and convincing that their followers were willing to die. Koresh was a shy psychopathic narcissist and Jones was overt, but each had enough charisma to weave a blend of fact, fiction, fantasy, and paranoia that played so strongly on the hopes and fears of their followers that each attained total power and control. They were also not afraid to use violence. The result in each case was catastrophe.

However, I am not talking about cults; I am talking about something in between a cult and a healthy church, something far stealthier and more difficult to identify.

Is it possible for the church itself to become narcissistic? Sadly enough, the answer is an unequivocal "yes." Healthy and unhealthy organizations tend to follow the patterns of their leaders. The term *leaders* includes not just the pastor(s), but also the lay leaders in the congregation. If the lead pastor is a narcissist and is able to pull other leaders into his circle of sickness, the church will begin a slide into its own version of Narcissistic Personality Disorder and will go deeper and deeper into it the longer these leaders remain in control. On top of that, the cycle has a way of becoming self-perpetuating: as healthier leaders leave due to discomfort and disagreement, new leaders who have stronger narcissistic tendencies will emerge along with a subgroup of kowtowing followers who get close to the leader in order to bask in his glory. When you understand what to look for, you begin to see and reclassify things that you have seen for years but have not been able to understand.[5]

---

4. Dyer, "Loving Thyself," 247.

5. Volkan and Fowler, "Large-group Narcissism and Political Leaders," 216.

Large-scale narcissism is nothing new. In fact, and when understood correctly, it is quite common and not necessarily negative or destructive—but it is powerful. The morality of organizations depends not just on their intentions and goals but also in the methods used to achieve those goals. The leaders of narcissistic organizations are often willing to use any means available to reach their goals, means that include isolation, propaganda, crushing any dissent, and even internal and external violence. They may be stealthy and hidden, but increasingly tend to come into the open as their power increases and they become more confident. Underneath you will find the same arrogance, sense of entitlement, grandiosity, lack of empathy, and all of the other attributes of the individual narcissist.

Take for example the national narcissism of Nazi Germany. Adolf Hitler was a charismatic psychopathic narcissist. At first people laughed at him but eventually, what he said began to strike deep chords within the German national psyche and he gained support as he repeatedly proclaimed what they wanted to hear. While there were pockets of resistance, the majority of the population over time saw Hitler as a savior from the humiliation and economic burden of the Treaty of Versailles cast after World War 1. In him, they saw the resurrection of a defeated people, prosperity, national pride, and renewed power. Over the course of only a few years, his message began to resonate so powerfully that he rose in rank from a discharged army corporal wounded in the trenches of World War I and convicted criminal to the elected chancellor of Germany. He then consolidated his power. Within a short time, those who dared to speak against Hitler were silenced through fear or force.

Hitler's narcissism was plain to see but the people craved the message he offered and saw in him their hope for the future. He created a compelling mythology of his own by drawing from Germanic and Scandinavian legends while weaving in the tale of a German master race destined to rule the world. His words and images were masterfully crafted into a compelling narrative of resurgence from moral humiliation and freedom from foreign oppression. He also identified his scapegoat: the Jews on whom he cast derision and blame for Germany's many woes. They were not truly human, he proclaimed, but subhuman, cunning and dangerous. Posters appeared with Jews portrayed as evil, subhuman caricatures who were a clear and present danger to all true Germans. With that focus, it became permissible and even logical to strip Jews of their rights and property, and eventually their lives. The holocaust Hitler brought into reality killed thirty to forty million people, including millions of Germans, and leveled almost every major city in Germany.

It is clear that a narcissistic message can be powerful to those who long for it. It is also clear that the narcissistic leader can, under the right circumstances, bring his or her followers into such a lock-step discipline that they will march into the abyss while singing a song of defiance and attempting to take everyone else with them. The problem is, "While one would like to see genocidal behavior as the product of demented or psychotic individuals it is increasingly apparent that genocide is perpetrated by largely normal leaders and their followers"[6] who succumb to their inherent narcissistic or codependent urges under a strong leader. If the leader has charisma, intelligence, and a strong enough narcissistic drive, he or she will find adherents who will do whatever they must to attain the goals the leader sets, and even die for the cause.

There is a counterpoint to Hitler's narcissism, and it brought the United States to full power. After the Japanese attack at Pearl Harbor and the declaration of war against Germany, Italy, and Japan, righteous but narcissistic fear and rage brought the country together into the tight focus of winning the war. Propaganda posters dehumanized both German and Japanese soldiers, sailors, and aviators into subhuman brutes, which then justified killing them in the same general manner that Hitler dehumanized and killed the Jews. We had no death camps, of course, but the mass slaughter of civilians at Dresden and Tokyo by fire bombing was justified as an unfortunate but necessary step in ending the war. Our soldiers and sailors were cast as heroic figures that were far more valuable than any Japanese or German, which then justified dropping the atomic bomb on the undefended cities of Hiroshima and Nagasaki. We still justify these annihilations of more than half a million unarmed civilians as necessary to save American lives.

This is simply the narcissistic psychology of war. Thankfully, in the United States, Canada, and Great Britain it was a temporary adoption necessary to refocus the people, industry, and economy to defeat a determined and utterly ruthless enemy. It has since subsided but still arises from time to time. In 2019, many would argue that the "exceptionalism" being propagated in the United States is such a narcissistic urge.

I am not comparing churches to Nazi Germany, Japan, or even to the United States during World War II; I am simply recasting how the psychological dynamics can be understood as narcissism in its most extreme forms and on a national scale.

Organizational behavior is predictable, and churches are organizations that fall under the same general rulebook in terms of seeking leaders that will grow and prosper the organization and the people in it. Churches rely

---

6. Shaw, "Narcissism, Identity Formations, and Genocide," 212.

on a professional leader (pastor) to guide them into the future. In many, perhaps most, cases, that leader is imbued with an aura that is different from and elevated above the rest of us, no matter how hard he or she may resist. While most people understand and accept the fact of pastoral fumbles and foibles, for others whatever the pastor says is holy writ. After all, he is an ordained man of God who is set aside by none other than God Almighty! This, of course, invites unrealistic expectations of the pastor, as well as abuses.

But a church is also more than a simple aggregation of individuals. The Apostle Paul described the church as a living, breathing, thinking, and discerning entity in what he termed the body of Christ. He was right, probably in more ways than he realized. Like people, every church has an image it projects into the surrounding community to gain attention and awareness. It has a unique flavor that it consciously enhances to attract new people who like that particular flavor. It has a purpose, which is what draws the individuals together into an interest group. It has a message and mission, which energizes them.

All of these in combination create levels of cohesion and stability in the congregation. Finally, it offers relationships that are deeper, richer, and more meaningful than those found in the secular world. Placing all of these together creates meaning in the lives of individuals and tightens the connections between them. If Jesus is kept at the center of all things, the church is likely to be relatively healthy, although it will experience levels of conflict. That changes when the pastor becomes the center in fact if not in image.

PERSONAL IDENTITY AND THE CHURCH

Part of entering and becoming part of a church involves the emergence of a new personal identity that says we belong to and are part of something greater than ourselves. We come to see ourselves as part of the church and the church as part of us in a shared-identity relationship. We find in this relationship a sense of belonging that we may not otherwise have. This new identity often has the ability to sustain us through dark times, which in turn motivates us to strengthen the identity and the relationships that created it. In this way the church is seen as legitimate and important.[7]

The church also has a life that is largely not seen. It is not hidden from view, but it operates in the background much like the operating system on a computer and thus is simply not very noticeable until it goes haywire. It is the identity of the church. Jay White of the University of Nebraska writes, "An organization's identity consists of the psychological makeup of current

7. Brown, "Narcissism, Identity, and Legitimacy," 664; Puls, *The Road Home*, 50–52.

and past organizational members. It is formed from people's psychological reactions to events within and outside organizations; events that are incorporated into their preconscious thoughts and influences their outward behaviors."[8] In other words, the church has a history that is alive in the present and influencing the current internal narrative about itself in proclaiming its uniqueness to those looking for a church. There simply are not many churches proclaiming that they are average, nothing unusual, run-of-the-mill places in which you will find little that challenges or inspires you. Couple the "uniqueness" message with the reality that the biblical church is one where personal narratives are retained but made subordinate to the collective narrative and ownership of each member by all the others, and the possibilities for abuse and predation arise.[9]

A church with a narcissistic pastor at its center quickly begins to veer off course towards treacherous shoals because "the narcissism of the chief executives often sets a similar tone for the corporation [church] as a whole."[10] Murray Hunter is an associate professor at University Malaysia Perlis. He writes, "[A]n organization can develop psychotic traits that influence perception, beliefs and values at an organizational level. Cognitive distortion is influenced by the psychotic traits of an organization along a continuum of various states which include paranoia, obsessive compulsive, dramatic, depressive, schizoid, and narcissistic tendencies."

He goes on to say that "everything that develops within a [church] including culture, management style, interpersonal relationships, rules and procedures, strategy, symbols and behavior will have some unconscious basis to it."[11] The unconscious basis consists of the internal identity the church creates for itself and the narrative the church holds as "truth." The problem lies in the fact that the "truth" of our narratives is often more about favorable interpretation than it is about factual reality—or scriptural integrity. When an internal narrative understood and accepted as true is confronted by outside resistance, in my experience it tends to strengthen the value placed on the story as it is rather than examining the resistance for bits of truth. The stronger the attack, the stronger is the resistance, the stronger the truth-story becomes, and a siege mentality often ensues. In other words, external forces rarely produce positive internal changes.

As stated above, an organization will reflect its leader, and the longer the leader is there the more accurate the reflection will be. I have found that

---

8. White, Review of Michael Diamond, *The Unconscious Life of Organizations*, 358.
9. Puls, *The Road Home*, 51–52.
10. Levinson, "Why the Behemoths Fell," 432.
11. Hunter, "The Psychosis of Organizations," 44–45.

to be true. However, I would also argue that the reflection is not just of the pastor in the case of churches, but the lay leaders as well, particularly if they are in strong support of a narcissistic pastor. In one case, a majority of the leadership group shared strong narcissistic tendencies to the point where strong narcissism was the character of that particular leadership group— and the primary reason the church was dying, which the leaders could not seem to comprehend.

CHARACTERISTICS OF THE NARCISSIST CHURCH

What are the characteristics of a narcissistic church? They are the same as the characteristics of the narcissist, only amplified and institutionalized. Also, please remember that almost every church will have some of these characteristics, but that does not make them narcissistic churches. Toxic narcissism is found in the combinations and intensities of these factors, and their positive or negative internal results.

Andrew Brown of the University of Cambridge argues in an extensive analysis of organizational narcissism that "collective entities, in the form of groups and organizations, literally have needs for self-esteem that are regulated narcissistically."[12] He goes on to say, "Organizational self-esteem consists of the collective self-esteem of individuals acting as the organization." He then goes to the heart of the matter in terms of how individuals become incorporated into a narcissistic culture and even allow their own identities to be swallowed by the organizational culture.

In effect, they become one with the organization and their organizational identity becomes dominant. "In an important sense, therefore, organizations exist in the minds of their members, organizational identities are parts of their individual members' identities, and organizational needs and behaviors are the collective needs and behaviors of their members acting under the influence of their organizational self-images."[13] In other words, as people become part of the church, the church becomes part of them in a reciprocal transfusion of culture, personality, and needs. Unhealthy people, then, are attracted to unhealthy churches, while the emotionally healthy will tend to either leave an unhealthy church or hunker down and make the best of it.

Much of what follows comes from Brown's analysis.

I must be clear about this: not all churches succumb to the narcissist pastor. Many resist powerfully enough that the strongly narcissistic pastor

12. Brown, "Narcissism, Identity, and Legitimacy," 649.
13. Brown, "Narcissism, Identity, and Legitimacy," 650.

is eventually forced out, but it usually takes a few years for the members to become convinced enough of the general "wrongness" of the situation to act. In other words, organizations do have the ability to resist effectively[14] —if they know what it is that must be resisted.

Denial

Brown states that organization members tend to conceal or simply deny any disagreeable truths from themselves about the organizations they belong to,[15] confirming philosopher Gregg Ten Elshof's contentions about how Christians are little different from others in having an amazing ability for self-deception. We tell ourselves lies and then believe the lies because they confirm what it is we want to believe when what we see is in opposition to what we wish to be true.[16] This is known as confirmation bias and is well documented.

The narcissistic church will conceal failures, blame "others" if they cannot be concealed, or simply deny them. If forced to acknowledge the failure, it will be recast into terms that are more positive, even heroic. If that is not possible, unnamed others, including satanic forces, will be blamed. The goal is never to have a failure of course, but that is not a reflection of reality. Every person and organization fails at some things. Healthy people and their organizations learn from the failure, incorporate their learnings into their general frameworks of interacting with the world, and move on.

Narcissistic organizations, on the other hand, hide their failures. They will hide or manipulate financial data, maintain an ongoing propaganda campaign in favor of itself, deny the existence of crises, and outright lie to its stakeholders in order to conceal internal problems, much the same as Jeffrey Skilling and Kenneth Lay did at Enron. Eventually, if the problems are not solved, the pastor will have to explain it to the entire congregation. Little could be more humiliating to the narcissist pastor than to stand before the people he sees himself as being superior to and then admitting failure, let alone intentional deception. Instead, he will wiggle and squirm to avoid taking personal responsibility, admitting nothing unless he has no other recourse, and even then, he will cast the blame elsewhere.

The narcissistic church will also create myths about itself that become entwined in its self-history and current truth narratives. While these myths

14. Godkin and Allcorn, "Organizational Resistance to Destructive Narcissistic Behavior."

15. Brown, "Narcissism, Identity, and Legitimacy," 654.

16. Ten Elshof, *I Told Me So.*

serve to foster denial, they also become part of the master story that the church tells itself and the outside world about its uniqueness, courage, resourcefulness, ingenuity, determination, and vitality. The myth is quickly absorbed into the master story as Truth. While it is a popular thing to do, it is also the organizational equivalent of pouring all of its resources into making a new and improved buggy whip.

Uniqueness

To claim uniqueness by necessity requires defining who we are, as well as defining the "other," which is who we are not. Jose Bruner argues, "Throughout history, as bonding has gone on and as identities have changed, the Other has been necessary in this process. Rome required barbarians, Christendom required pagans, Protestant and Catholic Europe required each other. Thus, while serving as a foundation of love among 'us,' the more pathological form of narcissistic collective self-love inevitably leads to rage against 'them,' that is, against those who fail to be part of 'us' because they differ in some significant way . . ."[17] Almost every church proclaims its uniqueness as a means of attracting new people. Branding, rebranding, and church growth have become a major industry. Every church needs members and every church tries to figure out how to attract new members, and so we ask ourselves, how are we unique? What's our brand? As I wrote earlier, no church I have ever seen advertises that it is dull, bland, and boring, and is probably a good fit for dull, bland, and boring people. However, some come close—one commentator recently suggested that the slogan for some mainline denominations could be, "Come back, because you were born here."

In looking at church slogans and tag lines, we see the effort to be different. Here are a few I found in a quick Internet search: "Church without the boring parts." "Real church, real people." "Love. Serve. Encounter." "Guidance in a misguided world." "A place where miracles happen." "Walking in faith; discovering a community." "Molding believers, influencing the world." "Transforming our city . . . one life at a time." "We're boldly going where no faith has gone before." "On our way to changing the world!" There is a certain amount of increasing grandiosity in each of these statements as they progress, particularly when a local church proclaims that it is influencing the entire world, transforming a city, going where no faith has ever gone before. You get the point.

The problem really is not in the slogan, but in the essence of the leaders and congregation and the intensity of belief in their uniqueness. Such

17. Bruner, "Pride and Memory."

as the church I pointed out earlier where the pastor regularly proclaimed how unique his church was and how many young pastors were (supposedly) coming to him for guidance. Many took his words with more than a few grains of salt, but many others believed him. They became proud and looked down at other churches in the area. Some still believe that it was special and unique, and even envied by others. Most of them have no idea how others in the community referred to them and their church as being "the Broadway church" for its many productions where the theology was "an inch deep and an inch wide" and where they preached "gospel lite." The reputation lingers today even though several years have passed and the congregation, pastor, theology, and even the name no longer resemble what they used to be.

A true quest for uniqueness can be a major spur to creativity, but it can also be a means of isolating the group from other churches and outside influences. See "Paranoia/Isolation" below.

Grandiosity

Every one of us has probably seen the phenomenon of a mediocre team unexpectedly winning a game and the players and bench sitters alike madly jutting their index fingers in the air while screaming "We're number one! We're number one!" Proclaiming yourself number one does not make it a reality. Unfortunately, churches are vulnerable to the same enthusiastic delusion.

One of the first things I do when called in to help a wounded church is visit its website. I look at the Statement of Faith, What to Expect, and What We Offer pages in particular to get the flavor they want you to have. I want to know the message the church is projecting to the world, and I often find some very interesting things.

Remember, to the narcissist, bragging about how exclusive his club is comes naturally and he is tone deaf about how it is received. It is no different for churches. One website proudly proclaimed that hundreds of people attended every Sunday, but only a few were actually members because the membership process was exhaustive and lengthy. The inference was that this was an exclusive club and only very special people were admitted. You had to be dedicated and willing to go through their initiation process. The senior pastor made the final decision on who was admitted into membership and who was not, so it was a clear possibility that you could give months of your time, energy, and study and still be denied. However, those selected were seen as favored by—but also obligated to—the senior pastor, which is a process ripe for abuse. While this sort of process will seem repugnant to many, it is actually quite attractive to a certain type of needy individual, particularly the narcissist who is having difficulty in finding something to brag about. In this sense, the church is appealing to narcissistic grandiosity. One man I know personally talks constantly about how his church is the best, most biblically accurate, friendliest, wealthiest . . . keep adding superlatives. His own narcissistic needs are met at least in part by being a member of this particular church.

We encourage pastors in self-aggrandizement by the ways in which we treat them, invite them into our most intimate and difficult moments, and place them on a higher plane than where we ourselves are confined. While a majority of pastors understand that this is not fair to them or us, the narcissist expects and demands it as his due. Remember, it is easy to proclaim how humbled we are by praise and attention while secretly gushing with pride.

Entitlement

If there is one place where entitlement should be loathed, it is the local church. Jesus had very strong words about entitlement.

> Then James and John, the sons of Zebedee, came to him. "Teacher," they said, "we want you to do for us whatever we ask."
>
> "What do you want me to do for you?" he asked.
>
> They replied, "Let one of us sit at your right and the other at your left in your glory."
>
> "You don't know what you are asking," Jesus said. "Can you drink the cup I drink or be baptized with the baptism I am baptized with?"
>
> "We can," they answered.
>
> Jesus said to them, "You will drink the cup I drink and be baptized with the baptism I am baptized with, but to sit at my right or left is not for me to grant. These places belong to those for whom they have been prepared."
>
> When the ten heard about this, they became indignant with James and John. Jesus called them together and said, "You know that those who are regarded as rulers of the Gentiles lord it over them, and their high officials exercise authority over them. Not so with you. Instead, whoever wants to become great among you must be your servant, and whoever wants to be first must be slave of all. For even the Son of Man did not come to be served, but to serve, and to give his life as a ransom for many." (Mark 10:35–45)

The North American culture is in many ways a culture of entitlement and church members bring that sense of entitlement with them. It is common for people to make various demands because they have been members for a long time or to withhold their tithes and offerings because they are unhappy with a decision made by the church leadership. When a narcissistic pastor comes together with members who also believe they are entitled, it can create a culture of entitlement in the church that exposes itself in sometimes-unexpected ways. Blake Coffee, who goes by the pseudonym the Church Whisperer, writes,

> Whatever the cause(s), the American church seems to me to have developed a sense of "entitlement" much more than a sense of "submission" such as Peter advocates in his letter. We are "outraged" by a Court ruling which takes away our right to pray over the intercom at a football game, while our own scheduled prayer meetings in our own facilities have tumbleweeds blowing through them. We are ready to take up arms to defend our "right" to receive tax exemptions on people's large financial gifts to us while our brothers and sisters in China are not even permitted to legally assemble in the first place. We will mobilize an army of voters to preserve the sanctity of marriage against gay rights advocates, but sit back quietly while 50% of the marriages within the church fall to divorce.[18]

The church at every level from the small group to the largest megachurch is called to one form expressed in many ways: servanthood. Like Christ, we are called to serve, not to be served (Mark 10:45).

The narcissistic church may serve, and serve very well. It may be exemplary in its service to those in need. That is not the point even as Jesus' words to James and John were not about service—they were about the attitude and spirit of service. So the question is, why do we serve? So that we can feel good about ourselves? So that we can get together and talk about how well and how much we serve, and then congratulate each other on our service? So that we collectively as the local church can proclaim our service as a reason for joining us? That is narcissism as it brings acclaim to us and not the Lord we serve. Jesus said in Matthew 6:3, "But when you give to the needy, do not let your left hand know what your right hand is doing."

There is a men's small group that reads and discusses various books. The group was reading Philip Yancey's wonderful *What's So Amazing about Grace?* and every week at the beginning of the meeting the leader would ask everyone how they offered grace to someone that week. Maybe it's just me

---

18. Coffee, "Entitlement and the Church."

and my Dutch German Reformed and fundamentalist background where we don't talk about these things, but it seems that in proclaiming our service graceful for the approval of others we have missed the point of what Jesus was calling us to, as well as the point of grace.

Paranoia/Isolation

Along with grandiosity and entitlement, the narcissistic church will experience a certain amount of paranoia that expresses itself through isolation. This will manifest as a sense of being superior to other churches, which then have nothing of value to offer. Instead, these churches should come to them to learn how to do church right. They wait and wait, but never figure out why it is that nobody comes. There are some that are hugely successful in this and have numerous conferences each year for pastors on preaching, church growth, and so on, but rarely participate when other churches offer similar programs. It's an interesting way of disguising internal narcissism under a cloak of service, but it is service with the background idea of "we are so good at this that you really need to copy what we do."

This is also manifested in more fundamentalist and cultic groups that believe contact with the outside world is polluting. In the dangerously narcissistic church, a warped gospel message proclaims that Truth can be found nowhere else. The twisted psychology of it provides for varying degrees of "We have a corner on the Truth as revealed through our charismatic pastor. To be part of us you have to accept that Truth exactly as we present it without question or challenge." As the church turns ever further inward, the message of paranoia and isolation grows stronger.

Lack of Empathy

Let's be honest: we all sin. Daily. Sometimes, we may fall into a major sin. So, what is the church to do? Galatians 6:1–2 states, "Brothers and sisters, if someone is caught in a sin, you who live by the Spirit should restore that person gently. But watch yourselves, or you also may be tempted. Carry each other's burdens, and in this way you will fulfill the law of Christ." The church is called to be a place of accountability and gentle restoration. It's not one or the other, but both.

You will probably not find gentle restoration in the narcissistic church. Instead, the narcissistic church will loudly proclaim the love and forgiveness of Christ even as it draws its members ever deeper into a cold, rigid, and unforgiving conformity.

Case in point: a young unmarried woman had an affair with a married man. Riddled with guilt, she went to her pastor and confessed. Her pastor counseled her that she had to stand up in front of the entire congregation and confess her sin. As humiliating as that would be, she cherished the relationships she had in this church, and so agreed. The following Sunday morning she quivered in fear and humiliation as she stood in front of the entire congregation and tearfully told her story. She expected biblical forgiveness and restoration. Instead, the pastor publicly told to her to leave and never come back and ordered the congregation to shun her. Amazing—a church proclaiming the gospel of Christ with no place for actual sinners! I would probably never be accepted into membership—but then again, I don't intend to try.

The lack of empathy usually is not that dramatic, but it is just as real. More often, people with questions or criticisms will be told privately that they would probably be much happier elsewhere, which is a shaded message to leave and never come back. Even more subtle are the places that begin a whispering campaign against someone that eventually cuts them off from all of their friends and makes it known that they simply are no longer welcome. Conformity is enforced in this way.

Little Awareness of External Perceptions

Just like the narcissist who has no understanding of how others see him, the narcissistic church will have little awareness of external perceptions. External criticisms are summarily dismissed because they do not comport with the existing internal master story and narrative of who we are, what we are about, and what it is that we do. By not engaging with other churches or limiting engagement with the community, there are fewer opportunities to become aware of outside perceptions. If the church is narcissistic enough, the people simply do not care what others think about them but are absolutely certain that the outside image is wonderful. In some, outside ridicule is seen as a badge of honor and of Gods' provenance (e.g., Westboro Baptist Church).

There is a flip side to this phenomenon. It is intentional, and it is used to isolate the church and its members into a more cohesive group: we are under satanic attack by outsiders who come to us with kind words and gestures but with terrible, evil intentions. There is nothing like believing a group is under attack to bring that group into tighter unity and deeper isolation. Again, all we need do is look at men like David Koresh and Jim Jones to understand the catastrophic consequences of paranoia among narcissistic leaders.

Rationalization

While secular organizations tend to rationalize their less-than-ethical actions both externally and internally, churches seem more inclined to internal rationalizations, and even those are very limited in terms of the congregation or the public. Where you will find the major rationalizations is in the upper strata of leadership: the pastor and his or her most trusted (as far as a narcissist can actually trust, of course) associates. Andrew Brown of the University of Cambridge says that policy makers are often more inclined to satisfy their own personal motives and emotional needs than the requirements of their organizations. The result is that decisions are made for egocentric reasons, which then must be justified/rationalized (often un-self-consciously) by means of "impressive-sounding reasons." This becomes possible because organizations allow "shadow places" to be created "in which nothing can be seen and no questions asked." The social order of organizations creates "selective principles" (rationalizations) that in turn highlight favorable events and obscure or cloak unfavorable events, "control memory, provide categories for thought, set the terms for self-knowledge, and fix identities."[19]

But doesn't every church do that in some respects? Probably, but again the objection misses the point, which is that the combination of these factors and their intensity determines whether or not a given church has narcissistic qualities or is intensely narcissistic. Witness the rise and fall of Harold Camping, who predicted the end of the world and the return of Christ. Many of his followers sold their homes, gave away their possessions, liquidated their assets, and gave them away because none of those things would be needed in heaven. They waited expectantly for May 21, 2011. Nothing happened. Camping then adjusted his prophecy to the date of October 21, 2011. Again, nothing happened.

Camping rationalized his narcissistic belief that he alone could "decipher" the "Bible code" that held the secret to the second coming and said on his radio program, "We're living in a day when one problem follows another. And when it comes to trying to recognize the truth of prophecy, we're finding that it is very, very difficult. There's one thing that we must remember. God is in charge of this whole business, and we are not. What God wants to tell us is his business. Amongst other things, I have been checking my notes more carefully than ever. And I do find that there is other language in the Bible that we still have to look at very carefully and will impinge upon this

---

19. Brown, "Narcissism, Identity, and Legitimacy," 656.

question very definitely." Notice the rationalization and refusal to admit that he was just plain wrong?

The *International Business Times* put it this way on November 2, 2011: "However, when Doomsday failed to materialize, the followers were left in the lurch. They did not fly off to heaven as promised and had exhausted their life's savings. When questioned about his moral responsibility to the followers, Camping deftly washed his hands off. He said he was not really responsible for anyone in particular."[20] He attributed favorable motives and outcomes to himself, blamed his followers for following him, and then blamed God for changing the second coming without notifying him! In Camping's May 21, 2011 spiritual judgment day predictions, he even claimed that God had stopped saving people who did not believe. He did apologize for that, but never actually retracted the statement.

Being leader of a church carries with it automatic prestige and power, and less often financial rewards. Being part of a church gives deeper meaning to who we are and why we exist; thus it offers the intrinsic reward of self-esteem—I am loved and cherished by none other than God Almighty. In maintaining this self-esteem, we also open ourselves to self-aggrandizement, and for the same reason—I am loved and cherished by none other than God Almighty! Brown aptly summarizes the dilemmas and traps that churches and their members are susceptible to. "These rewards encourage the individual to self-aggrandizement ('Because I am a member of a virtuous or worthwhile organization, I too am virtuous or worthwhile'), to deny moral improprieties and questioning of the individual's social utility ('Since I participate in a good organization, my actions must be good'), to rationalize actions ('My actions are prompted by virtuous motives'), to possess a sense of entitlement ('The virtuous should receive'), and to engage in attributional egotism ('Since I am good, so are the consequences of my actions')."[21]

Organizational Psychosis

Organizational paranoia can lead to organizational psychosis, where the organization loses its connections with reality and becomes more and more deeply enmeshed in its own self-deceiving truth-story to the point where all other truth-stories and inconvenient facts are summarily rejected. In normal organizations, knowledge is acquired and understanding and application sought through thought, word, and experience. Rational distortion in narcissistic organizations warps meaning and the understanding

20. Jijo, "Judgment Day 2011," *International Business Times*, October 16, 2011.

21. Brown, "Narcissism, Identity, and Legitimacy," 666.

of intentions, leading to incorrect, but thoroughly accepted, conclusions. Information that contradicts what we believe creates tension in our minds between what we believe to be true and authoritative information that contradicts that belief. "Cognitive dissonance" rests on the premise that people desire to view themselves as rational and uniform in both thought and action; therefore, they consciously choose how they respond to information or behaviors that challenge their way of thinking. Leon Festinger proposed three ways humans do this: minimize the importance of the dissonant thought, outweigh the dissonant thought with consonant thoughts, or incorporate the dissonant thought into one's current belief system.[22]

Organizational cognitive dissonance is the feeling of uncomfortable tension that spreads throughout an organization when what is expected and what actually happens are different. When there is cognitive dissonance between what the organization believes and what is observed outside the organization, the organization may tend towards such psychotic traits as "compulsion, anxiety, depression, attention seeking, fantasies, irrational fears, paranoia, shyness or narcissistic behavior."[23] This may be particularly true in churches. Paranoia is always focused on the present with fantasies of imminent attack or sabotage while the others have past-future components. The result is that the church withdraws further and further while becoming more and more cult-like.

Brown offers the following chart to help people understand how organizations operate in narcissistic ways.

22. Festinger, *A Theory of Cognitive Dissonance*.
23. Hunter, "The Psychosis of Organizations," 45.

TABLE 4: NARCISSISM IN ORGANIZATIONS[24]

Narcissistic Traits	Individual	Organization
Denial	Individuals deny the reality of demands and resource constraints, facts about themselves, and features of past occurrences.	Organizations deny facts about themselves through spokespersons, propaganda campaigns, annual reports, and myths.
Rationalization	Individuals rationalize decisions and actions to mitigate negative outcomes.	Organizations provide rationalizations that structure thought, post-hoc justify their actions, inaction, and responsibility.
Self-aggrandizement	Individuals engage in fantasies of omnipotence, exhibit grandiosity and exhibitionism, create cultures in their own image, narrate stories that flatter themselves, make nonsensical acquisitions, engage in ego-boosting rituals, and write immodest autobiographies.	Organizations endow themselves with rightness, make claims to uniqueness, commission corporate histories, and deploy their office layouts and architecture as expressions of status, prestige, and vanity.
Attributional egotism	Individuals blame external authority for their plight, and narrate stories that contain self-enhancing explanations.	Organizations use annual reports to blame unfavorable results on external factors and attribute positive outcomes to themselves.
Sense of entitlement	Individuals are exploitative, lack empathy, engage in social relationships that lack depth, and favor their interests over shareholders.	Organizations are structured according to principles of entitlement. Organizations assume entitlement to continued existence.
Anxiety/Paranoia	Individuals suffer internally, experience deprivation and emptiness, are paralyzed by personal anxiety and tension, and struggle to maintain a sense of self-worth.	Organizations suffer from social instability due to a breakdown of standards and values and alienation, requiring shared culture, moral order, a common sense of purpose, leadership attempts to secure commitment.

24. Brown, "Narcissism, Identity, and Legitimacy," 652–53.

Few churches consciously push people away, but the truly narcissistic church may take great pride in being ostracized and ridiculed, particularly when the members are completely convinced that theirs is the correct interpretation of Scripture and everyone else is plainly wrong. One need only observe the incredible destructiveness of the late Fred Phelps and Westboro Baptist Church that regularly picketed the funerals of soldiers killed in action with placards reading, "God loves dead soldiers." The narcissism behind this is quite clear and was stated on the church website: Westboro is so special in the eyes of God that God is killing US soldiers on the battlefield in retaliation for someone bombing Westboro in 1995.

We are called to more than that.

10

Healing the People

You will know that forgiveness and healing has begun when you recall those who have hurt you and feel the power to wish them well and pray for them.

—Dave Kreger

Many of you reading this book have been recoiling in horror as you began to recognize and understand a pastor that you know, have seen in action, or have been the victim of. The disbelief has been replaced first by bewilderment at how this could happen, anger that it did, and then the slow realization that your pastor may be deeply ill.

If you are the victim of a narcissist pastor, you have a lot of company. In fact, you have far more company than even I suspected.

You are not at fault if a narcissist pastor has victimized you! You were carefully and intentionally groomed, seduced, and manipulated to reveal some of your greatest hopes, weaknesses, and fears only to have them used against you by someone you trusted. You were blamed for things that were not your fault, accused of motives you did not have, and treated to one of the most discouraging emotional roller coaster rides imaginable. Even now you may be thinking that by your reaction you made things worse or that, with a bit more love and understanding, this would not have happened. In that you are wrong—there is nothing at all that you could have done to prevent it except break off the relationship. Even then, the narcissist's guilt-mongering is so effective that you likely would still have some small suspicion that you caused it. You didn't. Not at all!

One thing is clear: If the people do not confront themselves and each other in what has happened, there will be little if any healing at the congregational level. There are two things that we must do, and both are difficult: forgive and protect the church. You may have to do them simultaneously, but we will deal with them separately.

FORGIVING

Jesus commanded that we forgive others no matter what they do, which Paul says we must do in the same manner as Christ has forgiven us. It's a tall order, but not an impossible one.

I have been researching what forgiveness is, what it is not, and how to overcome our own internal barriers against forgiving, since 2004. I wrote about it in great depth in another book to help entire congregations forgive and reconcile following the destructiveness of a church conflict.[1] In particular, it was written to help narcissist-wounded congregations heal. Forgiving is ultimately up to each and every individual. No one can force it or command it. It is a decision you must make, and how it works is different for everyone but has the same general pattern of steps to follow.

If you are the victim of a narcissist pastor, then you have experienced severe psychological and spiritual trauma. You have been abused, used, betrayed, and thrown away like yesterday's trash. It is difficult to trust after that experience, and some resolve never to trust a pastor again, or blame the entire episode on religion itself. Both reactions are understandable, but unfair and unnecessary. Remember, most clergy want only to serve God and to help you. Many may have strong narcissistic tendencies but they keep them under control and channel them to further the kingdom of God and encourage others. They still love the praise and admiration, but it is more a result of ministry than it is the goal. For the true narcissist, it is the goal and he will use any means available to achieve it.

One of the more common responses to the idea of forgiving as God has forgiven us is an emphatic "I'm not God!" It's an honest exclamation and reflects the fact that we do not have godly powers. However, it also imagines that God just brushes off every evil thing we do and forgives instantly and

1. Puls, *The Road Home.*

joyously. I don't think so. If Scripture is accurate, God weeps and feels real pain at what we do to each other the same as we weep and hurt when it is done to us. If that is the case, then we can decipher how God forgives and apply it to ourselves.

First of all, forgiving does not require the person who harmed you to repent, however you understand the term (although true repentance does make it much easier). In fact, repentance and forgiveness are not even connected. Why do I say that? Just read Matthew 18:1–22. We are to forgive others no matter what they do and how many times they do it. Only Luke 17:3 talks about forgiveness having a connection to repentance, but the context is one of readmitting the repentant sinner to full church life. We call that reconciliation. Forgiveness and reconciliation are separate but connected actions.

Then there is what I term the Predicament of Reciprocity immediately following the Lord's Prayer in Matthew 6:14–15, "For if you forgive other people when they sin against you, your Heavenly Father will forgive you. But if you do not forgive others their sins, your Father will not forgive your sins." Those are hard but clear words: we are not forgiven if we do not forgive others. While repentance (confession, expressions of remorse, and changed behavior) makes it easier to forgive, it is not necessary. In fact, in this case, it will most likely never happen! Since the narcissist is never wrong and does not care that she hurt you, she sees nothing to repent from, and never will. Like the narcissist pastor we cited earlier, the most you are likely to get is something like this: "All right, I'll be the martyr. I'll accept your apology." That is normal thinking for the true narcissist. If you are waiting on repentance from a narcissist, you will have a very long wait.

Luke 17:7 is the only instance where Jesus might be interpreted as requiring some level of repentance prior to forgiveness between people and those who resist forgiving are quick to trot it out in triumph. Here Jesus is teaching about forgiveness and states that if a brother repents, he is to be forgiven. The logical obverse is no repentance = no forgiveness. Taken in isolation, Jesus' statement appears to require some level of repentance, of change, prior to forgiveness. However, Jesus immediately went on to say that if the same person sins 490 (70 x 7) times in one day and says that he repents 490 times, he or she must be forgiven. No one sins 490 times and then repents each time in a single day! Saying "I repent" is not repentance any more than Judas's "repentance" was real (Matt 27:23, KJV). Jesus is essentially saying that the behavior has not changed, and, even though the offender has engaged in false repentance multiple times, believers are to forgive anyway. What is even more important to note is that this is the only place in Scripture where Jesus mentions repentance in the context of believers forgiving others.

It is necessary then to define what we mean by forgiving someone else's sin against us. Biblically, the Greek word translated as forgive in the Lord's prayer is *aphiemi*. It is translated as forgive more than any other word. *Aphiemi* means to release, to let go of something. In forgiving, you must let go of something; you must release it—but what is the "it" you are to release? It comes down to this: human forgiveness as an internal series of decisions to release your own animosity, hatred, anger, fear, and the desire for revenge against another, replacing these emotions with more benevolent feelings, including love. Forgiving is a decision that you make to let go of your pain, anger, animosity, and desire for revenge even though the perpetrator has done absolutely nothing to deserve it. In essence, you drain your own internal toxins and release the person who caused them. Since these are our decisions alone, forgiveness is not dependent on the actions of the other. It can be that simple or more complex, depending on your emotional makeup, but the release you will experience is that of being set free from the pain and the person who inflicted it. It breaks the chains holding you bound in a miserable embrace.

The point of it is this: all of the emotions that come with being deliberately injured by someone else are designed for short-term survival. Anger numbs the pain, giving you the strength to survive, and dreaming about revenge feels good and can pull you out of depression for short periods of time. The problem is that over time they mar judgment, weaken the immune system, and cause high blood pressure along with increased risk of stroke and cardiovascular disease. Want a heart attack? Carrying a grudge for a long time triples the possibility. Same thing with a stroke. Dreaming of revenge can be addicting, as every time you think about it and experience that vicarious rush you are actually releasing powerful—and highly addictive—chemicals into the brain.

Have you ever been around someone who is perpetually angry? Couldn't get away from them soon enough, could you? So why would you want to become that same person? Forgiving is the antidote.

God did not design you to carry all of these toxic emotions within you for anything more than a very short period of time, because in the long run they can destroy your relationships and your health, and even kill you. When Jesus told us to forgive all things, *it had nothing to do with the people who harmed us but everything to do with our own well-being!* All of what I am writing here has been backed up by multiple clinical studies and Scripture—I'm not just making it up!

I have broken the forgiveness process down into five basic steps, which I will outline below. If you want greater detail or are going to help an entire congregation, then I recommend my book *The Road Home*.

I use a five-step forgiveness process that I remember under the acronym of TRUTH: Turning, Remembering, Understanding, Transforming, and Healing. In case you are interested, the process has been endorsed by the presidents of the American Association of Christian Counselors (Tim Clinton) and the Christian Association for Psychological Studies (Paul Regan). In fact, Everett Worthington, Jr., one of the world's leading researchers in forgiveness studies, wrote the introduction to the book.

THE TRUTH REALLY WILL SET YOU FREE

The entire forgiveness process generally follows a course outlined by Robert Enright of the University of Wisconsin: 1) an uncovering phase where one gains insight into how the wrongful act and subsequent injury have negatively impacted one's life; 2) a decision phase where the individual gains insight into forgiveness and commits to forgive; 3) a work phase where the individual reframes both the offender and the offense into a more positive light, thereby gaining and increasing empathy for the offender; and 4) a deepening phase where the individual feels more connected with others, finds decreased negative affect, and "at times, renewed purpose in life."[2] I have taken Enright's work and the works of many others and formulated the process into the TRUTH process.

Turning

The point of Turning is to reframe how we see and understand those who caused us injury in the same terms as we see ourselves: deeply wounded human beings who need the love and forgiveness of God in order to become who we were designed to be. It starts by praying for the person who has hurt you. I recommend that you pray that God will heal them and bless them beyond anything they can imagine. We are commanded to pray for and love our enemies, and you cannot pray for the welfare and healing of your enemies without beginning to see them as they are: so deeply wounded by life that they cannot function in any other way. You cannot pray for them in this way without the beginnings of empathy and sorrow for them. They are no less crippled emotionally than the quadriplegic is physically. In praying that

2. Enright, *Forgiving Is a Choice*, 68.

God will heal and bless them beyond their abilities to imagine we find ourselves beginning to see them much as we see ourselves: wounded creatures
in need of the grace and healing of God, instead of the monsters we may
have declared—or want—them to be. The realization that they cannot act
in truly benevolent ways because of their own deep emotional and spiritual
wounds enables us to release our anger in the decision to forgive. By the
way, is there someone who might pray that prayer for you?

To get there requires something we don't like to do: turn inward to
find those parts of ourselves that we share with those who have hurt us.
No amount of protest or avoidance will help. We must confront ourselves
squarely and honestly. Jesus said unequivocally that our thoughts count,
and it is here that we must confront them. Yes, we want to confront the offender and rip him a new one! We want to exchange pain for pain and hurt
them as badly as they hurt us (and perhaps a bit more as a warning to never
do it again). We want to verbally assassinate them and stand in front of the
world to declare their many sins. We want vindication! Instead, we discover
that, in many ways more than we want to admit, we are like them no matter
how strongly we wish to deny it. As someone once wrote, the truth will set
you free, but first it tends to make you miserable!

By praying for them and opening our eyes to their pain and woundedness, we become increasingly able to see them alongside us on a more equal
plane that was thrown out of balance by what they did. In turning inward,
we find our own capacity to abuse others. It is incredibly humbling suddenly
to realize that we are far more like those who harmed us than we are different. We desperately wish to be seen as different from those who oppress us,
but in believing the wish, we engage in a form of self-delusion.

We then find ourselves experiencing empathy for the offender, which
we may not want, but it is there nonetheless. To have empathy is to imagine
life and the incident from the perspective of the other. It means getting inside their skin to see him or her as a distinct individual with human needs
and weaknesses rather than as some "thing" less than me. Empathy helps us
see others in much the same way as we see ourselves, lessening the tendency
to exaggerate what they have done into who they are. Empathizing changes
our perspective from what mystic philosopher Martin Buber called the "I-
It" of seeing the other as an object to the more intimate, and equal, "I-Thou."
Instead of labeling them as thieves, we must wonder about why they needed
to steal. In inquiring about why they stole, we begin to see the human needs
that drove them and, in looking at them, we often see ourselves looking
back in a disturbing mirror image. When we first come to understand the
terror of exposure, the deep shame, and the humiliation that can only be
held back by victimizing others and living vicariously through those they

see as successful and powerful, we can begin to see the narcissism sufferer as a terrified child trapped in an adult body coping in the only manner he can. Dropping our self-justifying barriers makes forgiving not only easier, but attractive.

Shame says that we did something because we are defective; we are broken and bad people beyond help even from God, which in turn means that we cannot change no matter what. I *am* a thief, an unchanging state that leads to an angry helplessness, which in turn leads to the conclusion that since one *is* an offender, one can do nothing but continue offending. Guilt, on the other hand, is about what we have done, separating the act from who we are. Guilt says that I am a child of God who has done something sinful and harmful, but with forgiveness and help, I can change for the better. Guilt is healthy, freeing, and strongly pushes us to repentance and changing our ways, while shame is constricting and more likely to lead to self-destructive ways and dreams of revenge. Long-term shame is toxic to body and soul and finds its expression through physical, verbal, and symbolic aggression, indirect aggression through harming something important to the other person, malicious rumoring, and self-aggression. Guilt, however, pushes us to respond in conciliatory ways by seeking to forgive and renew a wounded relationship.[3]

Even though the narcissist pastor feels only shame and helpless rage, I must separate the person who victimized me from his sin in the same manner as God sees us as separate from our sin. I must see him as who he is and not for what he has done. He is loved and cherished by God not one bit less than I am. Like it or not, he is trapped in his own dilemma but, unlike us, he has little chance of escape.

In turning inward to locate how I am like him I find much more than I had anticipated or wanted, but it is part of God's great plan of repentance for us in that we can repent, change, and grow, where this is not even on the radar for the true narcissist.

It is so easy to lose hope when under such terrible attack, but the Holy Spirit restores lost hope (Rom 15:13), and hope allows empathy to grow. Without hope, we become stuck in the grave of depression, but as hope grows, empathy gains energy and strength until it changes to compassion and crests the last remaining barrier to my own repentance. Empathy says only that I feel for the offender, but compassion demands action: I must do what I can to alleviate the suffering; since the suffering in this case is mine, I must forgive. As we become more aware of our mutual woundedness, it becomes easier to allow love and compassion to re-enter our lives through

---

3. Tangney et al., "Relation of Shame and Guilt," 293.

the work of the Holy Spirit (Phil 2:12; Col 3:12; Rom 5:5). As compassion grows, hope grows stronger, and compassion grows again—they feed off each other while producing more than either consumes. The Holy Spirit is the catalyst to repentance, and is the key that opens each level. Thus, Turning is a change of mind from solitary suffering to mutual woundedness—and compassion begins to flow.

And so begins the increasingly intimate dance of forgiveness.

Remembering

Turning is an invisible step off the island and into a small boat and sailing in the safety of the harbor. However, one cannot enter a new harbor without risking the open sea. Turning propelled our little boats into the channel between harbor and sea, but will not go further. Remembering will take us through to the adventure of the open ocean.

Remembering first requires repenting from our own victimhood, then recognizing and acknowledging our own wrongdoing, which is almost always centered in what we thought, said, and did in return for the wounds we received. As much as we may not want to, we must remember and confront the truth of our own sin and own it through confession. In this, we confront the highest barrier to seeking or granting forgiveness, and the most common reason for refusing to forgive. Let's face the truth: we want the offender to suffer and to grovel before us in humiliating repentance. The narcissist knows what he did and the damage he caused, but he simply does not care. Waiting for an apology of any sort will mean waiting for the rest of your life.

Remembering is about repenting from our thoughts and behaviors through confession to God and asking God for forgiveness for harboring painful and hateful attitudes, no matter what we have suffered or how well-earned those attitudes may be. Repentance turns us from denial to acceptance, ownership, and admission of our own sin. It's easy to rebel here and proclaim that I am a victim, therefore I am *entitled* to my rage, but Scripture is plain that this is off course—we are to love and forgive our enemies no matter what it is they have done! We are called to a higher standard, and recovery from what we have experienced requires it: we must confess to God our own sin and seek forgiveness for it. We must confess our thoughts and repent from them. As I said, forgiving is not so much about the perpetrator as it is of freeing ourselves from his grip—and releasing our own death grip on his throat.

As it is used here, confession is simply a statement of truth and ownership, nothing more or less. It means telling the truth of what you thought, said, or did, and taking ownership for it. I thought it, I said it, I did it, and it was sin.

Confession requires an accurate assessment and accounting of sin, of truthfulness in taking ownership for what I thought and did—it is an admission against my own interests but it is also the gateway to purging those sins. It requires me to abandon the mask of victimization and self-righteousness that covers my sin. It is a step into true vulnerability. Once sin is admitted, it cannot be denied; it stays with me and only God can remove the stain.

We must turn from what others have done to us to what we have done to others, whether in thought, word, or deed. In a strange turnaround from common sense, seeing and confessing our own wrongdoing frees us from its grip. Jesus put it succinctly: "If you hold to my teachings, you are really my disciples. Then you will know the truth, and the truth will set you free." (John 8:31–32). Knowing the truth, however, is often unsettling. As noted, the truth will set you free, but first it tends to make you miserable. Knowing the truth allows us to make sense of events that were confusing, but also strips away our self-deceit and denial. Knowing the truth gives perspective where perspective was lacking, encouraging empathy to grow.

The most difficult element in the entire process is repenting from victimhood by confronting the truth of my own sin. Focusing on the sins against me and the person who committed them only leads to more pain, anger, and thoughts of revenge. Jesus was emphatic that we must look at our own actions first, not as a response to what someone else did, but in order to be freed from them. He used the comic image of someone with a log sticking out of an eye going around and pointing towards the speck of sawdust in someone else's eye (Matt 7:3–5). He also labeled it for what it is: hypocrisy.

Let's be honest: we are all hypocrites when it comes to this. To experience an attack of narcissistic rage is devastating (I speak from experience), but we do not have to stay in that shattered condition. We can decide to leave it behind, and finding my own rage tells me that, in many ways, I am little different from my attacker. We don't want to look at the "oppressor" and see ourselves, but, as German Pastor Dietrich Bonhoeffer wrote from a Nazi prison shortly before he was hanged, "Nothing that we despise in the other man is entirely absent from ourselves. We must learn to regard people less in the light of what they do or omit to do, and more in the light of what they suffer.[4]" And there lies the key for many: the narcissist suffers from a condition that is rarely successfully treated let alone "cured," and lives in a world limned by the terror and humiliation of being exposed and ridiculed. In understanding that she is operating in the only way she can, it becomes

---

4. Bonhoeffer, *Letters and Papers from Prison*, 10.

easier to let go of our pain as we begin to see her as a terribly wounded child of God, living in constant fear of exposure, who struggles to survive with inadequate coping skills.

In that small shared likeness, we find ourselves, and come closer to the miracle of forgiving.

The second part of this first step is prayer—prayer for our own forgiveness, and prayer for healing of the narcissist. I find that I cannot maintain my own angry attitude when praying the God will heal and bless my enemy beyond her wildest imaginings. It then becomes easier to confess my sin and seek holy forgiveness, and to grant it.

Understanding

Understanding comes with the dawning of just how much we and everyone around us have been hurt and what we have lost individually and collectively. It is a lament that cannot be contained, for it expresses all of our pain and bewilderment at the betrayal from someone we trusted. It is that sick feeling in the gut that churns when we realize that the pain was intentional and there will be no repentance.

But, it is also more than that. It is the wailing of grief too deep for words as we seek God to heal his church and people. It is the reality of having hurt others and having been hurt by them as we struggled to find a way through the shredding and pitiless thorns of dealing with a narcissist pastor. If there are many of us, it becomes a collective lamentation, for we are grieving all that has been lost, particularly trust and deeply held relationships.

The Apostle Paul writes that godly sorrow will never be rejected (2 Cor 7:10), but that means more than sorrow for what we have done; it also includes sorrow for what has been done to us. Godly sorrow seeks to heal and to be healed.

Understanding is the process of fully embracing our grief, for in the embrace we will find relief and renewed hope. For a large portion of people, it is here that they will choose to release their pain and anger, to be replaced by the sweet serenity of having forgiven in the face of the onslaught and with no expectation or even hope of reciprocity.

They key here is not only to acknowledge the grief and hurt, but also to embrace and experience them completely, to be awash in them. We must accept what has happened, that much of it was beyond our control, but also that we played a part by allowing it to go on as long as it did. We seek forgiveness from God and our friends in this deep lament and find that we are capable of forgiving far beyond what we thought possible. Yes, we have lost much, and we are disillusioned, but we have survived, and we will once again thrive.

A common objection at this point comes from fear: we don't want to go there because we don't want to experience it all over again. The counter is this: It is not real pain. It feels similar, but it is only the memory of pain and it cannot harm you.

This is a new beginning, a dawning of what is possible, of what can be. The past is gone and irretrievable, but the future has not yet been fully written, and our Lord calls us into it.

Transforming

We have confessed our sins of allowing it to go on, of not intervening sooner, of thinking and dreaming of revenge. We have found, felt, and expressed our sorrow in a lamentation that goes deeper than words can ever express. However, we must still commit to God and each other how we will relate to each other in the future and determine the boundaries of acceptable behavior for our (probably new) pastor and ourselves.

Changing the Wind

It is frustrating and even dangerous trying to sail directly into a strong headwind. As a sailor, I can attest that the wind drives steep waves straight into the bow of your boat and cold spray flies everywhere as the vessel shudders from each wave's impact. The boat bounces up and over the waves only to slam down hard into the next trough, burying the nose under tons of green water; as the boat recovers, the water gushes down the deck and straight into the cockpit with you. Within minutes, you are soaking wet, cold, and bruised. Now repeat this cycle a thousand times for every mile traveled. No wonder it's called "beating into the wind."

Conventional wisdom says that all we can do in the face of the storm is beat into the wind, change direction or trim the sails and hang on. Indeed, without Christ, those truly are the options when beating into the wind of unforgiveness. Jesus, however, has a life-altering alternative.

You see, Jesus knew what it was like to beat into the wind.

The crowds around Jesus were unrelenting, demanding that he teach and heal them. Seeking some peace and quiet, Jesus said to the disciples (my paraphrase), "Hey, guys, let's take the boat and go over to the other side of the lake." Everyone that could fit piled into the boat, and off they sailed. Within a few minutes, Jesus was sound asleep.

Ferocious squalls can come out of nowhere off the hills around a lake such as Galilee. One minute the water is calm and the next minute there is wind, rain, and spray in such a mix that you can't see where you are, where you were, or where you are going. Steep, choppy waves come at you from every direction at once. These squalls can be unpredictable, chaotic—and terrifying.

The wind was howling as the sharp and chaotic waves started coming over the sides and into the boat. The disciples were bailing, but the water was coming in faster than they could throw it back out. Jesus must have been exhausted, as he just slept on through the tumult. As the water in the boat rose, the small vessel rolled deeper and deeper into the wave troughs, which allowed even more water to come in over the sides. The disciples were in danger of sinking—and drowning. They were terrified.

Finally, one them shook Jesus awake, crying, "Master, Master, we're going to drown!"

The worldly solution at this point would be to trim the sails, reverse course and go with the wind. That is not what Jesus did.

Jesus looked at the frightened faces of his young followers, then at the raging lake. He got up and rather firmly told the wind to be still and the sea to be calm. Within a few moments, the wind was gone and the waves were again ripples. Jesus had changed the wind, taking away not the fear itself, but the root cause of their fear (Luke 8:22–25). It is an apt metaphor for the chaos and fear of conflict and narcissistic attacks and points us to an unexpected resolution. We must ignore the easy answer of trimming our sails and going with the flow, or even one of heaving-to and staying where we are; we must allow the Holy Spirit to change the wind that drives our fears and reluctance to let go. It is a change so revolutionary and profound that it forever alters the course of our lives, and is quickly visible to all around us.

We must commit to changing the winds that drive us. In this, we must further confront ourselves to identify those emotions and reactions that were not productive, and commit to changing them. It is a yielding to the Holy Spirit and it transforms us through what the Apostle Paul termed a "renewing of the mind" (Rom 12:2). It says to the world, "I am different than I was. I am transformed into something better and more trustworthy." The winds of anger drive our small boat towards the rocks without mercy, no matter what we do to control it. Repentance turns us from our anger. Remembering confesses what we have done. Understanding our mutual woundedness causes us to cry out in sorrow. Turning our lives over to the One who changes the wind and transforms and frees us to leave our fear behind and live redeemed lives.

The experiences you have been through have changed you against your will, and there was little you could do about it. No one can come through this experience unscathed. It burns us, cuts us, and make us wary. It also teaches us valuable lessons in living, for when we see and understand how everyone has been hurt, we begin to see new ways of responding rather than reacting. We "learn a lesson." There has been enough increasingly destructive fighting fire with fire; we must begin using water to put out the flames completely. Transformation pours water on the fire of broken trust. When placed on top of godly sorrow, repentance once again changes us from a past of anger and pain to a future full of promise. We are changed forever.

The Apostle Paul states that godly sorrow comes before, and causes, transformed behavior (2 Cor 7:9–10). The language of transformation says, "I have learned from this experience and I am committed to changing my life with the help of God." The message it sends is, "We have survived and now we must thrive together."

Though you will probably never hear sincere words of sorrow or repentance from the narcissist pastor, you find that you no longer need them. Together you can say, "We learned. We changed. Never again!"

In this way the decision to forgive is cemented into place.

If you find that you simply cannot let it go, there are still options that you can exercise.

It may simply be that you are not ready. If you find the memories still too chaotic and cannot make sense of them, there is a very effective technique that you can use. Though it is simple, it has proven to be powerful and effective in helping people organize what happened into something understandable, though not acceptable. Created by Dr. James Pennebaker, it is the healing power of writing.

Louise Desalvo, who has expanded on Pennebaker's work, writes,

> Writing that describes traumatic or distressing events in detail and how we felt about these events then and how we feel about them now is the only kind of writing about trauma that clinically has been associated with improved health. . . . [W]e can't improve our health by free writing . . . or by writing descriptions of our traumas or by venting our emotions. . . .. *We must write in a way that links detailed descriptions of what happened with feelings—then and now—about what happened.*
>
> In controlled clinical experiments, then, *only writing that describes traumatic events and our deepest thoughts and feelings about them, past and present, is linked with improved immune function, improved emotional and physical health, and behavioral changes indicating that we feel able to act on our own behalf.*[5]

---

5. DeSalvo, *Writing as a Way of Healing*, 25. Emphasis in original.

Desalvo offers a simple and specific guide to Pennebaker's kind of writing, which has proven tremendously effective in helping people understand the trauma that was inflicted upon them, and in releasing the subsequent toxic emotions.

Do:

1. Write twenty minutes per day over a period of four days. Do this periodically. That way you won't feel overwhelmed.

2. Write in a private, safe, comfortable environment.

3. Write about issues you're currently living with, something you're dreaming about or thinking about constantly, a trauma you've never disclosed, discussed, or resolved.

4. Write about joys and pleasures too.

5. Write about what happened. Write, too, about feelings over what happened. What do you feel? Why do you feel this way? Link events with feelings.

6. Try to write an extremely detailed, organized, coherent, vivid, emotionally compelling narrative. Don't worry about correctness, grammar, or punctuation.

7. Beneficial effects will occur even if no one else reads your writing. If you choose to keep your writing and not discard it, you must safeguard it.

8. Expect, initially, that in writing this way you will have complex and appropriately difficult feelings. Make sure you get support if you need it.

Don't:

1. Don't use writing as a substitute for taking action.

2. Don't become overly intellectual.

3. Don't use writing as a way of complaining. Use it instead to discover how and why you feel as you do. Simply complaining or venting will probably make you feel worse.

4. Don't use your writing to become overly self-absorbed. Over-analyzing anything is counterproductive.

5. Don't use writing as a substitute for therapy or medical care.[6]

The first day or two of writing is likely to produce a product that is chaotic and nonsensical to the outside reader. That's fine, as you are writing

6. DeSalvo, *Writing as a Way of Healing*, 26–27.

for no one other than yourself. It begins to organize itself as your mind sorts through the events, and by the fourth day generally brings the entire event into a framework that makes sense and tells you that this was not your fault, that you did nothing to deserve it, that there was little you could have done to stop it, and so on. One of the things known from research is that understanding the event makes it much easier to forgive and move on into a brighter future.

HEALING THE BODY OF CHRIST

Healing the narcissist-wounded church is so important that it gets its own chapter.

11

Healing the Church

Heal the wounds, heal the wounds. . . .
And you have to start from the ground up.

—Pope Francis, *A Big Heart Open to God*

The church pastored for several years by a narcissist is inevitably an emotional, relational, and spiritual shambles. It may also be financially devastated by internal fighting and people leaving, and its spiritual and relational foundations are severely weakened. Every church of this type I have worked with suffered from all of these.

Those who remain often have a bunker mentality—they have hunkered down in order to survive the storm. In many ways, they are like weary war refugees seeking only safety and shelter. Or, like Midwesterners trying to survive a tornado, they have gone as deep underground as they can to escape the winds of devastation.

HEALING

Healing begins with the admission of what you have been through. You must name it and claim it, more or less a reversal of some types of prosperity gospel. By naming it, the experience not only becomes more real, it also much more understandable, which in turn makes it easier to forgive and move on. In claiming it, you now have something definite and tangible to forgive and seek forgiveness from. The reality is this: you have been the victims of an extremely sick person who used you and God to promote himself above all others. You were in survival mode and doing the best you could, and you probably had no idea of what it was that you were trying to cope with. It now has a name: toxic narcissism. Naming it makes it easier to frame it.

Next, you must name and claim the behaviors that contributed to the problem, even though very few of those actions likely were intentional. What do I mean?

1. What behaviors did you tolerate even though they were demeaning or insulting?

2. What did you observe that you silently said, "That is just not right!" but then did not confront?

3. What did you rationalize as being nothing more than eccentric behavior even though you silently knew that it was more than that?

4. What fears held you and others back from confronting what you knew to be wrong? In other words, how did you and so many others aid and abet what happened?

Yes, I am talking once again of naming our communal and individual sins and confessing them.

There will be a temptation to just "forget about the past" and move on, basing the idea on the Apostle Paul's statement in Philippians 3:13–14: "Brothers and sisters, I do not consider myself yet to have taken hold of it. But one thing I do: Forgetting what is behind and straining toward what is ahead, I press on toward the goal to win the prize for which God has called me heavenward in Christ Jesus." Paul was not being literal here but was emphasizing the need to move from the past and not be frozen in it. But simply burying the past as if it never happened will not bring healing. The pain re-emerged recently in a church that tried to move forward with a new plan several years ago but without directly confronting its past. It doesn't work, because no one has the capacity to forget and so the past just travels with you like an ever-heavier baggage train. God just did not give us that ability. Our job is to remember, forgive—and change! Without that commitment everything will stay the same, wounds will not be healed, and trust will not be rebuilt.

Yes, you have to name the elephant sitting so proudly and powerfully in the middle of the room. Not only did it happen, it was allowed to happen, and the culpability is shared. To become an emotionally healthy church once again, you must confront your worst enemy: yourselves. It does not stop with confrontation, but instead moves forward to identifying and committing to new behaviors individually and communally that specify how you will work together in the future to prevent it from happening again.

The narcissistic pastor presents what novelist Susan Howatch calls the "glittering image" of herself, an image that denies and hides the blemishes of reality behind a curtain of self-aggrandizement the same as pancake makeup hides the zits and blemishes of an actor.

The church also takes on the makeup of something it is not over time, and this image must be deconstructed and replaced by what it is God is calling your church (and you) to become. The church of a narcissist pastor has been focused on its own story; the recovering church needs to find its unique place in God's ever-unfolding story. The difference is huge, for it shifts the focus from the uniqueness and specialness of the specific church to the master story of the Master, and the adventure of finding the new place of the church within it.

To do this the church must break the power of the past. Our history is powerful and has a way of holding us in place unless we confront it. Peter Scazzero writes in *The Emotionally Healthy Church* that we must stand "naked in the icy wind" of self-examination to identify which parts of the past are holding the church in place so that a conscious decision may be made to discard them.[1] If the church has been an inch wide and an inch deep in its theology, it must decide to go wider and deeper. If it has been projecting a glittering image of itself, it must look honestly inward and upward towards God to find its real self, in which it will find its new true image.

Self-examination is never fun. The twelve-step programs call it "making a fearless moral inventory." By that they do not mean that there is no fear in the search, for there is, but to overcome our fears against overturning all the rocks to expose what lies under them, and then to morally clean house. Though the temptation will to be to rationalize what happened and diminish our part in letting it happen, we must confront who we are, what we have allowed and done, and then commit to change. Without this step, the church is likely to wallow in moral stagnation even though it may say all the right words.

---

1. Scazzero and Bird, *The Emotionally Healthy Church*, 88.

What I am describing here is the refocusing of the church from the past with its pain to a future full of promise by changing it at the deepest levels.

The narcissist pastor inevitably runs what can only be called a personality-driven church. Though the sermons and teachings may have been focused on Christ, the church itself is focused on the personality of the pastor. Unfortunately, and as we found, this style of church appears to be common and popular. Ask yourself, "Where would Rivers Edge Church be without Pastor Ted?" If the answer is that it would not exist in its present form, then it may be a personality-driven church. Unfortunately, we live in a society that praises and rewards the narcissist pastor who can win a huge following, never examining the driver behind it all: Jesus, or self-aggrandizement? Then there is the persona of the church itself: Jesus, or its own uniqueness? These are what I believe to be the fundamental identifiers between the narcissistic church and the healthy church.

The church victimized by a narcissistic pastor is likely to have a sense of abandonment and loss of identity once he is gone, but it is just as likely not to recognize the narcissistic patterns it has taken on. The church must move deeper into the existential questions of "Who are we?" and "Who is God calling us to become?" You must redefine who you are as a church, and you must redefine the dynamics of relationships within the church. Moreover, you must now find your new place in God's story, and you must identify the boundary-violating characteristics that are endemic in narcissism—and change them.

There is one thing that history tells us that we know is true: churches that do not change tend to die slowly. Though the message of Christ does not change, the churches that spread the message and preach the gospel must change or they are quickly bypassed as irrelevant. Once that happens they are existing on borrowed time.

Getting There

You have already read bits and pieces leading to the rest of the story. Within a year after Pastor Dave came under attack and resigned, there was an uprising in the church that lasted for another year.

The forced retirement of the covert narcissist pastor who had led it for decades was catastrophic. The damage was immense, and the congregation showed many of the patterns of psychological and emotional woundedness found in war refugees. The congregation dwindled as the pastor's supporters and opponents alike fled for safer ground.

Multiple major issues had to be resolved. As a body, the church had believed its own story that it was unique and special to the point where it was being copied and emulated in many places, all of which pointed back to the "wonderful and amazing" pastor. None of this was true, but there was a false sense of pride. Their annual Christmas production was (and still is) a well-known, huge, and high-quality production, but the focus of telling the Christ-story to the community was diluted within the church by pride over how well they did it. It was not all negative, of course. The annual production pulled the congregation together and forged wonderful, long-lasting relationships, and it reached thousands every year with the Christmas message.

Since the pastor had been the focus of so much, the church lost its identity when he left, and many of those who had gone through the decades with him left as well. It was an exceedingly difficult time. Those who remained did not know who they were and had no idea of where they were going as a body. Then there were the issues of boundaries, unhealthy communication patterns, and entitlement. Some of those who remained seemed to believe that they were entitled to special privileges and treatment simply because they were still there. Finally, they had to deal with the monumental task of changing the course of the church, something the former pastor had sworn he would never do; he did, however, state many times that he would rather see the church destroyed if it began to stray from the path on which he and God (in that order) had set it.

These were powerful dynamics for they defined who they were as a church and as a people of God. The new pastor and remaining leaders chose not to attack the issues head-on but to use the opportunity of this massive transition to find a new vision and path into the future. They brought in an experienced outside facilitator. Even though there were trained and highly experienced professional facilitators within the congregation, they realized that this work could not be done from the insiders' perspective. Only an outsider could challenge them to become who God was calling them to be. The past was honored and properly mourned, but the past could not be changed. Their future was in finding their new place in God's story.

The facilitator used a discernment process that takes the church leaders and all else who chose to participate through a focusing process of examining, revising, and perhaps adopting a new mission statement, identifying a written list of core values to help them find their new center by prioritizing what is it that they did well, less well, not so well, and what could be discarded. They then developed benchmarks that would measure progress.

It started chaotically enough: more than 100 people showed up on a Saturday morning to spend the entire day (and many ensuing evenings and Saturdays) trying to discern the will of God for themselves and for the church they served. They were a wounded church, much of the congregation was gone or leaving, there were unhealthy boundaries and relationships, and there was an unhealthy self-view. Using these realities, they sought to determine what it was God was calling them to become in order to heal each area. With the facilitator as guide, they spent a lot of time in prayer at every level, as they knew it would be easy to get off track. They were extremely vulnerable to spiritual attack and they knew it.

They spent time in action planning to determine what it was they needed to do, and then in what was necessary in order to accomplish it. They were preparing themselves for an unpredictable future rather than planning it, as following God leads to unexpected places.

They examined leadership styles individually and collectively, deciding to use only their individual strengths, creating teams that backfilled the strengths of others where they were weakest.

Finally, they had to pull it all together. God was clearly in the middle of it, as the new mission statement seemed to appear out of nothing. It would guide them for the next seven years, at which time a new mission was visualized and formed. They went on to define specific core values; these would become the benchmarks against which church would measure everything. Otherwise their mission statement would be like so many others: essentially meaningless.

Each core value was assigned to a small team. The teams met, prayed, talked, prayed some more, and finally all came back together. It was a Saturday morning and probably a hundred people were in the room as each team began to present its value statement. It had seemed that it could not all come together as they had been all over the map before, but the Holy Spirit was in it: everything fell into place. They suddenly had a new mission and sense of who they were. They had clear statements of their core values against which they would measure everything that they did. In that, they found a new purpose and began rebuilding.

The re-centering progression took six months to accomplish, but the results guided the church through the transition process of seven years. But they never confronted each other, honestly acknowledged their past, confessed, or sought forgiveness and reconciliation, and so vestiges of past pain remain. Though there are still sticking points and rough spots, the personality and character of the congregation have changed. One of the more obvious signs of it happens between Sunday morning worship services. It used to be that the people left immediately as if to escape something noxious and bothersome, but now they stay, carrying on animated conversations until well after the next service has started.

The dark presence of anger and resentment were still present, however, and recently came again to the fore. The biblical path set by Jesus of holy confrontation and forgiveness has not been followed as a congregation. It seems to present too much risk, as well as an underlying belief that time by itself heals all wounds. It does not. They have overcome bumps and road-blocks, of course. No one will deny that it was difficult, but then it probably would not have much value or buy in if it had been easy. Without risk and challenges, there is no adventure. Nor will anyone proclaim that everything is perfect, for the growth process never stops. But the internal abscess re-mains and will not be healed without following the path Jesus set forth.

If you are tempted to begin the rebuilding process on your own, please reconsider. If you have been in a narcissist-victimized church then you need to deal with your own personal psychological and spiritual wounds, which may include betrayal, verbal brutality, spiritual and emotional manipula-tion, and grief. You cannot help but inject your own issues into the process if you have been through this and are trying to lead the restructuring ef-fort. You need a highly trained, compassionate outside facilitator to lead the work.

12

Prevention

The best form of defense is attack.

—Carl von Clausewitz, *Principles of War*

It is crucial that church leaders become aware of the tell-tale symptoms of Narcissistic Personality Disorder and act accordingly when evaluating their current pastor or seeking a new pastor. Admittedly, in some denominations, the local church does not have much say about who will be its pastor but that is not a valid reason to sit back and passively take who is sent to you. One of the most basic functions of a church leader is to protect the local church and that means not blindly accepting what is given to you. Governing board members must be made aware of their legal responsibilities to protect the church as fiduciaries. In that function we must be like well-trained sheepdogs: we stay between the sheep and the wolves and we sometimes have to take on the wolves, but more often we have to nip at the heels of, and even face down, the sheep.

Protecting the local church begins long before beginning the pastoral search with ads in various publications, and it certainly must begin long before you begin to sift through a hundred or so applications for the pastor position. The best form of defense is not found in reacting to what happens, but in keeping it from happening in the first place. This requires aggressive preventative action.

SEMINARIES AND BIBLE COLLEGES

The primary factors considered before admitting a ministry candidate to most seminaries and Bible colleges are a combination of good grades, recommendations, and agreeing to the institution's faith statement. That is probably as it should be, as the natural winnowing process will eliminate a substantial number of students along the way, but there needs to be more winnowing prior to graduation, as to whether or not ordination will be conferred or recommended. Placing the school's divinity degree imprimatur on a student generally means more to a congregation than the candidate met minimum standards. For many it means that the budding minister has been thoroughly vetted and judged worthy of the moral endorsement conferred by a divinity degree, even though some seminaries may deny this moral validation as being part of their process (which would seem to be a moral problem in and of itself).

I argue that all seminary and Bible school faculty and administrators should be trained to recognize narcissistic behavior when they see it and that there should be an ongoing assessment of the student's emotional health. Dealing purely with academics is beyond foolish in a profession that will expose the narcissist to his victims' every weakness. It is too easy to judge candidates based on their grades, enthusiasm, and proclamations of God's call. By placing so much on these criteria (whether consciously or not) we allow the wolves to pass directly into the pen with the sheep. They talk the talk and even walk the walk under normal circumstances, but normalcy is neither the test nor the benchmark. What matters is how they act and react under pressure, personal criticism, and failure. The extraverted narcissist cannot stand strong criticism and will react to it with rage and indignation, while his shy counterpart will be bewildered and convincingly play the victim role. Both overts and coverts tend to be mediocre students full of self-promotion and excuses why projects are not completed on time and blame others or external events for their shoddy work.

Some denominations require that all candidates for ordination undergo detailed and lengthy psychological testing under the direction of a licensed psychologist. Only after they have passed professional scrutiny are they allowed to apply for ordination. I applaud those denominations, but they are too few. Even in that vetting process, the stealthiest covert narcissists may get through, as no current system is foolproof. For those not comfortable with psychology we recommend Everett Worthington Jr.'s book *Coming to Peace with Psychology*.[1] Worthington is a Christian clinical psychologist and professor at Virginia Commonwealth University, and one of the world's foremost Christian psychological clinicians and researchers.

Is it "fair" to deny someone a career based on psychological testing? It's a good question and we should pause in the process to consider it. I argue that it is, as redirecting a narcissistic candidate into a different field does far less harm than letting him or her into ordained ministry. It is not a guarantee—police departments routinely test the mental health of potential officers and deny the opportunity to those who fail, but some still get through—but it certainly lessens their frequency in the ordination gene pool.

LOCAL CHURCHES

The local church is where this is most important, particularly independent churches that have no denominational resources to use or to fall back upon in winnowing candidates. It also appears that independent churches are where those with predatory narcissism would be most attracted. The reasons are not complex: where there is no denominational oversight or power and the local church controls the entire hiring/call process, the predator narcissist is most likely to succeed in pushing for extraordinary freedom and control. Even so, and as I have so graphically shown, denominations that do no psychological testing are much more vulnerable to narcissists and offer them ample feeding on unsuspecting congregations.

A few years ago, several hundred churches left their denominations and banded together in a loose confederation. They no longer had a central clearinghouse for assistance and advice on legal, structural, and ecclesiastical matters. It did not take long to discover that they had also left behind their entire infrastructures of bishops, processes, appeals, financial assistance, and conflict resolution services. Where the denomination had appointed pastors, the local congregations were now faced with the task of seeking and selecting their own. Never having had to swim these waters before, they had no idea what to look for beyond a seminary degree, a general agreement on theology, and to check the references the candidates gave them. Many had followed traditional wisdom by appointing business people to their selection committees, who then applied traditional business practices to their church, often with disastrous results.

1. Worthington Jr., *Coming to Peace with Psychology.*

One of the trademarks of the narcissist candidate is that everything is about him. He did this, he did that, he created this incredible program, that wonderful idea was his . . . In business that is called marketing and is expected in a candidate. In Christianity it is called pride. Depending on how intensely it is presented, it can cross over into dangerously high levels of narcissism. Very few churches have any level of understanding of what they are up against in the predatory narcissist as pastoral candidate. Nor do most churches that select their own clergy know how to screen for this mental disorder or even consider it.

So, what can you do?

GETTING STARTED

The starting point for most churches, which should be prayer for guidance, is to decide on the qualities they want in a candidate and place ads in various publications and websites announcing the opening and inviting applications. They get out the job description, dust it off, and perhaps make a few minor changes. They then connect with unemployed or unhappy pastors who are looking to leave something behind and gain something in the process. Do you see the problem here? There is a fundamental flaw. One of the most important and essential questions you should ponder for yourselves is one that is never asked: *Why are you looking for a pastor who is looking for a job?* There are reasons behind his or her job search, and you need to know what they are, and not only from him or her, but also from those they wish to leave behind—or who forced them out. All of us try to make negatives into positives when on a job search but the narcissist will be particularly adept at it, will tell you about it, and then try to draw you into his story so that you will agree that he was unfairly treated, misunderstood, targeted by jealous colleagues or a cabal of fundamentalists or liberals . . . or whatever else he comes up with. Just understand that all candidates will "spin" the narrative to their own advantage, and that narcissists do it better than the rest. The intention is to bias you in their favor so that you will discount any negatives you will hear when you speak with the people most knowledgeable of their past behaviors. The true narcissist, of course, cannot conceive of anyone speaking badly about him except out of jealousy.

Candidate Winnowing

First, slow down! Take the time to breathe, pray, and debrief your most recent experience with the pastor who is leaving or has left. What did you learn? How will you use what you learned? Too many churches panic at the idea of not having a permanent pastor and ignore their own internal resources. Even the smallest churches have untapped assets that can sustain the congregation over the short term, and even over the longer term—I know of one church that was self-sustaining for six years.

Begin with prayer. You know what you would *like* in a pastor, but what is it the congregation *needs* in a pastor? These are totally different questions. Too often we decide on the minimum qualifications for the new pastor before knowing what God is telling us what it is we need rather than what we want. They may be the same or they may be completely different, but we will never know unless we spend adequate time and intensity in prayer.

Once you are certain of God's leading, decide on the minimum qualifications to fill that need. In doing that, you define the absolute minimum educational and pastoral qualifications that you will consider and the reasons behind them. One caveat: these are more changeable than you may think. Does the position require a Master of Divinity degree? A Bible school certificate? How many years of pastoral experience are the absolute minimum (and why)? The key here is to create a baseline of unconditional minimums on which there must be no compromise. If that is done well it will be much easier to know when it is time to repost the position rather than settle on the candidate who comes closest to the minimum standards while still missing them. However, the minimum qualifications must also be realistic. A small church in the hinterlands is unlikely to attract a PhD biblical scholar who is a dynamic preacher and Mr. Rogers personified in pastoral care. If it does, then you might want to look very closely at why this person wants to be your pastor as it may be a response of fleeing an unpleasant current reality. After all, she probably would not be an applicant if everything were wonderful where she is . . . It is important to investigate the reality behind their stories as you may uncover a dragon where you were told you would find a gecko.

There are exceptions, of course. It is entirely possible that he or she wants out of the endless demands of an urban church in favor of a slower pace in the countryside. We know of a gifted surgeon who left a big city practice to live in the mountains of northwest Oregon simply because he wanted the slower pace and the beauty that is now all around him. He now practices surgery at a small community hospital, and both he and the hospital benefit. It is up to you to find out what is truly behind the application and the applicant.

Use the normal questionnaire about previous employment, reasons for leaving, and so on, but include a requirement for a ten-page double-spaced essay on why the candidate is uniquely qualified to be your pastor. For one, that will automatically eliminate the lazy ones who will see it as too much work while the overt narcissist may love it as a chance to extol his or her amazing virtues. It will also give an example of their writing abilities, but you must also beware of plagiarized stories. Yes, it happens. If the verbiage seems too good or it tone and style varies noticeably, copy and paste the suspect sentence into Google and see what pops up. You may be surprised at what you find.

Carefully examine the applications for cues and clues once the application period is closed. Immediately set aside those that do not meet your minimum requirements.

You are likely to have at least one who claims that God revealed to them that they are specifically called to be your next pastor and can't wait to get started. Really? As we said earlier, one church had several of those. God is calling someone, but not twenty, and the one God is calling may not know it or may not even be looking for a new church. Claiming to be the "called one" appeals to the narcissist. After all, who are you to argue with God's call?

Read the essays carefully, looking for the narcissistic marker of "I" rather than "we." There is a huge difference between the two, though the covert narcissist will be more difficult to detect as he is more adept at camouflage through the use of the inclusive "we," but he is also quite likely to emphasize that it was under his leadership, thereby taking credit. Once you have narrowed the field down to eight to ten, have a licensed Christian psychologist read their essays specifically to look for the markers of narcissistic, borderline, and sociopathic personality disorders. These are detectable in their writing and you need someone trained in the art of that detection. Why?

Craig and Amernic put it this way: if the written language "shows evidence of destructive narcissism, then . . . such language should be regarded as disturbing: it signals potential for an organization to follow a path of destructive narcissism."[2] They note that the narcissist tends to use powerful hyperbolic language persistently to exaggerate their importance and visionary leadership qualities (grandiosity and superiority/invincibility).[3] For example, he may say something like, "Under my leadership the congregation doubled in size, the Sunday school grew so fast we had to add on new classrooms, and we streamlined our staff by bringing in only top-notch leaders." One candidate wrote that he was "laser-focused on creating a world-changing church," which is the narcissistic fantasy of unlimited success. Everything that they do is "great" or "world-class," and their sermons have been downloaded around the world from the church website. Or, they

---

2. Craig and Amernic, "Detecting Linguistic Traces," 563.
3. Craig and Amernic, "Detecting Linguistic Traces," 569.

may want you to believe that their "passion for Christ" is so powerful that others cannot help but become energized. One of the more revealing ways of understanding their core psychological makeup is in how they use metaphors, particularly what are termed "master metaphors" about themselves. Over the course of nineteen years, one corporate CEO described himself in annual reports to shareholders variously as a pedagogue, physician, architect, commander, and saint.[4] Really? They want you to believe that you cannot go wrong with them as your pastor but that also begs the question: If he is so successful, why is he looking for a job?

Reference Checks

Doing extensive background checks is rapidly becoming a matter of legal "due diligence." The Merriam-Webster Collegiate Dictionary defines due diligence as:

1. the care that a reasonable person exercises to avoid harm to other persons or their property, and

2. research and analysis of a company or organization done in preparation for a business transaction (as a corporate merger or purchase of securities).

USLegal.com defines it this way: "Due diligence in a broad sense refers to the level of judgement, care, prudence, determination, and activity that a person would reasonably be expected to do under particular circumstances."

In these days of lawsuits over careless hiring practices and the damage done by hiring incompetent or predatory employees, doing due diligence in hiring has become a legal issue if things do go wrong and church staff and members are harmed. It begins with checking their references.

Check their references well before initial contact. A crucial caution: *never stop with the primary references.* Contact the primary references and have a short conversation with each, but your purpose is to get the names and contact information for more people to speak with. He would not have listed the primary references unless he was sure they would give glowing reviews (although one narcissist was so convinced of his own incredible gifts that he was totally unaware that his references fairly screamed "Do not hire this man!"). Do that with each person you call. By the time you have dug to the third or fourth levels you will have reached reality. Always ask the hard questions at each level: How does she take criticism? How quick

4. Craig and Amernic, "Detecting Linguistic Traces," 573.

is he to admit a mistake? How often—and well—does she apologize? How important does he see himself as being? You get the picture.

By this time, you have narrowed it to between three and five and you are determining whom to bring in for an interview. This is where a licensed Christian psychologist or therapist experienced with NPD becomes invaluable. You can have the candidates tested, you can have the psychologist/therapist on the interview team, or you can do both, which is what I recommend. With the saturation of narcissists in the candidate pools, *not* doing this is what Dietrich Bonhoeffer would call "cheap grace"—it's all grace and no accountability—which can lead to disaster. It also may fail due diligence under the fiduciary responsibilities of elder and deacon board members.

Interviews

Next, choose a selection/interview team that is not dominated by one type of person, e.g., successful business owners. Now don't get me wrong, as I love business people. In fact, below I will relate how one highly successful CEO quickly learns what he needs to know about every executive and engineer he hires. It's just that business people tend to think and perceive in certain ways that emphasize some attributes but totally miss others. Balance it out with a cross section of personality types.

Leave nothing to chance. Have a written list of questions, but forget the softball stuff (How do you get along with people? How do you deal with conflict? What are your greatest assets? What is your vision? What are your weaknesses? Etc.). Assign each question to a team member. That person will ask the question, but everyone has the right to ask follow-up questions. A common frailty here is the idea that Christians must always "be nice" and so they never get to asking hard questions as that would not be polite. Really? This is not a welcoming reception; it is an intentional process of finding the right pastor while protecting the church! Jesus was downright antagonistic at times. Sometimes the only way to drill down to the core of who narcissists are is to goad them into an angry retort. You do not want to make interviews into a collegial interchange of banalities—you want to have hard questions asked by someone not afraid to confront and follow any threads of evasion to their source. The reason is simple enough: the narcissist is likely to respond to confronting questions with confusion, hostility, or by simply shoving them aside with a minimalist answer, all of which are red flags. You want to "push their buttons" in order to see how they react.

Typical interview questions are not only widely known, they are published. But if asked, their answers call for careful interpretation. For example, the following question and recommended answer play directly into the hands of the manipulating narcissist:

> Q: Why should we hire you? *A: This interview question seems forward (not to mention intimidating!), but if you're asked it, you're in luck: There's no better setup for you to sell yourself and your skills to the hiring manager. Your job here is to craft an answer that covers three things: that you can not only do the work, you can deliver great results; that you'll really fit in with the team and culture; and that you'd be a better hire than any of the other candidates."*[5] Or this: What do you consider to be your weaknesses? *What your interviewer is really trying to do with this question—beyond identifying any major red flags—is to gauge your self-awareness and honesty. So, "I can't meet a deadline to save my life" is not an option—but neither is "Nothing! I'm perfect!" Strike a balance by thinking of something that you struggle with but that you're working to improve. For example, maybe you've never been strong at public speaking, but you've recently volunteered to run meetings to help you be more comfortable when addressing a crowd."*[6]

A common twist is an answer is something like this: "Well, my greatest weakness is also my greatest asset. I work too hard and too much, which is of course great for the company . . ." I recommend that probing weaknesses be a required part of the essay. The narcissist is likely to describe one or two events but will always deflect blame to circumstances, someone else, or even satanic forces. I was once a member of an interview team where a candidate declared that he had never failed at anything. When challenged, he said it again. He did not make the cut.

And now for the "different" part of interviewing. Dr. Carl Cadwell is founder and President of Cadwell Laboratories, which is a world leader in developing and manufacturing equipment for diagnosing and monitoring the brain and nervous system. Dr. Cadwell also owns two health clubs, a physical therapy practice, and other health-related companies. As busy as he is, he is part of the interview team for every critical position hiring process.

They start with the normal questions but quickly deviate from the "normal" interview processes into something the candidates are not prepared for.

Cadwell says that the hardest part of hiring is getting great people. How do we get around the polished façade that they all have and their polished

---

5. The Daily Muse, "How to Answer the 31 Most Common Interview Questions."
6. The Daily Muse, "How to Answer the 31 Most Common Interview Questions."

answers, he asks? Cadwell attended a conference several years ago where the main speaker was Adam Bryant, author of the book *Quick and Nimble*.[7] Cadwell came away with a unique set of questions that are designed to cut quickly through the polished veneers that all candidates present. He has since modified some and created new ones.[8] What would your answers be?

1. What is your natural strength, the thing that comes so easy to you that others may struggle? How did you do that so easy? What are you in the top 5 percent in the world at? What is your ninja power? *These first questions will quickly bring out latent narcissism.*

2. How do you define success for yourself? *This will quickly bring out the desires for prestige, power, recognition, etc.*

3. On a scale of 1–10 how weird are you? *It is not so much the number; it is more seeing how candidates react to a question. Because our whole belief is that everyone is a little weird.*

4. If time, money, and talent were not part of the equation, what would you do? *This leaves a lot of people at a loss, but the one who smiles and says "Exactly what I'm doing now" is worth further investigation. On the flip side, someone who immediately gives the impression of hating what they do should raise a cautionary flag. Attitude is self-constructed and a bad attitude tends to transfer with the person.*

5. What is the biggest misperception that people have about you? What is the difference between perception and misperception? How self-aware are you? *The first question asks them to define how misunderstood they feel they are. These are measures of paranoia, self-image, anger, etc.*

6. If there were no humans on the planet, only animals, what kind of animal would you be? *Beware the* solitary *predator. Animals with strong social bonds, including predators, are a positive.*

7. How would you describe who you are in the core of your DNA, in one word? *This always throws them. Explore the answer.*

8. What qualities do you like most and least in your parents? *Parents influence you. You want to not be like them or you want to be like them. The question is why?*

9. What is the meaning of life? *Again, this is an exercise in deeper thinking processes.*

---

7. Bryant, *Quick and Nimble*.
8. Email from Carl Cadwell to Darrell Puls, March 19, 2016.

10. What is something you believe that nearly no one agrees with you on? *This is an interesting way to get at a sense of isolation, grandiosity, and even paranoia.*

11. Describe a moment when you are most beautiful, when you are at your best. *This tends to reveal their passions in life.*

12. Do you feel lucky? *Only one right answer: YES! It is a good attitude.*

13. Personality test. *There are no right answers, but tests like the Meyers-Briggs Type Indicator or the Keirsey Bates Temperament Sorter II are useful. Just don't place too much trust in them. Also, be wary of someone who immediately tells you their typology and uses it to explain why they are the way they are, as that tends to shirk responsibility and becomes an excuse not to change.*

14. You are about to go on a long journey. You have five animals and have to leave one behind. Horse, rabbit, lion, cow, monkey. Rabbit stands for love, lion for courage, cow for friendship, horse for work, and monkey for family. Which one are you going to leave behind? Why? *The healthiest answer seems to be horse/work!*

Think of it as an investment in a healthy church rather than as a cost that the church cannot afford. The reality is this: the cost of *not* doing this can quite literally close the church doors!

Once you have narrowed it down to a couple of candidates and they pass psychological testing, send a team to the place where he or she is currently or was located, and dig! Ask the hard questions instead of the sloppy, easy kind of questions church selection teams are noted for.

Am I trying to frighten you? Yes, I am. I am trying to shake you from the naiveté that so often permeates the church when it comes to hiring pastors where we believe that every candidate declaring himself to be a man of God really is a man of God. Too many are not, but they are experts at wearing the camouflage of godliness.

These truly are wolves wearing the skin and disguise of sheep. They are very sick, and the evidence is that you cannot help them. But then, your calling is not to help them; it is to protect the flock that the narcissistic pastor simply sees as a food source.

TERMS OF EMPLOYMENT

The United States Supreme Court has ruled in more than one case that it will not get involved in employment dismissals where the employee is designated as a minister, pastor, clergy, or priest. Therefore, it is possible in every state of the US to employ a pastor as an "at will" employee, meaning that the pastor serves at the will of the employer (the local church) and may be dismissed at any time for any reason, and for no reason at all as long is the reasons for termination do not violate various anti-discrimination laws. With a few denominations as exceptions, this is not a tenured position or appointment for life we are talking about. For the sake of the church, have a qualified lawyer draw up an employment contract or letter of call that states the pastor serves at the will of the church, can be dismissed at any time and has no right or expectation of an appeal or judicial process upon termination, whether that termination is with or without cause.

It needs to contain a fair notice timeline to allow a semi-graceful transition, but it must give the church the right to dismiss immediately if the church determines that this is necessary to protect the church, its property, or people.

Denominational churches need to follow the requirements set by the denomination. Be sure to research them carefully and discuss the matter with denominational officials before acting.

Canadian law is similar in many ways except that it requires written notice of termination prior to the actual termination date and payment of additional wages. Both the amount of time in the dismissal notice and the amount of termination pay are based on length of service. Have a qualified lawyer draw up the notice to stay within the requirements of the law. In most instances, the employer is not required to give specific reasons for the termination, only adequate notice and severance pay as required by statute. The Provinces may have minor variations, so always check with a knowledgeable lawyer/solicitor before any decision to terminate the pastor.

Employment Policies

Even the smallest church needs to have written employment policies that detail acceptable norms of behavior for everyone, but in particular the pastor(s), employees, and leaders. Once the Employment Policies Handbook is developed it should be formally adopted by the governing board of the church and given to every employee and leader (whether appointed or elected), who *must be required to sign and date a statement that they have received it.* Some employers have tried to have the employee sign a statement saying that they received and understood it, but that has failed in some legal challenges. Receiving something is one thing, but requiring someone to state in writing that they fully understand it is an entirely different standard.

The handbook is necessary as it places the employee on notice from the outset about acceptable and unacceptable behaviors and practices. Yes, I know, you are a church, and this feels too much like a business practice. The reality is that the church is a legal corporation in every state and province, so this is for the legal protection of the church should you find yourselves in a situation where you must discipline or dismiss an employee, including a pastor. Members of governing boards have a "fiduciary responsibility" to act on behalf of the church to protect it from liability and they are generally protected from being sued personally if they follow the written procedures.

The importance of written policies, rules, and procedures must not be minimized. Craig and Amernic state point blank:

> A narcissist CEO presumes he is blessed with everlasting immortality, sees little need for succession planning, and is probably contemptuous of the executive talents of underlings. . . . A narcissist CEO is prone to be overconfident, obsess about his sense of entitlement, resent constraints on his (self-evaluated) superior leadership, and regard corporate governance checks and balances as impeding his masterful, inspired, and "divine right" leadership. Consequently, boards of companies with a narcissist CEO should apply closer attention to corporate governance mechanisms. *If they do not, they are likely to be browbeaten by the CEO into tolerating supine executive directors, few genuinely independent non-executive directors, and a weak audit committee.*"[9]

There are numerous free employee handbook templates on the Internet containing standard language that you can modify for your specific circumstances, but there are several sections that you might want to pay more specific attention to as protection for both the pastor and the church. Again, there are templates for each of these that can be modified to fit your needs.

Intellectual Property Rights (Copyright)

Narcissists have a way of claiming ownership of anything and everything that might be even remotely connected to their work. The underlying question to be answered is this: Who owns the intellectual property rights (the copyright) for works he or she developed as part of employment? Generally, work developed for the church on church equipment is the property of the church, not the author. Even so, I recommend specific provisions that clearly state ownership of what is termed "intellectual work product."

9. Craig and Amernic, "Detecting Linguistic Traces," 564–65. Emphasis added.

Examples: who owns the sermons that the church paid her to write as part of her employment? Who owns the copyright to a book of her collected sermons? Who owns the rights to a book written by the pastor on church computers during work hours? What if the book is written on his personal computer at home? These are important issues that most churches ignore to their potential detriment.

Employee Conduct and Work Rules

It is imperative that prohibited conduct is spelled out clearly, but with this warning added: "It is not possible to list all forms of behavior that are considered unacceptable in the workplace. Each employee is expected to be responsible for his or her own behavior and make smart choices. The following are some examples of conduct that may result in disciplinary action, up to and including termination of employment. This list is not exclusive and is used for illustrative purposes only." That's called a safety valve. It allows the church to deal with issues not specifically covered in the list but which are still prohibited. Even so, the narcissist will argue that he did not know because it was not specifically stated.

Examples: theft or inappropriate removal of church property; falsification or misrepresentation of official records; working under the influence of drugs or alcohol; making verbal or written threats or engaging in threatening behavior; possession of illegal weapons or explosives; actions demeaning the reputation of the church; insubordination or other disrespectful conduct; violation of health or safety rules; excessive absenteeism; improper or unauthorized use of church property; improper use of electronic media (computers, tablets, cell phones, etc.); biblically immoral conduct; and conduct that is inconsistent with the individual's job description.

Several items need to have their own detailed sections.

Drug and Alcohol Use (and Marijuana in Some States)

This issue has become more common than many realize. This section should answer the following questions: Are employees subject to drug and alcohol testing? Are employees prohibited from being on the premises or working while under the influence of drugs (prescribed or illicit) or alcohol? What are you going to do with a pastor who has an addiction and shows up at work drunk or high? Are you going to pay for rehabilitation services? How does the Americans with Disabilities Act play into all this? Again, consult with an experienced employment attorney.

Sexual Harassment and Hostile Work Environment

A narcissist pastor will almost always create a hostile work environment through his temper tantrums, unpredictability, constant sniping at subordinates, vindictiveness, refusal to apologize, and arrogance. You must fully investigate any and all claims of sexual harassment or hostile work environment whether the claims are formal or verbal. It is wise to hire a confidential trained investigator if you do not have anyone qualified to conduct such an investigation. The church that does no investigation or only a poor one is opening itself to huge liability in the event of a lawsuit. This is also true of the church that does not take effective measures to prevent or stop sexual harassment or hostile work environment situations. Having worked with these cases for almost thirty years in a variety of settings, including churches, I can tell you that this is one area where you *must be vigilant and proactive in protecting the church*. Just ignoring it or rationalizing it can be a violation of the legal responsibility of being a fiduciary (board member or officer) in the church, which can leave board members open for a lawsuit that may not be covered by board errors and omissions insurance policies.

Ministerial Sexual Misconduct

According to some research data, up to one-third of pastors have engaged in sexual contact with a parishioner. While they almost always claim that it was between consenting adults, it also leaves the church open for a lawsuit if there is no policy against it. You also need to know that the pastor is in a power position over vulnerable parishioners by virtue of his office and, its pastor, and the governing board can be sued if the pastor uses that power to exploit a vulnerable person.

Staff Relations

This is the catchall "be nice" requirement for all staff. You cannot require that everyone likes each other but you can require polite and respectful behavior at all times. The narcissist may scoff at this as he or she believes that engaging in aggressive and angry behavior is normal and acceptable—but is outraged when he or she is the recipient. This is one way of placing pressure on the narcissist to rein in his "normal" tendencies.

Problem Resolution

I highly recommend a problem resolution policy that is specific in process and timelines. This is not a grievance policy but a means of expressing concerns and problems within a clear and safe framework. This is beneficial to the narcissist as she has difficulty in expressing concerns in ways that others can hear. Creating a clear process provides her with a guidebook and the church with a process. It also provides staff with an avenue that bypasses the pastor if the pastor is seen as the problem. A helpful adjunct to this process is to bring together a group of spiritually mature people who are experienced in working with interpersonal conflicts to act as a neutral *ad hoc* or standing committee in hearing, investigating, and deciding the merits of complaints and conflicts.

Contracts

Independent churches in particular may want to create a formal employment contract with the pastor. It may be termed a letter of call, a contract, a covenant, or something else. What matters in a court of law is called *offer* and *acceptance*. *Offers* consist of written promises and agreements regarding his or her employment, while *acceptance* means that the candidate formally accepts the offer by signing the document. These contracts typically spell in detail the hours, wages, benefits, working conditions, expectations, and everything else surrounding the employment relationship. The problem with contracts is that they are enforceable by the courts or arbitrators and need to be carefully crafted by people with specialized training in appropriate fields. Unless there is a specific clause allowing it, neither party can break the contract or declare it invalid without the specific written permission of all the other parties. Likewise, a common contract clause allows for either party to cancel the contract on ninety days' written notice to the other party.

In other words, once you sign a contract you are stuck with it in all of its conditions until it expires after a specific period of time, usually two or three years unless it is cancelled by giving timely written notice. Forcing someone out while a contract is in effect usually results in having to pay the wages and benefits remaining for the entire period of the contract, unless there is clear language in the contract itself that allows early termination without paying out the entire contract.

Contracts do not become a important until there are problems. I recently was working with a church having difficulties with the pastor. The church board turned to the pastor's contract, but it was so poorly written that it was largely meaningless and unenforceable by either board or pastor—a board member had written it. Unless the contract is drawn up by a lawyer or another experienced professional, I recommend against a formal employment contract in favor of good policies and procedures.

Church Discipline and Restoration Policy

Very few churches have a formal church discipline and restoration policy, particularly independent churches and those already pastored by a narcissist. It is admittedly uncomfortable to create an official policy and process for receiving and investigating formal complaints against a pastor, employee, leader, or member. Many churches have subscribed to the idea that they have never needed such a policy and so the policy itself is not needed. Then they find themselves without any policy or prescribed process when a formal complaint is received. Under pressure, they tend to create it on the fly and later find themselves being sued for violating someone's right to a clear, fair, and formal investigation, hearing, and opportunity to defend themselves before being disciplined.

Church discipline is one of the most unpopular ideas I have encountered across the United States. It is resisted because churches do not want to appear "judgmental" even when Jesus and Paul clearly and repeatedly told us to guard the flock and judge those whose sin is destructive to the body of Christ. A well-crafted church discipline policy is an insurance policy, the same as any other insurance policy. It is designed to protect the church and everyone in it. As so many churches have discovered, not having one can be disastrous.

13

Now What?

The enemy is infiltrating the church in North America through the egos, shame, and insecurities of her pastors and people. Given the characteristics of the predatory narcissist and the characteristics looked for in pastoral candidates, the odds are that every church will have a toxic narcissist pastor at some point in its life span. There is no foolproof methodology to pinpoint and exclude them before they are hired, but that must never become an excuse not to try.

The first step in protecting the church is for church leaders, seminaries, denominational leaders, and anyone else with a stake in this to become aware of the scope and reality of this challenge. This would necessarily include being familiar enough with the symptoms of toxic narcissism to be able to detect them based on the criteria used for diagnosis, and then take the necessary precautions. This would include some manner of mental health screening before ordination of seminarians, Bible school students, and others on the path to pastoral ministry, and certainly before hiring or calling them to a church. While it is unlikely that a candidate could be excluded at the student level, this would make it possible to at the very least counsel them towards a different direction. The church, however, is not under any such restrictions.

Churches naturally want to grow and so seek candidates who are charismatic, full of energy, and overflowing with ideas. While there are balanced narcissists who fit these criteria and who are wonderful pastors, these are also the characteristics that describe those with Narcissistic Personality Disorder. In seeking these qualities, we inadvertently create an invitation for the narcissist to join us. There is nothing wrong with church growth, but we must become more aware of how we play into the game plan of the narcissistic pastor in our search for greater visibility and more members within the community. We want charisma, charm, energy, and creativity, all of which the narcissistic pastor is all too happy to present to us. For them it is a thin veneer, but it seems real enough that they are able to move from church to church, leaving devastation in their wakes while blaming all of it on ungrateful parishioners and satanic forces.

I recommend that individual churches, particularly independent churches, take a hard look at their internal health as it relates to narcissistic tendencies. Are they telling themselves a story that is self-aggrandizing by focusing on their uniqueness? Does their story grow bigger and better with each telling? Is it important that they are "saving the world one soul at a time"? It is too easy for the church itself to adopt a narcissistic persona, which in turn will attract the narcissist pastor—who will then compound the problem.

Churches in the hiring process have more options available to them than do the seminaries and Bible schools, and have a greater ability to identify the narcissist candidate before the hiring/call decision is made. While every candidate will promote him- or herself in the written documents and oral interviews, the narcissist stands out in his claims, pride, and grandiosity. This gives the search team the ability to examine carefully whatever the candidate submits for the markers of narcissism.

Search teams must dig when checking references and not stop at the first or second levels; they must burrow deeper and ask the harder questions of how the candidate deals with failure, anger, and so on. I have recommended that all candidates submit a written essay that explains why they are far above the rest of the field, and then submit the most promising essays to a licensed Christian counselor who is familiar with NPD for analysis. I have also recommended that the interview team not be comprised entirely of business people, and should include a person whose job is to poke and prod the candidate to see how they react to this breach of our traditional—and politically correct—culture of politeness. As noted previously, narcissists are notoriously bad at masking their indignation and outrage when they are provoked. I also recommend that finalists be interviewed and tested by a licensed Christian psychologist and, if possible, have that psychologist on the actual interview team.

No process can guarantee detection of the narcissist pastor before hiring. Therefore, Letters of Call and employment contracts should be very clear that the pastor serves at the pleasure of the church, however the church is governed, and that calling or hiring them is not an automatic appointment for life. Likewise, every church no matter its size needs to have comprehensive written policies on every aspect of the employment relationship. These are available free on the Internet and can easily be modified to meet the specific needs of any church. Next, those policies must be enforced. We may not like this aspect, but any reading of the Pauline letters makes it clear that the church (and individual churches) must guard against predators and must take action when they are detected. Paul's words ring as true today as they did then, and for good reason: the predator is always trying to get at the flock.

All I am proposing in this book is how to keep the narcissist out in the first place, and to make the readers aware of their options should they discover a predatory narcissist already in place.

Bibliography

Acosta, Regis. "Envy—The Forgotten Narcissistic Issue." *Psychiatric Times* 24.10 (1990) 52.

Akhtar, Salman. "Love, Sex, and Marriage in the Setting of Pathological Narcissism." *Psychiatric Annals; Thorofare* 39.4 (April 2009) 185–91.

American Psychiatric Association. *Diagnostic and Statistical Manual of Mental Disorders 5*. Washington, DC: American Psychiatric Association. 2013.

Amernic, J. H., and R. J. Craig. "Accounting as a Facilitator of Extreme Narcissism." *Journal of Business Ethics* 96 (2010) 79–93. https://doi.org/10.1007/s10551-010-0450-0.

Ashmun, Joanna M. "Narcissistic Personality Disorder (NPD): Traits Discussed." 2008. http://www.halcyon.com/jmashmun/npd/traits.html.

Atlas, Gordon D., and Melissa A. Them. "Narcissism and Sensitivity to Criticism: A Preliminary Investigation." *Current Psychology* 27.1 (2008) 62–76.

Augsburger, David. *Helping People Forgive*. Louisville: Westminster John Knox, 1996.
————. "The Private Lives of Public Leaders." *Christianity Today* (November 20, 1987). https://www.christianitytoday.com/ct/1987/november-20/private-lives-of-public-leaders.html.

Barna Group. "Pastors Rate Themselves Highly—Especially as Teachers." https://www.barna.com/research/pastors-rate-themselves-highly-especially-as-teachers/.

Baron-Cohen, Simon. *The Science of Evil: On Empathy and the Origins of Cruelty*. New York: Basic, 2009.

Baumeister, Roy F., and Kathleen D. Vohs. "Narcissism as Addition to Esteem." University of Minnesota. http://www.carlsonschool.umn.edu/assest/71519.pdf.

Behary, Wendy T. *Disarming the Narcissist*. 2d ed. Oakland, CA: New Harbinger, 2013.

Bennett, C. Susanne. "Attachment Theory and Research Applied to the Conceptualization and Treatment of Pathological Narcissism." *Clinical Social Work Journal* 34.1 (2006) 45–60.

Besser, Avi, and Beatriz Priel. "Grandiose Narcissism versus Vulnerable Narcissism in Threatening Situations: Emotional Reactions to Achievement, Failure and Interpersonal Rejection." *Journal of Social and Clinical Psychology* 29.8 (2010) 874–902. https://doi.org/10.1521/jscp.2010.29.8.874.

Blair, Carrie A., Brian Koffman, and Katherine R. Helland. "Narcissism in Organizations: A Multisource Appraisal Reflects Different Perspectives." *Human Performance* 21.3 (2008) 254–76.

Bland, Earl D. "Finding Self, Forming Virtue: The Treatment of Narcissistic Defenses in Marriage Therapy." *Journal of Psychology and Christianity* 29.2 (2010) 158–65.

Bleiberg, Efrain. "Normal and Pathological Narcissism in Adolescence." *American Journal of Psychotherapy* 48.1 (Winter 1994) 30–51.

Blue, Ken. *Healing Spiritual Abuse: How to Break Free from Bad Church Experiences.* Downers Grove, IL: InterVarsity, 1993.

Bogart, Laura M., Eric G. Benotsch, and Jelena D. Pavlovic. "Feeling Superior but Threatened: The Relationship of Narcissism to Social Comparison." *Basic and Applied Social Psychology* 26.1 (2004) 35–44.

Bonhoeffer, Dietrich. *Letters and Papers from Prison.* Edited by Eberhard Bethge. New York: Touchstone, 1997.

Bradbury, Ray. *Something Wicked This Way Comes.* New York: Avon, 2006.

Bradshaw, Samuel L. "Ministers in Trouble: A Study of 140 Cases Evaluated at the Menninger Foundation." *Journal of Pastoral Care* 31.4 (1977) 230–42.

Braun, Suzanne, Aydin Nilu, Dietr Frey, and Claudia Peus. "Leader Narcissism Predicts Malicious Envy and Supervisor-Targeted Counterproductive Work Behavior: Evidence from Field and Experimental Research." *Journal of Business Ethics* 151 (2018) 725–41. https://doi.org/10.1007/s10551-016-3224-5.

Brown, Andrew. "Narcissism, Identity, and Legitimacy." *The Academy of Management Review* 22.3 (July 1997) 643–86.

Brown, Todd A., John A. Sautter, Levente Littvay, Alberta C. Sauter, and Brennen Bearnes. "Ethics and Personality: Empathy and Narcissism as Moderators of Ethical Decision Making in Business Students." *Journal of Education for Business* 85 (2010) 203–8.

Brubaker, David R. *Promise and Peril: Understanding and Managing Change and Conflict in Congregations.* Herndon, VA: Alban Institute, 2009.

Brunell, Amy B., and W. Keith Campbell. "Narcissism and Romantic Relationships: Understanding the Paradox." APA PsychNet, 2011. http://psycnet.apa.org/record/2011-16529-030.

Bruner, Jose. "Pride and Memory: Nationalism, Narcissism and the Historians' Debates in Germany and Israel." *History and Memory* 9.1/2 (1997) 256–300.

Bryant, Adam. *Quick and Nimble: Lessons from Leading CEOs on How to Create a Culture of Innovation.* Rev. ed. New York: St. Martin's Griffin, 2014.

Burijon, B. N. "Narcissism and Grace Inherent Incompatibility." *Pastoral Psychology* 49.3 (2001) 181–86.

Buss, David, and Lisa Chiodo. "Narcissistic Acts in Everyday Life." *Journal of Personality* 59.2 (1991) 179–215.

Campbell, Ken. *When You Love a Man Who Loves Himself.* Naperville, IL: Sourcebooks Casablanca, 2005.

Campbell, W. K., and C. A. Foster. "Narcissism and Commitment in Romantic Relationships: An Investment Model Analysis." *Personality and Social Psychology Bulletin* 28 (2002) 484–94.

Campbell, W. Keith, and Joshua D. Miller, eds. *The Handbook of Narcissism and Narcissistic Personality Disorders: Theoretical Approaches, Empirical Findings and Treatments.* Hoboken, NJ: John Wiley and Sons, 2011.

Capps, Donald. *The Depleted Self: Sin in a Narcissistic Age*. Minneapolis: Fortress, 1993.

———. "Don Quixote as Moral Narcissist: Implications for Mid-Career Male Ministers." *Pastoral Psychology* 47.6 (1999) 401–23.

———. "God Diagnosed with Narcissistic Personality Disorder." *Pastoral Psychology* 58.2 (2009) 193–206.

Capps, Donald, and Allan Hugh Cole, Jr. "The Deadly Sins and Saving Virtues: How They Are Viewed Today by Clergy." *Pastoral Psychology* 54.6 (2006) 517–34.

———. "The Deadly Sins and Saving Virtues: How They Are Viewed Today by the Laity." *Pastoral Psychology* 37.4 (1989) 229–53.

Capps, Donald, and Melissa Haupt. "The Deadly Sins: How They Are Viewed and Experienced Today." *Pastoral Psychology* 60.6 (2011) 791–807.

Carr, Darren. "Relationship among Overt and Covert Narcissism and Vocational Interests with Respect to Gender." PhD Diss., Florida State University, 2008.

Carroll, Lynne, Natalia Hoenigmann-Stovall, Alan King, Janice Wienhold, and George Whitehead III. "Interpersonal Consequences of Narcissistic and Borderline Personality Disorders." *Journal of Social and Clinical Psychology* 17.1 (1998) 38–49.

Cataldo, Lisa M. "Religious Experience and the Transformation of Narcissism: Kohutian Theory and the Life of St. Francis of Assisi." *Journal of Religion and Health* 46.4 (2007) 527–40.

Chrnalogar, Mary Alice. *Twisted Scriptures: Breaking Free from Churches that Abuse*. Grand Rapids: Zondervan, 2000.

Clark, Malissa, Ariel Lechon, and Marcie Taylor. "Beyond the Big Five: How Narcissism, Perfectionism, and Dispositional Affect Relate to Workaholism." *Personality and Individual Differences* 48.7 (May 2010) 786–91. https://doi.org/10.1016/j.paid.2010.01.013.

Cloud, Henry, and John Townsend. *Boundaries: When to Say Yes, When to Say No to Take Control of Your Life*. Grand Rapids: Zondervan, 1992.

Coffee, Matt. "Entitlement and the Church." The Church Whisperer, 2014. Accessed June 9, 2014. http://churchwhisperer.com/2013/10/31/103113/.

Cohen, Orna. "On the Origins of a Sense of Coherence: Sociodemographic Characteristics, or Narcissism as a Personality Trait." *Social Behavior and Personality* 25.1 (1997) 49–58.

Collins, Jim. *Good to Great: Why Some Companies Make the Leap and Others Don't*. New York: Harper Collins, 2001.

Cooper, Marjorie, Chris Pullig, and Charles Dickens. "Effects of Narcissism and Religiosity on Church Ministers with Respect to Ethical Judgment, Confidence, and Forgiveness." *Journal of Psychology and Theology* 44.1 (March 2016) 42–54.

Cooper, Marjorie, and Chris Pullig. "I'm Number One! Does Narcissism Impair Ethical Judgment Even for the Highly Religious?" *Journal of Business Ethics* 112.1 (2013) 167–76.

Corbitt, Elizabeth M. "Narcissism from the Perspective of the Five-factor Model." In *Personality Disorders and the Five Factor Model of Personality*, 2d ed., edited by Paul T. Costa Jr. and Thomas A. Widiger, 293–98. Washington DC: American Psychological Association, 2002.

Cornelison, Robert T. "Losing Oneself to Gain Oneself: Rethinking God in a Narcissistic Age." *Union Seminary Review* 52 (1998) 67–84.

Craig, R., and J. Amernic. "Detecting Linguistic Traces of Destructive Narcissism at-a-Distance in a CEO's Letter to Shareholders." *Journal of Business Ethics* 101 (2011) 563–75.

Crawford, T. N., P. Cohen, J. G. Johnson, S. Kasen, M. B. First, K. Gordon, and J. S. Brook. "Self-reported Personality Disorder in the Children in the Community Sample: Convergent and Prospective Validity in Late Adolescence and Adulthood." *Journal of Personality Disorders* 19.1 (2005) 30–52.

Crisp-Han, Holly, Glen Gabbard, and Melissa Martinez. "Professional Boundary Violations in the Clergy." Institute for Spirituality and Health at the Texas Medical Center. Accessed April 21, 2016. http://www.ishtmc.com/sites/default/files/ Mentalizing_and_Professional_Boundaries_Gabbard_Crisp_Han.pdf.

The Daily Muse. "How to Answer the 31 Most Common Interview Questions." The Daily Muse. https://www.themuse.com/advice/how-to-answer-the-31-most-common-interview-questions.

Daniel, Victor. "Ethan Couch, 'Affluenza Teen' Who Killed 4 While Driving Drunk, Is Freed." *New York Times,* April 2, 2018. https://www.nytimes.com/2018/04/02/us/ethan-couch-affluenza-jail.html.

Delaney, Jason, and John Winters. "Sinners or Saints? Preachers' Kids and Risky Health Behaviors." *Journal of Family Economics* 35 (2014) 464–476. https://doi.org/10.1007/s10834-013-9388-6

DeSalvo, Louise. *Writing as a Way of Healing: How Telling Our Stories Transforms Our Lives.* Boston: Beacon, 1999.

Donaldson-Pressman, Stephanie, and Robert M. Pressman. *The Narcissistic Family: Diagnosis and Treatment.* San Francisco: Jossey-Bass, 1994.

Dragioti, Elena, Dimitrios Damigos, Venetsanos Mavreas, and Mary Gouva. "Effects of Childhood Trauma on Hostility, Family Environment and Narcissism of Adult Individuals." *International Journal of Caring Sciences* 5.2 (2012) 137– 46.

Duchon, Dennis, and Brian Drake. "Organizational Narcissism and Virtuous Behaviour." *Journal of Business Ethics* 85.3 (2009) 301–8.

Duncan, Ryan. "10 Warning Signs of a Spiritual Narcissist." Crosswalk.com, 2018. https://www.crosswalk.com/faith/spiritual-life/10warning-signs-of-a-spiritual-narcissist.html

Duthie, Alexander. *The Greek Mythology: A Reader's Handbook.* Westport, CT: Greenwood, 1979.

Dutton , Donald G., Matthew K. Denny-Keys, and Joanna R. Sells. "Parental Personality Disorder and Its Effects on Children: A Review of Current Literature." *Journal of Child Custody* 8.4 (Nov 2011) 268–83. doi.org/10.1080/153 79418.2011.620928.

Dyer, Jennifer E. "Loving Thyself: A Kohutian Interpretation of a 'Limited' Mature Narcissism in Evangelical Mega Churches." *Journal of Religion and Health* 51.2 (2012) 241–55.

Eagly, Alice H., Reuben M. Baron, and V. Lee Hamilton, eds. *The Social Psychology of Group Identity and Social Conflict.* Washington DC: American Psychological Association, 2004.

Edling, Dave. "The Greatest Danger to Your Pastor's Spiritual Growth—Narcissism." *The Aquila Report,* 2013. Accessed Feb 13, 2015. http://theaquilareport.com/the-greatest-danger-to-your-pastors-spiritual-growth-narcissism.

Enright, Robert D. *Forgiving Is a Choice: A Step-by-Step Process for Resolving Anger and Restoring Hope.* Washington, DC: American Psychological Association, 2019.

Enright, Robert D., and Richard P. Fitzgibbons. *Helping Clients Forgive: An Empirical Guide for Resolving Anger and Restoring Hope.* Washington, DC: American Psychological Association, 2002.

Erlich, Shmuel. "On Loneliness, Narcissism, and Intimacy." *American Journal of Psychoanalysis* 58.2 (1998) 135–62.

Exline, J. J., R. F. Baumeister, B. J. Bushman, W. K. Campbell, and E. J. Finkel. "Too Proud to Let Go: Narcissistic Entitlement as a Barrier to Forgiveness." *Journal of Personal and Social Psychology* 87.6 (2004) 894–912.

Federman, Russ. "The Relationship Between Narcissism and Bipolar Disorder: Distinctions, Similarity and Synergy between Narcissism and Bipolar Grandiosity." *Psychology Today,* 2013. Accessed December 15, 2015. https://www.psychologytoday.com/blog/bipolar-you/201310/the-relationship-between-narcissism-and-bipolar-disorder.

Festinger, Leon. *A Theory of Cognitive Dissonance.* Stanford, CA: Stanford University Press, 1957.

Firestone, Lisa. "Self-esteem versus Narcissism." *Psychology Today,* 2012. Accessed July 17, 2015. http://www.psychologytoday.com/blog/compassion-matters/201206/self-esteem-versus-narcissism.

Francis, Perry C., and Tracy D. Baldo. "Narcissistic Measures of Lutheran Clergy Who Self-Reported Committing Sexual Misconduct." *Pastoral Psychology* 27.2 (1998) 81–96.

Francis, Leslie, Mandy Robbins, Peter Kaldor, and Keith Castle. "Psychological Type and Work-related Psychological Health Among Clergy in Australia, England, and New Zealand." University of Warwick, 2009. Accessed April 21, 2016. http://business.highbeam.com/62578/article-1P3-1885092681/psychological-type-and-workrelated-psychological-health.

Freis, Stephanie, Ashley Brown, Patrick Carroll, and Robert Arkin. "Shame, Rage, and Unsuccessful Motivated Reasoning in Vulnerable Narcissism." *Journal of Social and Clinical Psychology* 34.1 (2015) 877–95

Fritz, Robert. *The Path of Least Resistance.* New York: Fawcett Columbine, 1989.

Glieg, Ann "The Culture of Narcissism Revisited: Transformations of Narcissism in Contemporary Psychospirituality." *Pastoral Psychology* 59.1 (2010) 79–91.

Godkin, Lynn, and Seth Allcorn. "Organizational Resistance to Destructive Narcissistic Behavior." *Journal of Business Ethics* 104 (2011) 559–70.

Greenberg, Elinor. "Narcissistic Love Patterns: The Romantic." *Psychology Today,* 2017. Accessed June 4, 2018. https://www.psychologytoday.com/us/blog/understanding-narcissism/201705/narcissistic-love-patterns-the-romantic.

Greenfield, Guy. *The Wounded Minister: Healing from and Preventing Personal Attacks.* Grand Rapids: Baker, 2001.

Grubbs, Joshua, and Julie J. Exline. "Humbling Yourself Before God: Humility as a Reliable Predictor of Lower Divine Struggle." *Journal of Psychology and Theology* 42.1 (2014) 41–49.

Gumpel, Thomas, Vered Wiesenthal, and Patrik Soderberg. "Narcissism, Perceived Social Status, and Social Cognition and Their Influence on Aggression." *Behavioral Disorders* 40.2 (February 2015) 138–56.

Guthrie, Shirley C., Jr. "The Narcissism of American Piety: The Disease and the Cure." *Journal of Pastoral Care* 31.4 (1977) 220–29.

Halligan, Fredrica R. "Narcissism, Spiritual Pride, and Original Sin." *Journal of Religion and Health* 36.4 (1997) 305–19.

Hall, Julia. "Narcissism 101: A Glossary of Terms for Understanding the Madness." Narcissist Family Files. 2017. https://narcissistfamilyfiles.com/2017/09/19/narcissism-101-a-glossary-of-terms-for-understanding-the-madness/.

Hall, Todd W., and Keith J. Edwards. "The Spiritual Assessment Inventory: A Theistic Model and Measure of Assessing Spiritual Development." *Journal for the Scientific Study of Religion* 4.2 (2002) 341–57.

Hammond, Charles. "Second Generation Korean American Presbyterians Revitalizing Their Faith by Adapting To North American Culture." DMin diss., Trinity Theological Seminary, 2014.

Hands, Donald R., and Wayne L. Fehr. *Spiritual Wholeness for Clergy: A New Psychology of Intimacy with God, Self, and Others.* Herndon, VA: The Alban Institute, 1993.

Harbinson, Adam. *Savage Shepherds: One Man's Story of Overcoming Spiritual Abuse.* London: Authentic Media, 2006.

Harvard Business Press. *Dealing with Difficult People.* Boston: Harvard Business Press, 2005.

———. *Managing Difficult People.* Boston: Harvard Business Press, 2008.

Haugk, Kenneth C. *Antagonists in the Church: How to Identify and Deal with Destructive Conflict.* Minneapolis: Augsburg, 1988.

Hess, Carol Lakey. "Echo's Lament: Teaching, Mentoring and the Danger of Narcissistic Pedagogy." *Teaching Theology and Religion* 6.3 (2003) 127–37.

Hoffman, Thomas. "The 'It's All About Me' Syndrome." *Computerworld* (2008) 32–33.

Hotchkiss, Sandy. "Key Concepts in the Theory and Treatment of Narcissistic Phenomena." *Clinical Social Work Journal* 33.2 (2005) 127–44.

———. *Why Is It Always About You? The Seven Deadly Sins of Narcissism.* New York: Free, 2003.

Howatch, Susan. *Glittering Images.* New York: HarperCollins, 2012.

Howland, Marcia. "Correlation of Attachment Styles and Conflict Responses: Reflective Model and Method for Clergy." PhD diss., Trinity Theological Seminary, 2015.

Hunter, Murray. "The Psychosis of Organizations." *Contemporary Readings in Law and Social Justice* 5.1 (2013) 44–57.

Ingersoll, Alicia R., Christy Glass, Alison Cook, and Kari Joseph Olsen. "Power, Status and Expectations: How Narcissism Manifests Among Women CEOs." *Journal of Business Ethics: Dordrecht* (2017) 1–15. https://doi.org/10.1007/s10551-017-3730-0.

Irvin, Lisa. "Ethics in Organizations: A Chaos Perspective." *Journal of Organizational Change Management* 15.4 (2002) 359–81.

Jijo, Jacob. "Judgment Day 2011: 'You Will Quietly Die' on Oct. 21, Camping Warns." *International Business Times,* October 16, 2011. https://www.ibtimes.com/judgment-day-2011-you-will-quietly-die-oct-21-harold-camping-warns-323694.

Johnson, David, and Jeff Van Vonderen. *The Subtle Power of Spiritual Abuse.* Minneapolis: Bethany House, 1991.

Katz, Neil, Katherine Sosa, and Suzette Harriott. "Overt and Covert Group Dynamics: An Innovative Approach for Conflict Resolution Preparation." *Conflict Resolution Quarterly* 33.3 (2016) 313–48. https://doi.org/10.1002/crq.21159.

Kaufman, Scott Barry. "Do Narcissists Know They Are Narcissists?" *Psychology Today* (2011) 2–15. http://wwww,psychologytoday.com/blog/beautiful-minds/201103/do-narcissists-know-they-are-narcissists.

———. "How to Spot a Narcissist." *Psychology Today*, 2011. Accessed November 14, 2015. https://www.psychologytoday.com/articles/201107/how-spot-narcissist.

———. "23 Signs You're a Secret Narcissist." *Scientific American*, 2013. http://www.salon.com/2013/0827/stoptellingmeyoureasensitiveintrovertpartner.

Kealy, David, and Brian Rasmussen. "Veiled and Vulnerable: The Other Side of Grandiose Narcissism." *Journal of Clinical Social Work* 40 (2012) 356–65.

Keller, Peggy S., Sarai Blancoe, Lauren Gilbert, C. Nathan DeWall, Eric Haak, and Thomas Widiger. "Narcissism in Romantic Relationships: A Dyadic Perspective." *Journal of Social and Clinical Psychology* 33.1 (2014) 25–50.

Keller, W. Philip. *Predators in our Pulpits: A Compelling Call to Follow Christ in These Perilous Times*. Eugene, OR: Harvest House, 1988.

Kernberg, Karen. "The Cracked Mirror: Features of Narcissistic Personality Disorder in Children." *Psychiatric Annals* 39.3 (2009) 147–55.

Kernberg, Otto F. *Aggression in Personality Disorders and Perversions*. New Haven, CT: Yale University Press, 1992.

Kernberg, Otto F., and Frank Yeomans. "Borderline Personalities Disorder, Bipolar Disorder, Depression, Attention Deficit/Hyperactivity Disorder, and Narcissistic Personality Disorder: Practical Differential Diagnosis." *Bulletin of the Menninger Clinic* 77.1 (2013) 1–22.

———. *Severe Personality Disorders: Psychotherapeutic Strategies*. New Haven, CT: Yale University Press, 1986.

Kernberg, P. F. "Narcissistic Personality Disorder in Childhood." *Psychiatric Clinicians of North America* 12.3 (1989) 671–94.

Kohut, Heinz. *The Analysis of the Self: A Systematic Approach to the Psychoanalytic Treatment of Narcissistic Personality Disorders*. New York: International University Press, 1976.

Konrath, Sara, Olivier Corneille, Brad Bushman, and Olivier Luminet. "The Relationship Between Narcissistic Exploitativeness, Dispositional Empathy, and Emotion Recognition Abilities." *Journal of Nonverbal Behavior* 38 (2014) 129–43.

Kowalski, Robin M. *Behaving Badly: Aversive Behavior in Interpersonal Relationships*. Washington, DC: American Psychological Association, 2001.

Krahe, Barbara. *The Social Psychology of Aggression*. 2d ed. London: Psychology, 2013.

Krejcir, Richard. "What is Going on with Pastors in America? Statistics on Pastors." Francis A. Schaeffer Institute of Church Leadership Development, 2007. Accessed May 3, 2016. http://www.intothyword.org/apps/articles/?articleid=36562.

Lachkar, Joan. *How to Talk to a Narcissist*. New York: Routledge, Taylor and Francis, 2008.

Lancer, Darlene. "All You Should Know About Narcissistic Love Bombing." *Psychology Today*, 2018. https://www.psychologytoday.com/us/blog/toxic-relationships/201811/all-you-should-know-about-narcissistic-love-bombing.

Larson, Janet Karsten. "The Rhetoric of Narcissism: Language and Survival of American Culture." *Christian Century* (September 9, 1981) 859–64.

Lasch, Christopher. *The Culture of Narcissism: American Life in an Age of Diminishing Expectations*. New York: Norton, 1979.

———. *The Minimal Self: Psychic Survival in Troubled Times*. New York: Norton, 1984.

Lasine, Stuart. "Divine Narcissism and Yahweh's Parenting Style." *Biblical Interpretation* 1 (2002) 36–56.

———. *Knowing Kings: Knowledge, Power and Narcissism in the Hebrew Bible*. Atlanta: Society of Biblical Literature, 2001.

Lawless, Chuck. "8 Reasons Pastors Struggle with Doing Spiritual Discipline." Chucklawless.com. http://chucklawless.com/2016/01/8-reasons-pastors-struggle-with-doing-spiritual-disciplines/

Lawrence, Constance. "An Integrated Spiritual and Psychological Growth Model in the Treatment of Narcissism." *Journal of Psychology and Theology* 15.3 (1987) 205–213.

Leary, Mark, and Rick Hoyle, eds. *Handbook of Individual Differences in Social Behavior*. New York: Guilford, 2009.

Lee, Kibeom, and Michael C. Ashton. *The H Factor of Personality: Why Some People Are Manipulative, Self-entitled, Materialistic and Exploitive—And Why It Matters for Everyone*. Waterloo, ON: Wilfred Laurier University Press, 2012.

Leonard, Erin. "Co-Parenting with a Narcissist." *Psychology Today*, 2018. https://www.psychologytoday.com/us/blog/peaceful-parenting/201807/co-parenting-narcissist.

Lerner, Rokelle. *The Object of My Affection Is in My Reflection: Coping with Narcissists*. Deerfield Beach, FL: Health Communications, 2009.

Levinson, H. "Why the Behemoths Fell: Psychological Roots of Corporate Failure." *American Psychologist* 49.5 (1994) 428–36. https://doi.org/10.1037/0003-066X.49.5.428.

Lopez, Frederick G., Mark Gover, Jennie Leskela, Eric M. Sauer, Lisa Schirmer, and James Wyssmann. "Attachment Styles, Shame, Guilt, and Collaborative Problem-solving Orientations." *Personal Relationships* 4 (1997) 198. https://doi.org/10.1111/j.1475-6811.1997.tb00138.

Lowen, Alexander. *Narcissism: Denial of the True Self*. New York: Simon and Schuster, 1985.

Martens, Willem H. J. "Shame and Narcissism: Therapeutic Relevance of Conflicting Dimensions of Excessive Self Esteem, Pride, and Pathological Vulnerable Self." *Annals of the American Psychotherapy Association* 8.4 (2005) 10–17.

Malkin, Craig. "5 Early Warning Signs You're with a Narcissist." *Psychology Today*, 2013. Accessed March 26, 2016. https://www.psychologytoday.com/blog/romance-redux/201306/5-early-warning-signs-youre-narcissist.

Masterson, J. F. *The Search for the Real Self: Unmasking the Personality Disorders of Our Age*. New York: Taylor & Francis, 1988.

Mayo, Marya. "What Does the Bible Really Say About Forgiveness?" *Huffington Post*, July 29, 2011. https://www.huffpost.com/entry/forgiveness-in-the-bible_b_911562.

McDonald, Craydon D. "Clarifying Several Nuances of Narcissism and Their Implications for Pastoral Care." *The Journal of Pastoral Care* 45.2 (1991) 149–56.

McWilliams, Warren. *Christ and Narcissus: Prayer in a Self-centered World.* Scottsdale, PA: Herald, 1992.

Meyers, Seth. "Narcissistic Parents' Psychological Effect on Their Children." *Psychology Today,* May 1, 2014. https://www.psychologytoday.com/us/blog/insight-is-2020/201405/narcissistic-parents-psychologicaleffect-their-children.

Miller, Joshua D., Ally Dir, Brittany Gentile, Lauren Wilson, Lauren R. Pryor, and W. Keith Campbell. "Searching for a Vulnerable Dark Triad: Comparing Factor 2 Psychopathy, Vulnerable Narcissism, and Borderline Personality Disorder." *Journal of Personality* 78.5 (2010) 1530–64.

Miller, Joshua D., Brian J. Hoffman, Eric T. Gaugham, Brittany Gentle, Jessica Maples, and W. Keith Campbell. "Grandiose and Vulnerable Narcissism: A Nomological Network Analysis." *Journal of Personality* 79.5 (2011) 1013–42.

Miller, Theodore, and Roger Davis, with Carrie Millon, Luis Escovar and Sarah Meagher. *Personality Disorders in Modern Life.* New York: John Wiley and Son, 2000.

Miller, William. *Integrating Spirituality into Treatment.* Washington, DC: American Psychological Association, 2000.

Millon, Theodore, with Roger Davis, Carrie Million, Andrew Wenger, Maria H. Van Zuilen, Marketa Fuchs, and Renee B. Millon. *Disorders of Personality: DSM-IV and Beyond.* New York: John Wiley and Son, 1996.

Moreford, Mark P. O., and Robert J. Lenardon. *Classical Mythology.* New York: David McKay Company, 1971.

Morf, Carolyn C., and Frederick Rhodewalt. "Unraveling the Paradoxes of Narcissism: A Dynamic Self-Regulatory Process Model." *Psychological Inquiry* 12.4 (2001) 177–96. https://doi.org/10.1207/s15327965PLI1204_1.

Namaka, Lynne. "Selfishness and Narcissism in Family Relationships." 2005. Accessed April 20, 2016. http://www.angriesout.com/grown17.htm.

Nauta, Reinhard. "Self, Sin and the Sacred: Some Elements of a Select Psychology for the Care of Souls." *Pastoral Psychology* 56.6 (2008) 585–92.

Nauta, Reinhard, and Leon Derckx. "Why Sin? A Test and an Exploration of the Social and Psychological Context of Resentment and Desire." *Pastoral Psychology* 56 (2007) 177–88.

Oates, Wayne. *Behind the Mask: Personality Disorders in Religious Behavior.* Louisville: Westminster, 1987.

Ogrodniczuk, J. S., W. E. Piper, A. S. Joyce, P. I. Steinberg, and S. Duggal. "Interpersonal Problems Associated with Narcissism among Psychiatric Outpatients." *Journal of Psychiatric Research* 43 (2009) 837–42.

O'Reilly, Charles A. III. Bernadette Doerr, David F. Caldwell, and Jennifer A. Chatman. "Narcissistic CEOs and Executive Compensation." University of California, Berkeley. 2016. Accessed April 20, 2016. http://haas.berkeley.edu/faculty/papers/chatman_narcissism.pdf.

Ornstein, Paul. "Chronic Rage from Underground: The Treatment of a Patient with a Severe Narcissistic Disorder." *Psychiatric Annals* 39.3 (2009). https://doi.org/10.3928/00485713-20090301-07.

Ovid. *The Metamorphoses Book III.* Translated by A. S. Kline. "Poetry in Translation." 2000. Accessed March 4, 2015. http://poetryintranslation.com/PItBr/Latin/Metamorph3.htm.

Pan, Shinhwan. "Pastoral Counseling of Korean Clergy with Burnout: Culture and Narcissism." *Asian Journal of Theology* 20.2 (2006) 241–55.

Patrick, James. "Working with a Narcissistic Leader." *Leadership*, 2010. Accessed April 20, 2016. http://www.christianitytoday.com/le/channel/utilities/print.html?type=article&id=90117&source-article.

Paulhus, Delroy L., and Kevin M. Williams. "The Dark Triad of Personality: Narcissism, Machiavellianism, and Psychopathy." *Journal of Research in Personality* 36.6 (2002) 556–63. https://doi.org/10.1016/s0092-6566(02)00505-6.

Pennebaker, James. *Opening Up: The Healing Power of Expressing Emotions.* New York: Guilford, 1990.

Pinsky, Drew., S. Mark Young, with Jill Stern. *The Mirror Effect: How Celebrity Narcissism is Endangering our Families—and How to Save Them.* New York: Harper, 2009.

Poling, Edward L. "Spiritual Direction in an Age of Narcissism." *Brethren Life and Thought* 43.3–4 (1998) 81–97.

Puls, Darrell. *The Road Home: A Guided Journey to Church Forgiveness and Reconciliation.* Eugene, OR: Cascade, 2013.

Rainer, Thomas. "The Top Ten Things Church Members Want in their Pastor." 2013. https://thomrainer.com/2013/01/ten-things-church-members-desire-in-a-pastor/.

Randall, Robert L. "Narcissism and the Use of Fantasy." *Journal of Clinical Psychology* 46.4 (July 1991) 490–99.

———. "Religious Ideation of a Narcissistically Disturbed Individual." *Journal of Pastoral Care* 30.1 (1976) 35–45.

Randall, Robert L., Jill Novacek, and Robert Hogan. "Narcissism, Self-esteem, and Defensive Self-enhancement." *Journal of Personality* 59.1 (1991) 19–38. https://doi.org/10.1111/j.1467-6494.1991.tb00766.x.

Randall, Robert L., and Robert Shaw. "Narcissism and the Use of Personal Pronouns." *Journal of Personality* 56.2 (1988) 393–404. https://doi.org/10.1111/j.1467-6494.1988.tb00892.x.

Raskin, R. N., and C. S. Hall. "A Narcissistic Personality Inventory." *Psychological Reports* 45.2 (1979) 590. https://doi.org/10.2466/pro.1979.45.

Rijsenbilt, Antoinette, and Harry Commandeur. "Narcissus Enters the Courtroom: CEO Narcissism and Fraud." *Journal of Business Ethics* 117.2 (2013) 413–29.

Ronningstam, E. *Identifying and Understanding the Narcissistic Personality.* Oxford: Oxford University Press, 2005.

Ronson, Jon. *The Psychopath Test: A Journey Through the Madness Industry.* New York: Penguin, 2011.

Rowat, Wade, Linda Kang, and Megan Haggard. "A Social-Personality Perspective on Humility, Religiousness, and Spirituality." *Journal of Psychology and Theology* 42.1 (2014) 31–40.

Ruffing, Elizabeth, David R. Paine, Nancy G. Devor, and Steven J. Sandage. "Humility and Narcissism in Clergy: A Relational Spirituality Framework." *Pastoral Psychology*, 2018. https://doi.org/10.1007/s11089-0180830-4.

Ryan, Kathryn M., Kim Weikel, and Gene Sprechini. "Gender Differences in Narcissism and Courtship Violence in Dating Couples." *Springer Science and Business Media* 58 (2008) 802–13.

Ryan, Kathryn M., Kim Weikel, Laura Widman, and James K. McNulty. "Sexual Narcissism and the Perpetration of Sexual Aggression." *Archives of Sex Behavior* 39 (2010) 926–39. https://doi.org/10.1007/s10508-0089461-7.

Sandage, Steven, Peter Jankowski, Sarah Crabtree, and Maria Schweer. "Attachment to God: Adult Attachment, and Spiritual Pathology: Mediator and Moderator Effects." *Mental Health, Religion & Culture,* 2015. https://doi.org/10.1080/136746 76.2015.1090965.

Sandage, Steven, Peter J. Jankowski, Cheryl D. Bissonette, and David R. Paine. "Vulnerable Narcissism, Forgiveness, Humility, and Depression: Mediator Effects for Differentiation of Self." *Psychoanalytic Psychology,* 2016. https://doi.org/10.1037/ pap0000042.

Sandage, Steven, and Shane Moe. "Narcissism and Spirituality." In *The Handbook of Narcissism and Narcissistic Personality Disorder: Theoretical Approaches, Empirical Findings, and Treatments*, edited by W. Keith Campbell and Joshua D. Miller, 32–33. San Francisco: Wiley, 2012. https://doi.org/10.1002/9781118093108.ch37.

Sandage, Steven, David Paine, and Peter Hill. "Spiritual Barriers to Humility: A Multidimensional study." *Mental Health, Religion & Culture,* 2015. https://doi.org/10.1080/136746.2015.1038229.

Sandage, Steven, Everett Worthington Jr., Terry Hight, and Jack Berry. "Seeking Forgiveness: Theoretical Context and an Initial Empirical Study." *Journal of Psychology and Theology* 28.1 (Spring 2000) 21–35.

Scazzero, Peter, and William Bird. *The Emotionally Healthy Church: A Strategy for Discipleship that Actually Changes Lives.* Grand Rapids: Zondervan, 2003.

Schiffer, Irvine. "The Role of Illusion in Mental Life." *Union Seminary Quarterly Review* (1981) 83–93.

Schiff, Stacy. *The Witches: Salem, 1692.* New York: Little Brown, 2015.

Schwartz, Tony, Mark Gerzon, Holly Weeks, and Amy Gallo. *Dealing with Difficult People.* Boston: Harvard Business Press, 2005.

Schwartz-Salant, Nathan. *Narcissism and Character Transformation: The Psychology of Narcissistic Character Disorders.* Toronto: Inner-City, 1982.

Seibel, Cory. "It's All About Me, Jesus: The Narcissistic Worship Leader." *Direction Journal* 38.2 (2009) 246–53.

Shaw, Jon A. "Narcissism, Identity Formations, and Genocide." *Adolescent Psychiatry* 22 (1998) 211–26.

Shepperson, Vance L. "Jacob's Journey: From Narcissism toward Wholeness." *Journal of Psychology and Theology* 12.3 (1984) 178–87.

Shults, F. Leron, and Steven J. Sandage. *The Faces of Forgiveness: Searching for Wholeness and Salvation.* Grand Rapids: Baker Academic, 2003.

Simon, George, Jr. *In Sheep's Clothing: Understanding and Dealing with Manipulative People.* Little Rock, AR: Parkhurst Brothers 2010.

Simpson, Austin J., Anthony D Hermann, Mark Lehtman, and Robert Fuller. "Interpersonal Transgressions and Interest in Spiritual Activities: The Role of Narcissism." *Current Psychology: Research and Reviews* 35.2 (2016) 195–206. https://doi.org/10.1007/s12144-015-9393-z.

Sosik, John, Jae Uk Chun, and Weichun Zhu. "Hang On to Your Ego: The Moderating Role of Leader Narcissism on Relationships between Leader Charisma and

Follower Psychological Empowerment and Moral Identity." *Journal of Business Ethics* 120.1 (2014) 65–80.

Sprechini, Gene. "Gender Differences in Narcissism and Courtship Violence in Dating Couples." *Sex Roles* 58 (2008) 802–13. https://doi.org/10.1007/s11199-008-9403-9.

Stackhouse, Max L. "On the Boundary of Psychology and Theology." *Andover Newton Quarterly* 15.3 (1975) 196–207.

Streep, Peg. "Are We Raising a Nation of Narcissists?" *Psychology Today*, 2012. Accessed April 20, 2016. http://www.psychologytoday.com/blog/tech-support/201204/are- we-raising-nation-narcissists.

Szalavitz, Maia. "Wealthy Selfies: How Being Rich Increases Narcissism." *Time*, 2013. Accessed April 20, 2016. http://healthland.time.com/2013/08/20/wealthy-selfies-how-being-rich-increases-narcissism.

Tangney, J. P., P. E. Wagner, D. Hill-Barlow, D. E. Marshal, and R. Gramzow. "Relation of Shame and Guilt to Constructive Versus Destructive Responses to Anger Across the Lifespan." *Journal of Personality and Social Psychology* 70.4 (April) 797–809. https://doi.org/10.1037//0022-3514.70.4.797.

Ten Elshof, Gregg. *I Told Me So: Self-Deception and the Christian Life*. Grand Rapids: Eerdmans, 2009.

Thomaes, Sander, Brad Bushman, Bram Orobio De Castro, and Hedy Stegge. "What Makes Narcissists Bloom? A Framework for Research on the Etiology and Development of Narcissism." *Development and Psychopathology* 21 (2009) 233–47. https://doi.org/10.1017/s0954579409990137.

Thompson, Curt. *The Soul of Shame: Retelling the Stories We Believe About Ourselves*. Downers Grove, IL: InterVarsity, 2015.

Tracy, Jessica L., Joey T. Cheng, Richard W. Robins, and Kali H. Trzesniewski. "Authentic and Hubristic Pride: The Affective Core of Self-esteem and Narcissism." *Psychology Press* 8 (2009) 196–213. https://doi.org/10.1080/15298860802505053/

Trzesniewski, Kali H., M. Brent Donnellan, and Richard W. Robins. "Do Today's Young People Really Think They Are So Extraordinary? An Examination of Secular Trends in Narcissism and Self-enhancement." *Psychological Science* 19.2 (2008)181–88. https://doi.org/10.1111/j.1467-9280.2008.02065.x.

———. "Is 'Generation Me' Really More Narcissistic than Previous Generations?" *Journal of Personality* 76.4 (2008) 903–917. https://doi.org/10.1111/j.1467-6494.2008.00508.x.

Tyrer, Peter, ed. *Personality Disorders: Diagnosis, Management and Course*. 2d ed. Oxford: Butterworth-Heinemann, 2000.

Twenge, Jean M. *Generation Me: Why Today's Young Americans are More Confident, Assertive, Entitled—and More Miserable than Ever Before*. New York: Free, 2006.

———. "How Dare You Say Narcissism is Increasing?" *Psychology Today*, 2013. http://www.psychologytoday.com/blog.the-narcissism-epidemic/201308/how-dare-you-say-narcissism-is-increasing.

Twenge, Jean M., and W. Keith Campbell. *The Narcissism Epidemic: Living in the Age of Entitlement*. New York: Free, 2009.

Urban Ministry Institute. "Interesting Statistics about Pastors." 2007. https://www.tumi.org/index.php/94-harvest-field-cat/138-interesting-statistics-about-pastors.

Vaknin, Sam. *Malignant Self-Love: Narcissism Revisited*. Skopje, Macedonia: Narcissus. 2013.

———. "The Self-Deprecating Narcissist." http://samvak.tripod.com/journal39html.

Vandeven, Kyle. "Are Narcissists Always Extroverts, or Can They Be Introverts?" Quora.com, 2012. https://www.quora.com/Are-Narcissists-always-extroverts-or-can-they-be-introverts.

Vitz, Paul, and Jennifer Meade. "Self-forgiveness in Psychology and Psychotherapy—A Critique." *Journal of Religious Health* 50 (2010) 248–63.

Volkan, Vamik. *Blind Trust: Larger Groups and Their Leaders in Times of Crisis and Terror*. Charlottesville, VA: Pitchstone, 2004.

Volkan, Vamik, and Christopher Fowler. "Large-group Narcissism and Political Leaders with Narcissistic Personality Disorder." *Psychiatric Annals* 39.4 (2009) 214–23. https://doi.org/10.3928/00485713-20090401-09.

Wallace, Harry M., Benjamin R. M. Scheiner, and Andrew Grotzinger. "Grandiose Narcissism Predicts Willingness to Behave Badly, Without Proportional Tolerance for Others' Bad Behavior." *Current Psychology* 35 (2016) 234–43. https://doi.org/10.1007/s12144-016-9410-x.

Waska, Robert. "Striving Toward Useful Interpretation While Managing Countertransference Enactments: Encounters with a Thick-skinned Narcissistic Person." *The American Journal of Psychoanalysis* 71 (2011) 246–63.

Watson, P. J., Ralph W. Wood, and Ronald J. Morris. "Religious Orientation, Humanistic Values and Narcissism." *Review of Religious Research* 25.3 (1984) 257–64.

Whitbourne, Susan Krauss. "Revisiting the Psychology of Narcissistic Entitlement." *Psychology Today* Online, 2014. Accessed April 20, 2016. http://www.psychologytoday.com/blog/fulfillment-any-age/201402/revisiting-the-psychology-narcissistic-entitlement.

White, Jay. Review of Michael Diamond, *The Unconscious Life of Organizations*. *Public Administration Review* 57, no. 4 (July/August 1997) 358–60.

Widman, Laura, and James K. McNulty. "Sexual Narcissism and the Perpetration of Sexual Aggression." *Archives of Sexual Behavior* 39 (2010) 926–39. https://doi.org/10.1007/s10508-008-9461-7.

Wilson, Marc Stewart, and Chris G. Sibley. "Narcissism Creep? Evidence for Age-related Differences in Narcissism in the New Zealand General Population." *New Zealand Journal of Psychology* 40.3 (2011) 89–95.

Wink, Paul, Michelle Dillon, and Kristen Fay. "Spiritual Seeking, Narcissism and Psychotherapy: How are They Related?" *Journal for the Scientific Study of Religion* 44.2 (2005) 143–58. https://doi.org/10.1111/j.1468-5906.2005.00272.x.

Worthington, Everett, Jr. *Coming to Peace with Psychology: What Christians Can Learn from Psychological Science*. Downers Grove, IL: InterVarsity, 2010.

Zagano, Phyllis. "Spiritual Wisdom, Narcissism, and Healthy Humility." *Journal of Pastoral Counseling* 39 (2004) 19–34.

Zondag, Hessel. "Between Imposing One's Will and Protecting Oneself: Narcissism and the Meaning of Life among Dutch Pastors." *Journal of Religion and Health* 44.4 (2005) 413–26.

———. "Involved, Loyal, Alienated, and Detached: The Commitment of Pastors." *Pastoral Psychology* 49 (2001) 311–23. https://doi.org/10.1023/A:1004823606194.

————. "Just Like Other People: Narcissism Among Pastors." *Pastoral Psychology* 52 (2004) 423–37.

————. "Motivation for the Pastoral Profession in the Netherlands." *Journal of Psychology and Religion* 28 (Summer 2000) 109–18.

————. "Narcissism and Motivation for the Pastorate." *Journal of Empirical Theology* 19 (2006) 227–43. https://doi.org/10.1163/157092506778884481.

————. "Still Knocking on Heaven's Door: Narcissism and Prayer." *Journal of Empirical Theology* 24 (2011) 19–35.

————. "Unconditional Giving and Unconditional Taking: Empathy and Narcissism among Pastors." *The Journal of Pastoral Care and Counseling* 61 (2007) 85–97.

Zondag, Hessel, Cor van Halen, and Joanna Wojtkowiak. "Overt and Covert Narcissism in Poland and the Netherlands." *Psychological Report* 104 (2009) 1–10.

Zondag, Hessel, and Marinus H. E. van Uden. "I Just Believe in Me: Narcissism and Religious Coping." *Psychology of Religion* 32 (2010) 69–85. https://doi.org/10.1163/008467210X12626615185702.

————. "My Special Prayer—On God, Self, and Prayer." *European Journal of Mental Health* 9 (2014) 3–19.

Made in the USA
Las Vegas, NV
15 January 2021